# Ageing selves and everyday life in the North of England

MANCHESTER
1824

Manchester University Press

# New
# Ethnographies

*Series editor*
Alexander Thomas T. Smith

## Already published

# Ageing selves and everyday life in the North of England

## Years in the making

Cathrine Degnen

Manchester University Press

The right of Cathrine Degnen to be identified as the author of this work has been
asserted by her in accordance with the Copyright, Designs and Patents Act 1988.

Published by Manchester University Press
Oxford Road, Manchester M13 9PL, UK
www.manchesteruniversitypress.co.uk

British Library Cataloguing-in-Publication Data
A catalogue record for this book is available from the British Library

ISBN 978 0 7190 8308 2 hardback

First published 2012

The publisher has no responsibility for the persistence or accuracy of URLs for any
external or third-party internet websites referred to in this book, and does not guarantee
that any content on such websites is, or will remain, accurate or appropriate.

Typeset
by Action Publishing Technology Ltd, Gloucester

# Contents

# List of figures and maps

## Figures

## Maps

# Acknowledgements

I owe an enormous debt of gratitude and thanks to the many people in Dodworth that took part in this research. Additionally, there are some very special people that I wish to thank for their friendship and kindness, making me, a rootless academic immigrant, feel at home for the first time since I had left it ten years prior: Lucy Senior, Joyce Prigmore, Nellie Grindy, Phyllis and Horace Hirst, Fred, Jackie and Jo-Anne Prigmore, Jane Jowitt-Pickering, Olly and Anthea Bullough, Jean, John and Barbara Hirst, Norah and Harry Harrison, Phyllis Mulrooney, Norah Dickenson, Elsie Nixon, Tom and Blanche Tipping, Gill, Ray, Nerissa and Jake France, Roger Kilner, Sandra and Mick O'Connor, Sue Staples and Margaret Holderness.

I would also like to extend my great thanks to colleagues and friends who have in various guises provided their support over the years in developing this book. This includes Michaela Benson, Maggie Bolton, Thom Brooks, Andrew Dawson, Colin Duncan, Jeanette Edwards, Elizabeth Hallam, Tim Ingold, Steph Lawler, Sharon Macdonald, Kristen Norget, Raksha Pande, Mike Savage, Colin Scott, Simon Susen, two anonymous peer reviewers with MUP press and the entire MUP team. I would especially like to thank Katharine Tyler and Peter Phillimore for their invaluable comments on the entire manuscript as well as for their unstinting support and friendship.

Funding from a McGill FGSR Social Sciences Research Funding Grant, a McGill Department of Anthropology and Faculty of Graduate Studies Award, the Radcliffe-Brown Trust Fund for Social Anthropological Research, STANDD/ AGREE at McGill University and the Faculty REF fund at Newcastle University are all gratefully acknowledged.

I also gratefully acknowledge permission from the publishers to use elements of work that have previously appeared in print in the following: Degnen, C. (2007) 'Minding the gap: the construction of old age and oldness amongst peers', *Journal of Aging Studies* 21(1): 69–80; Degnen, C. (2007) 'Back to the future: temporality, narrative and the ageing self', in *Creativity and Cultural Improvisation,* Elizabeth Hallam and Tim Ingold (eds), ASA Monograph Series, Oxford: Berg; and Degnen, C. (2005) 'Relationality, place and absence: a three-dimensional perspective on social memory', *The Sociological Review* 53(4): 729–44.

My doctoral supervisor, Ellen Corin, deserves a special mention. Many of the ideas in this book are indebted to nascent conversations we had in Montreal; without her guidance and support I am not sure I would have ever managed to arrive in Dodworth in the first place. She has always led by example, being a dedicated, inspirational, elegant and ethical scholar. I feel exceptionally fortunate to have had the chance to study with her and hope that I am now passing on a small fraction of what she taught me to my own students.

Finally, I would like to thank Hugh and Leo for everything else. You have made it possible for me, also, to be years in the making.

Dedicated to Joyce, Nellie, Lucy, Horace and Phyllis

# Series editor's foreword

At its best, ethnography has provided a valuable tool for apprehending a world in flux. A couple of years after the Second World War, Max Gluckman founded the Department of Social Anthropology at the University of Manchester. In the years that followed, he and his colleagues built a programme of ethnographic research that drew eclectically on the work of leading anthropologists, economists and sociologists to explore issues of conflict, reconciliation and social justice 'at home' and abroad. Often placing emphasis on detailed analysis of case studies drawn from small-scale societies and organisations, the famous 'Manchester School' in social anthropology built an enviable reputation for methodological innovation in its attempts to explore the pressing political questions of the second half of the twentieth century. Looking back, that era is often thought to constitute a 'gold standard' for how ethnographers might grapple with new challenges and issues in the contemporary world.

The *New Ethnographies* series aims to build on that ethnographic legacy at Manchester. It will publish the best new ethnographic monographs that promote interdisciplinary debate and methodological innovation in the qualitative social sciences. This includes the growing number of books that seek to apprehend the 'new' ethnographic objects of a seemingly brave new world, some recent examples of which have included auditing, democracy and elections, documents, financial markets, human rights, assisted reproductive technologies and political activism. Analysing such objects has often demanded new skills and techniques from the ethnographer. As a result, this series will give voice to those using ethnographic methods across disciplines to innovate, such as through the application of multi-sited fieldwork and the extended comparative case study method. Such innovations have often challenged more traditional ethnographic approaches. *New Ethnographies* therefore seeks to provide a platform for emerging scholars and their more established counterparts engaging with ethnographic methods in new and imaginative ways.

Dr Alexander Thomas T. Smith

**1**

# Introduction

Ageing and older age present some of the most pressing social and political issues of our time. They have justifiably received extensive scientific attention from both the medical sciences and the social sciences. What often becomes lost in these studies, however, are the everyday experiences of the older people themselves who are at the heart of such enterprise. This book inverts this relationship. It asks instead what can be learned about older age by focusing on the fine-grained and multiple ways in which ageing and selfhood are experienced in daily life.[1] In particular, it focuses on the links between everyday experiences, subjectivity and ageing selfhood. It does so through the lenses of narrativity, memory practices, profound social transformation and temporality.

Ageing and older age are paradoxical issues in both daily life and in academia. In daily life it is a truism to state that older age and older people are discriminated against in Western[2] societies. Such discrimination is based on the profound stigmatisation of older age. Both are key components of how older people are continually made and remade as 'Other' in many Western settings. Ordinary members of the public feel at their ease exerting casual impatience in the queue at the supermarket when the older man ahead of them struggles to find the correct change in his purse, or when the older woman moves too slowly for their liking on the crowded pavement outside. Older people are the butt of jokes, are assumed to be out of touch and are often portrayed solely as a social burden. Public discourse is another site where subtle (and sometimes not) negative messages about older people are exerted. One of the most common tropes describes old age as a demographic time bomb waiting to go off. Consider as an example the language used in the autumn of 2010 to advertise a Royal Society of Medicine conference entitled 'Our Changing Expectations of Life: What Do We Really Want?':

> In 2031, 23% of the population will be of pensionable age and 17% will be under sixteen. Even now there are more pensioners than youngsters under 16. 20% of the UK's population is over 65 and as research on ways to increase survival continues this percentage is very likely to increase.

The call goes on to point out that this can be seen both positively – Britons can look forward to living longer – but also that Britons do not seem to want a better old age but rather to live a longer youth. In either case, the language used evokes fearsome statistics of a booming population of older people, no longer working, who are poised to overwhelm national resources. The comparison in the text of 'pensioners' with 'youngsters' heightens this effect. Such a framing of old age in terms of exponential growth and claims on resources is a standard rhetorical device in public discourse, what Katz has called 'alarmist demography' (1992). It centres on an economic conceit – who will pay the pensions? – that damningly frames older people as unproductive burdens instead of equal members of society.

The irony here and in the previous examples is that older people are not simply irritants in public places, a social demographic to fear the growth of or bundles of health problems to be solved: rather, older people are *people* first and foremost. Furthermore, older people are not Other: old age is the shared destination for the vast majority of the younger and middle-aged people alive today. As such, one might expect to witness patterns of social empathy for older people rather than social indifference and belittlement. And yet, it is the opposite that more often holds sway.

Social scientists have developed a wide range of models to explain the denigrated position of older people, including modernisation theory (Cowgill and Holmes, 1972), disengagement theory (Cumming and Henry, 1961) the political economy of old age (Estes *et al.*, 1979; Walker, 1981) and structured dependency theory (Townsend, 1981) as well as models that resist these earlier theories such as the third age (Laslett, 1989) and critical gerontology (Luborsky and Sankar, 1993; Moody, 1988). My goal here is not to revisit in detail such theories, nor to develop a new explanatory model of these social dynamics. Instead, my starting point is the proposition that at the heart of those dismissive social gestures mentioned just now towards older people is where a particular cultural threshold is revealed, one where empathy dries up and where the other in oneself (Jackson, 1983: 336) is denied. *Ageing selves* seeks to develop a fuller account of the experiences of this cultural threshold from the perspective of older people themselves as they go about their everyday lives.

The second irony, one at the centre of academic enterprise on ageing, is that despite a vast literature dedicated to the study of older age there has been a marked absence of accounts that address core disciplinary questions in anthropology about knowledge and practice, subjectivity, self and representation in regards to older age. It strikes me that in many instances, real people and the rich complexity of their lives as lived is strangely muted in the literature. Also absent, with some very important exceptions, are ethnographic accounts of older age and especially those based not in institutional settings but in everyday realms of life in the community.

One reason for this state of affairs is that many researchers in the field characterise themselves as 'social gerontologists', whether they be anthropologists, sociologists, psychologists, social workers or human geographers. This disciplinary marker is one way of indicating the level of collaboration among social scientists in a range of specialities. It also, however, sets anthropologists who work on issues of older age apart from the rest of the anthropological discipline, in what Lawrence Cohen has called a 'subdisciplinary limbo', replete with its own creation myths about itself and its own rituals of self-perpetuation (1994: 155). For his part, Cohen argues that the lack of anthropological theory in social gerontology is linked to 'the institutional history of professional gerontology and its embeddedness in ideologies of applied sociology and social work', which consequently means that for many anthropologists working on ageing, 'the term *anthropology* becomes less an epistemological than a professional marker' (1994: 139 emphasis in original). This book takes heed of Cohen and is set firmly within an anthropological framework. I seek to interrogate mainstream cultural practices and epistemological assumptions about old age from the perspective of older people. I use theoretical anthropological perspectives on selfhood, narrativity and temporality to inform and shape my account presented here of experiences of ageing. In so doing, I seek to reinsert ageing into larger anthropological debates about the conditions of being and meaning-making within which life unfolds. Reciprocally, I also seek to demonstrate how such bodies of literature might be enriched by considering the distinctive positionality of older people and what light their experiences shed on some taken for granted assumptions in the existent literatures on selfhood, temporality and narrativity.

My approach to these issues is reflected in the sub-title of this book, *Years in the making*. This turn of phrase is inspired by and borrowed from Jon Hendricks' article 'Coming of age', published in a special edition of the *Journal of Aging Studies* (2008) in which critical gerontologists reflect on their own ageing experiences. Hendricks, in his third decade of a professional life dedicated to better understanding ageing, ruminates on the recalibration he has recently experienced in regards to what matters and to his own comportment. Both are in light of his own ageing and a recent cancer diagnosis. Such experiences have made clearer to him than ever before that 'human beings do not live life two variables at a time, but come as complex, often times messy packages lodged in lifeworlds that have been years in the making' (2008: 113). Hendricks' reflections and expression 'years in the making' crystallise a number of points this book puts forward: that the experience of older age is an incremental process which occurs over time; that the ageing self is constituted in the present day but also cumulatively through past experiences; that 'old age' is not a boundary that once crossed one is irrevocably immersed in – it is instead a much less discrete category of being and one with porous and blurred edges; and that oldness, like the self, is achieved intersubjectively and via social interactions. We are, all of us, years in the making. It is this richness and complexity of life as lived that I focus on in this account of experiences of older age.

Crucially, *Years in the making* is also a detailed ethnographic account of life as lived by older people in a northern English village called Dodworth. My research in Dodworth set out to examine what old age 'is', what the markers of 'old age' are and what the experience of the older self is like from the perspectives of the people living it. Dodworth is not incidental to what I have come to understand about ageing, the self and what I wish to argue about them in this book. Instead, being based in Dodworth is absolutely central. This book draws on research data from fourteen months of fieldwork conducted in multiple registers of everyday life in both public and private settings between 1999 and 2001, a second period of fieldwork in 2003–4, ongoing residence in the village for a period of five years and continuing connections since I moved away in 2005.[3]

Dodworth, located two miles west of Barnsley in South Yorkshire, is a former 'pit village' in the region's coalfields. Until the late 1980s, coal was still being mined on a large scale in and around Dodworth. In many ways this part of the north of England is a place now known for what it was – a major centre of the UK coal mining and steel industries – rather than what it is (Degnen, 2006). As in many other parts of deindustrialising Britain, the past twenty years in this locale have witnessed profound social upheaval with the disappearance of heavy industries. How people make sense of their lives under the erasing pressures of post-industrialism is a question that runs alongside and fundamentally intersects with my interest in the experiences of ageing. Issues of selfhood become particularly relevant within this context as the excruciating lurch out of heavy industry into post-industrialism threatens the collective foundations on which the self is written and understood locally. This in turn augments in unpredictable ways the reorientations simultaneously being experienced by individuals due to the ageing process itself. Post-industrial rupture is thus a key grounding aspect of *Years in the making*. Equally significant is the extent to which multiple intersecting networks (of kin, work, school and sociality) overlap and tie people to Dodworth and to each other. Dodworth, a village of about 5,700 people when I lived there, is a place where the majority (but not all) of older residents have lived as children, worked, socialised and, in turn, raised their own families either immediately in the village or in a neighbouring one. Circulating in these networks, Dodworth is not a place in which to be easily anonymous for either anthropologist or Dodworthers. This also becomes a significant factor for experiences of self, as I shall elaborate.

The public spheres where my fieldwork was based include tea and bingo afternoons, luncheon clubs and whist drives held explicitly for older people. Private spheres include events such as shopping, visits from family and friends, hospital appointments, domestic chores, chatting with neighbours, gardening, watching television and going on walks. It is through these various encounters and sites of everyday meaning that the reader gains important insights into the vivid realities of daily life from the perspective of older people themselves. Growing older is a complicated mixture of bodily and social change and this book explores how negotiating these shifts has crucial implications for one's sense of self and subjectivity. Owing to the challenges in marking when 'old age' begins that I discuss more fully in Chapters 2 and 4, I did not wish to prejudge the category of old age nor demarcate my research population in the conventional sense by chronological age. Instead, as 'being old' is situationally contingent, one of my research objectives was to attend to the ways in which markers of old age varied and were employed.

Ethnographic studies of old age in Western locales are usually based in institutional settings such as day centres and nursing homes (e.g. Diamond, 1992; Farmer, 1996; Gubrium, 1993, 1975; Hazan, 1980, 1984; Henderson and Vesperi, 1995; Hockey, 1990; Johnson, 1971; Johnson and Grant, 1985; Kayser-Jones, 1981; Myerhoff, 1979; Reed-Danahay, 2001; Ryvicker, 2009; Savishinsky, 1991; Shield, 1988). While these works have made a substantial contribution to knowledge, only a small percentage of older British people actually live in an institutional setting: just one per cent of people in their late sixties and only 12 per cent of men and 20 per cent of women over the age of eighty-five (Arber and Evandrou, 1993: 17). As has been well documented, institutional life is subjected to very different sets of regimes and power relations than life outside them. Thus, accounts of ageing based exclusively in institutional settings risk distorting the experience of old age as lived by the majority of elderly people.[4] It is my hope that *Years in the making* will provide a useful counterbalance to this body of work, based as it is in a non-institutional setting.

Ethnographic fieldwork has allowed me to focus on the ways in which the social interactions I observed in these private and public spheres reveal how the social category of old age is constructed, used, negotiated and experienced by older people themselves, both as individuals and as members of groups. In the experience of ageing, cultural assumptions about what old age 'is' (decline, decay and social irrelevance) and where it begins (magically, at the stroke of retirement) are contradicted by everyday experiences. The actual lived reality of the people I interacted with does not correspond with these stereotypes. Subsequent stages of fieldwork permitted me to explore in much more depth individual and reflective perspectives on older age in more private realms of life. Ethnography, which permitted me as researcher to share multiple dimensions of people's lives as far as is possible, is extremely well suited to these research topics. Being immersed in the life world of the people I came to know allows me to examine the gross disparity between subjective experiences of older age and the negative social stereotypes of what old age 'is' and who is thought to be old. As I argue in this book, it is at the complex juncture of narrativity, temporality, memory and subjectivity that the ageing self at times resists such damning social assumptions and at others succumbs to them.

Anthony Cohen, exploring the genesis of his ethnography of Whalsay, perfectly describes the sense of inadequacy provoked by attempting to write the 'truth' about a place and the people living there in the face of their intricacy and heterogeneity. He also, however, determines that his is one version of the truth, no versions of which are ever absolute (Cohen, 1987: 3–5). So it is with my version of Dodworth presented here. In the daunting task of 'writing it down', I offer one interpretation, a perspective that I hope will not be unfamiliar to those who also know Dodworth. Writing it down entails for me, however, looking and thinking through an anthropological lens. Perhaps Dodworth will thus appear here in ways which will not always be familiar to those who also know the places and people I describe. However, I, like Cohen with Whalsay, do not claim to be the arbitrator of ultimate truth on Dodworth. This is simply my version of it, but

I have always remained as faithful to the accounts and lives of the people I knew there as I could possibly be. I describe Dodworth's history and contemporary circumstances in much greater detail in the following chapter, but wish first to more fully detail my own approach to ageing that I present in this book.

## Opening the frame: selfhood, subjectivity, temporality and narrativity

A central premise of this book is to develop a fuller sense of what is at stake for older people in their daily lives as they come to embody a category of selfhood that is socially devalued. I explore how it is that old age comes to be attributed to older people, given the plurality of the category of age itself (it is possible to speak of chronological age, social age, mental age, physical age and emotional age), and the resistance of people to self-identity as 'old' (c.f. Thompson *et al.*, 1990). Despite this, old age is something everyone agrees exists. How then does it become real? To answer this, I draw from anthropological theory on the self, subjectivity, narrativity and temporality, bringing them into conversation to reflect on the experiences of the older people I came to know in Dodworth and to problematise the category of old age.

Narrativity is the vibrant process of storying lives (our own and those of others), recounting who we are, how we place ourselves in the world and what our relationships are in, and to, that world. It is a core element of how we make sense of the world we are immersed in (Ochs and Capps, 2001) and is a profoundly social, interpersonal, activity. Narrativity is not simply a representative form of knowledge; it is instead 'an ontological condition of social life' (Somers, 1994: 614) and is intimately bound up in our very selfhood.

Temporality, the experience of and within the passage of time, also figures powerfully in the creation of self. This is because the storying of the self occurs repeatedly through time. It is also a way of reflecting on the experience of change and continuity across the passage of time, experiences that are ongoing with a past, present and future. The practical and conceptual meanings of time are not given, but instead are produced in an ongoing process. It is within these temporal frameworks that people live and create meaning (Bender and Wellbery, 1991). Narrativity is thus inextricably interwoven with our understanding and experiences of self and time, which in turn necessarily implicate each other. The construction of self can thus be conceptualised as the intersection of two mutually informing axes. The first axis is composed of the everyday experiences and interactions (culturally framed and informed) of an individual with other social actors, in which narrativity plays a prominent role. The second axis is that of history and temporality.

Some researchers have been explicit about how culturally constructed negative stereotypes of old age and older people's self concept are mutually constitutive (Pickard, 1995: 20; Vesperi, 1985: 131). Integrating this insight with anthropological theory on how the self is made, particularly that selves are contextually dependent, multivocal and are created in social interaction, opens up new space to consider both experiences of old age and how concepts of selfhood are rendered more complex by ageing. What I argue throughout this book is that given the extent of bodily, social and affective changes experienced by older people, it is not unreasonable to anticipate shifts in the parameters of selfhood owing to older age. As one's subjective position in the world changes (due to a range of social, cultural and physical circumstances), new sets of demands and pressures on the ageing self emerge that are unique to this part of the life course. As I demonstrate, both narrativity and temporality are elements of selfhood that are at times differently weighted for older people than younger people. Rather than perceiving this as a negative categorisation of self, more consideration needs to be paid to the possibility of the different temporal rhythms and flows that older people may enter into.

However, despite the rich body of anthropological scholarship on the self that I examine in more detail below, insufficient anthropological consideration has as yet been paid to the constitution of the ageing self and ageing subjectivities. As Lamb, a rare exception to this trend, points out, 'except for studies of death … the ways people may be transformed … in later life' (1997: 281) are absent in theoretical reflections on the self. Another contention I make in this volume is that regardless of the cultural setting under discussion, it is an implicitly middle-aged, universalised self that has become the baseline norm in the literature.[5] Experiences of 'unprecedented seriousness … (such as) retirement … death of lovers, friends and kin' (Thompson, 1992b: 27) and the embodied transformations faced more persistently by older people than those younger demand more careful attention for the effect they have on the constitution of self. *Years in the making* considers these shifts particularly in relation to narrativity and temporality, examining the ways in which older people at times engage in narrative and temporal relations that distinguish them from younger people. While there is much in the experience of the middle-aged self that parallels older selves, there are trends in the presentation and creation of the older self that at times challenge a model of self based primarily on middle-aged adults. In juxtaposing these, I wish to explore how a normative middle-aged self comes to be the standard against which older people are measured in their everyday lives. I wish to call attention to the ways in which older age takes shape in relation to younger age. When younger, individuals are thought to have a great deal of agency (even if this is illusory) over life choices, economic circumstances, mobility and corporeality. Deviation away from this norm is interpreted by others as a shift away from full adulthood into a less-than-full-adulthood position. This is the normative governing power of a middle-aged subjectivity; idealised, no doubt, but also one that frames social expectations. Older people, as fully socialised members of society, are themselves at once inside and outside these processes, at times enacting these norms and at others getting caught in them as I demonstrate. In this regard, my work also seeks to highlight the complex tension of, on the one hand, confronting social stereotypes of old age – emphasising the resilience of people subjected to these stereotypes – but on the other hand also to acknowledge some of the distinctiveness of older age in comparison with younger age.

Such juxtaposition also permits me to draw out a set of considerations that enrich anthropological perspectives on self and subjectivity by taking the ageing self into account.

Crucially, the juxtaposition of the ageing self with middle-aged norms is not a neutral social practice. It is precisely the departure from narrative and temporal norms that is often interpreted in social interactions as a manifestation of a less-than-full adulthood. So, for instance, as we see in Chapter 6, I describe what happens when one woman I came to know (named Olive) finds herself in an anxiety producing situation. As her narrative cohesion begins to evaporate, her behaviour is interpreted as evidence of her 'oldness' rather than being down to the stress of the events she is experiencing, as it might have been had she been a younger woman. Such practices once again reveal the cultural threshold where empathy for the older person as *person* evaporates and becomes replaced instead by the label of '*old* person' discussed earlier in this chapter.

In order to begin building the theoretical framework that I wish to pursue in this book on the ageing self, narrativity and temporality, I turn now to a detailed account of anthropological approaches to self and subjectivity. Before I do so, however, two caveats on my approach to the ageing self are necessary. The first is that, as I explain in greater detail in Chapter 5, dementia has been a persistent focus in the sociological, anthropological and human geography literatures with regard to ageing and selfhood. While this is a devastating condition, it in actual fact afflicts only a minority of older people. It has, however, for understandable reasons centring around the ontological crisis provoked by such diseases, attracted a great deal of popular and social scientific attention. In *Years in the making*, worries about 'losing the self' are expressed by older people I worked with, but my focus in discussing the ageing self is not primarily about the extreme end of experience that dementia represents. Instead, I am more concerned with the 'unremarkable', the non-sensational, elements of selfhood in older age. It is these that are the daily experience and concern of the majority of older people in Britain and therefore deserve more considered attention.

The second caveat is that in this book I resist the notion that impending death is the overarching trope that informs how the ageing self is constituted and which, in turn, organises subjectivity (see Alexander *et al.*, 1991 as an example). A corollary to this trope is the idea that older people experience some sort of profound, reflective insight into their lives as they come closer to death. A brief passage from an article by Freeman published in the journal *Ageing and Society* is a good example of this sort of discourse: 'our lives are themselves like journeys and as a rule – a tragic rule indeed – only as we approach death may we find ourselves in the position of being able to see, in some whole sense, what it's all been about' (Freeman, 1997: 378). I do not dispute the relevance of death to older people's life experiences. Indeed, older people do tend to talk more openly about death than younger people. They also tend to have more direct experience of it via the loss of close friends and family and are frank about the unpredictability of the immediate future, often meeting my 'See you next week' when departing with 'All being well'. However, my research experiences in Dodworth do not lead me to believe the spectre of death is the single most potent informing factor in the daily lives of the older people I came to know, nor to their sense of self. Cultural assumptions about the inherent pressures of death being the central background-ing issue for older people's notion of self and self-making are misleading. The idea that older age and death go hand in hand is part of the larger problem of othering and fear that cluster around this part of life, in large part coloured by Western societies' deep-seated fear of death, which is assumed to link 'naturally' with older age. Visions of ageing selfhood which speculate that faced with death the self consolidates its forces and gains privileged insight into its true character were not born out in my fieldwork experiences. In practice, what is more pressing to my research participants[6] than death, and which they were a great deal more reflective about, was the less certain and less predictable threat of 'losing' oneself and 'real' old age. I argue that it is the threat of these that represent what Dawson identifies as a 'threat of temporal discontinuity' to the self (2002: 36), not just the 'impending death' that he refers to.

## The self and subjectivity from an anthropological perspective

Anthropological approaches attuned to the self and to subjectivity permit insight into 'how people (try to) act on the world even as they are acted upon' (Ortner, 2005: 34), offering a 'view of the subject as existentially complex, a being who feels and thinks and reflects, who makes and seeks meaning' (*ibid.*: 33). They are part of a long tradition of anthropological enquiry into cross-cultural differences in notions of self, which has a long and illustrious pedigree, including seminal contributions to the field by figures such as Mauss (1985[1938]) and Hallowell (1955). When I refer to the self, I draw from this long intellectual history and do not simply mean 'identity' or 'social roles' (although these are clearly bound up in issues of selfhood), but refer instead to the subjective 'I', the constellation of subjective realities created through interaction (Morris, 1994) that binds us to the social world and permits us to act in it.

The peculiarities of Western notions of self have also been widely written about and debated by philosophers, psychologists, historians and sociologists. These perspectives offer a useful conceptual framework for my own research. It is, however, worth bearing in mind that the dominant understanding of 'the Western self as autonomous and integrated is mostly derived from ... Western written philosophical traditions and not from analysis of experiences of people in the West' (Sökefeld, 1999: 418). It is also worth bearing in mind that Western notions of self are a product of a particular social history, cultural context and form of social organisation (Carrithers, 1985). Taylor (1989) reminds us of this historical specificity in how the Western self is conceptualised. One of the key aspects that he highlights is the notion of an inner/private self and external/public self. This opposition plays a significant role in self-understanding in many Western cultures:

> There is a sense of 'inside' which designates the thought or desires or intentions which we hold back for ourselves, as against those which we express in speech

and action. When I refrain from saying what I think about you, the thought remains inner and when I blurt it out, then it is in the public domain. (Taylor, 1989: 113)

The notion of a hidden, inner, true self is one that permeates Western notions of self (M. Rosaldo, 1984: 147) and is an important building block in my discussion here.

A second and related key aspect of the Western self is how it can be simultaneously perceived as both object and subject. Hollan, drawing from Hallowell, tells us that 'the self is that part of consciousness that comes into play when a human being begins to take him or herself as an object' (Hollan, 1992: 284). Kaufman (2000) argues that authors including G. H. Mead and Foucault have demonstrated how the individual self in Western societies is conceptualised as both object and subject to itself and that 'self-determination arises because the individual can distance itself from itself. Relationships, events and social and historical processes are considered external to the self, which is seen to be freestanding and autonomous. The self is intentional and conscious and not identified with the physical body' (Kaufman, 2000: 77). Taking both of these aspects into account, what emerges is a paradigm of selfhood whereby not only is there a profound division between mind and body (due to the legacy of Cartesian dualism), there is also the possibility that we can both secrete our inner, 'true' self and intentions from the public gaze (and whatever it may read on to us by interpretations of external signs) and even secrete our true motivations and desires from ourselves. Such a model also clearly has Freudian overtones.

Freudian psychoanalytic principles have come to hold a powerful place in Western understandings of self and psyche. Freudian concepts include that of the unconscious and of repression as well as a belief in the significance of childhood events for adult lives. This means that 'it is almost impossible for contemporary Westerners to think of themselves as anything other than containing some "depth" – some element of the self which is not immediately accessible' (Lawler, 2008: 80–1). Not only have Freudian principles entered into commonplace understandings of selfhood in many Western contexts, some have also argued convincingly that psychoanalysis can be usefully put to work by social scientists. This is particularly the case for those interested in conceptual tools that 'giv(e) us a way to consider the place of fantasy, repression and desire in the formation of the self and a way to understand the non-conscious, non-rational, emotional elements of identity' (Lawler, 2008: 83), identities such as gender and sexuality. However, where Freudian principles – underlying as they do Western notions of self – might be more problematic are in regards to *age* identities.

As some commentators have pointed out, Freud virtually ignored ageing in his theories of self (Silver, 2003: 381, citing Woodward, 1991) and he perceived a growing rigidity of self linked to a presumed growing fixity of the libido in old age (Silver, 2003: 382). Older women are especially problematic for Freud, being described by some as 'a missing person' in psychoanalysis (Woodward, 1995: 86), due in no small part to Freud's interpretation of older women as having had 'their psychic energy ... used-up in childbirth and mothering' which in turn made it difficult for them, he posited, to undergo psychoanalytic treatment (Silver, 2003: 382). The prominence of Freudian perspectives on the self provides a partial element of explanation as to why the normative middle-aged self has emerged in Western cultural contexts: while childhood experiences are understood as relevant to the development of the adult self, this development at a certain point in an individual's life becomes perceived as, in effect, seizing up. Within a Freudian perspective ageing's contribution to conceptualising the self then becomes only a series of losses and injuries to the self rather than something worth considering in its own right for how it interacts with experience and subjectivity.

A third prominent characteristic of Western notions of self, and one alluded to by Sökefeld and Kaufman above, is that of individualism. Geertz's oft-cited description of the category of person is a useful one to illustrate the union of these concepts:

> The Western conception of the person as a bounded, unique, more or less inte-grated motivational and cognitive universe, a dynamic center of awareness, emotion, judgment and action organized into a distinctive whole and set contrastively both against other such wholes and against its social and natural background, is, however incorrigible it may seem to us, a rather peculiar idea within the context of the world's cultures. (Geertz, 1984: 126)

Geertz's account usefully calls attention to the culturally specific character of Western understandings of self but may also obscure more complex experiences. Indeed, other authors such as Hollan (1992) have challenged the absolute rigidity of the notion of Western individualism as often portrayed in popular accounts and by social scientists, arguing instead that researchers have been too ready to assume that simplified cultural ideals of self are closely correlated with subjective experience. It is important to point out that cultural notions of what is accepted as 'the self' also shift. Several authors (resisting earlier work in the school of culture and personality studies) make this explicit by problematising the notion that there is a 'unitary discourse of selfhood pervasive in an entire society' (Kondo, 1987: 241). Similarly, Abelmann (1997) argues that 'by assuming various and blurred epistemologies in the (traditional anthropological) field against a unified selfhood in advanced capitalist societies ... we impoverish our under-standing of selfhood everywhere' (Abelmann, 1997: 789).

This then brings us to a two-fold problem that has arisen historically in the anthropological literature on self. First, a dominant understanding gradually emerged which reified a binary between 'Western' selves, taken to be highly indi-vidualistic and autonomous, and 'Eastern' selves described as socio-centric and relational (see for example, Dumont, 1980; Geertz, 1984; Marriott, 1990). The second problem stems from this binary. It masked internal cultural variation in concepts of self as well as the scope for concepts of self to be simultaneously relational (socio-centric) *and* individualistic (Hollan, 1992; Kusserow, 1999b). A significant body of work has addressed many of these concerns, particularly in regards to problematising a uniquely socio-centric 'Eastern' self and to producing a more nuanced account of difference in accounts of American selves (c.f. Ewing, 1990; Holland and Kipnis, 1994; Kusserow, 1999a; Lamb, 1997; McHugh, 1989; Mines, 1994; Murray, 1993; Spiro, 1993).

Recent scholars with interests in the self and subjectivity have thus paid careful attention to cross-cultural differences in how the self is understood, presented and experienced and the ways in which the self in Western worlds is made in relation with others. They have also attended to the complicated inter-section of factors such as gender, ethnicity and class with selfhood such as Mageo (2002) and Kusserow (1999a). Indeed, Kusserow (1999a) has demonstrated how accounts of the 'Western self' in the anthropological literature have tended to be based on middle-class white Americans and tended to promote a generic model of 'Western individualism'. Kusserow's work has sought to explore the processes through which various class positions differently inflect and shape what forms 'individualism' comes to take and also to show how both individualistic and socio-centric tendencies coexist in these various forms of individualism. She conducted ethnographic fieldwork in four different preschools in Manhattan and Queens in three different American class areas (upper-middle class, lower-working class, upper-working class). Kusserow focused on both verbal and non-verbal socialisation processes of self-concepts of four-year-olds, attending to 'the ways cultural and class construction[s] of the self were embedded in everyday discourses and social interactions' (1999a: 214) among teachers, children and parents. Based on her findings, she argues for a spectrum of indi-vidualisms that children are socialised into in the various communities that range from 'hard' to 'soft', as well as a spectrum of interpretation of what kind of self to encourage, from 'defensive'/'tightening up' to 'offensive'/'opening up', thus de-homogenising classed accounts of descriptions of selfhood in this part of America. My works sits within this tradition, developing it by examining a Western but non-American cultural setting and also takes into account lessons from this body of literature about the difficulty in defining the 'West' as a cultural locale and consequently the problem of discussing 'Western selves'. While these have been important developments in anthropological perspectives on selfhood, I believe that what has not yet sufficiently been examined are the normative assumptions that the literature makes about selfhood (and consequently narra-tivity and temporality as these are so closely bound to the self), which takes a middle-aged adult as its baseline. Additionally, while I take class and gender into account wherever possible, the prominence of these categories comes in and out of focus in my analysis, much as they do in life as lived.

## A processual approach to the ageing self

My approach to better understanding the ageing self is predicated on a processual and interpretive framework. Processual paradigms consider people as social actors who are actively engaged in shaping 'the conditions of their existence' and yet who are equally shaped by the cultural, social and historical contexts in which they live (R. Rosaldo, 1993: 92–103; c.f. Bourdieu, 1977). A processual approach emphasises how meaning and experience emerge in interaction with others and the world, forged through ongoing series of negotiations among social actors (Turner, 1985: 153–4). This is a framework that, as Turner succinctly noted, is concerned less with being and more with becoming. A processual perspective resists systems based analysis (which perceives social action and behaviour to be dictated by rules and norms) and perceives life and culture to be more disordered than predictable. And yet, processual analysis does not completely reject these paradigms of structure. Indeed, as Turner points out, 'process is intimately bound up with structure and ... an adequate analysis of social life necessitates a rigorous consideration of the relation between them' (Turner, 1985: 156).

Following from authors such as M. Rosaldo (1980, 1984) and White and Kirkpatrick (1985), I take the self to be forged through experience, action and interaction with others in a highly social world. The self is created in its telling, in its performance and in its reception by others (E. Bruner, 1984a; Ochs and Capps, 1996) intersubjectively across multiple moments in time, varying circumstances and as embedded in particular socio-cultural contexts. From this perspective, self-formation is not a uniform nor necessarily chronological process (Boyarin and Boyarin, 1995: 28) but is rather experienced as a cyclical and, at times, contradictory relational process. What is emphasised in one's presentation of self depends importantly on the context of interaction and the other social actors present. Consequently, the self is not a unitary, stable, fixed entity. While a model of the self as continuous and integrated is highly valorised in many Western settings, the self is more fractured and contradictory than this (Ewing, 1990). By narrating experience, we create self-representations which are not unitary nor fixed, but rather fragmented and partial as well as perpetually under construction (E. Bruner, 1984b, 1986; Peacock and Holland, 1993). Indeed, great effort is expended to project, as Ewing says, an 'illusion of wholeness' on to the self and to maintain a sense of continuity. This version of self-formation has recently been criticised for overemphasising the symbolic and self-representation as evidence of an 'over-commitment' to theoretical vision of self as partial, fragmented and changing (Quinn, 2006: 363), but broadly speaking an approach to the self that valorises a consideration of 'the temporal flow of experience ... (and how) individuals are continuously reconstituting themselves into new selves in response to internal and external stimuli' (Ewing, 1990: 258) is taken to be a key tenet of cultural theory on the self.

Within this processual approach to the ageing self, I integrate both narrativity and temporality in my analysis as stated above. In this, I have been influenced by Ricoeur and his work on 'narrative imagination [which in his] thought exercises a[n] ... "ontological" function: it is only by virtue of narrativity that human temporality comes to expression' (Vanhoozer, 1991: 42). Narrativity is profoundly significant to our experiences of the world and the processes of becoming as discussed above. Narrativity is a part and parcel of the ways in which the ageing self is forged dialectically via social interaction with others. In this book, I consider narrative in terms of the *content* of the daily narrative flows I was immersed in as well as their *style*. I pay considerable attention to social interaction and subjective reflection in conversational detail, narrative accounts of self and other, as well as the fine threads of meaning which play out at the level of everyday life. The banal, the revelatory, the what is in between and my own reactions to situations have all been sources of information. Such an approach allows me to examine the affective component of the disparity between the subjective experience of the self in old age and the social expectations of what old age 'is'.

The way we story our lives, however, is also subject to norms and social expectations of comportment. Given the close link between narrativity and self, if these narrative conventions are disrupted, the integrity of the self can be thrown into jeopardy. In order to reveal more closely this process, I pay careful attention to narrativity in regard to the narrative styles employed by the older people I came to know. As I demonstrate in Chapter 6, these styles can diverge from middle-age norms and this divergence then be interpreted by interlocutors as characteristic and emblematic of 'old age' itself. Narrative style itself then becomes another element in both the experience of older age, but also the ways in which old age is made and assigned.

Narrative action and selfhood are intimately acquainted with temporal considerations. Narrative is cumulative in the sense that it draws from the past through memory and nostalgia, with both selective remembering and forgetting at play.[7] Turner, citing Dilthey's structures of experience, calls our attention to how an experience is not a self-contained entity 'since it carries within it direct relations with the past' (1985: 211). If we extend this concept and replace 'experience' with 'the self' in Turner's formulation above, the self can be conceived as always having a particular relation with the past – it is not fixed or wholly determined by the past, but is informed by how the past is remembered and brought into the present moment. As Luckmann reminds us however, 'human beings order their course of life prospectively and retrospectively' (Luckmann, 1991: 163) and while self-representations are cumulative because they draw from the past through memory and nostalgia (with both selective remembering and forgetting at play), the production of self also hinges importantly on the future (in addition to the past) through anticipation, desire and expectation. What the future and the past actually signify to my research participants, however, is an important distinction and one that Luckmann's model, based on an assumed middle-aged adult, does not take into consideration. A universalised normative middle-aged self is linked to a certain set of assumptions about people's relationships with time that may or may not map onto the experiences of older people. I turn my attention now to a deeper consideration of the intersection between temporality and older age.

## Time, temporality and older age

There is a richness and complexity to the experience of time and the experience through time that marks my research participants' lives. Both aspects of temporality inform the construction of the ageing self and challenge the simplistic notion, alive in commonplace stereotypes, that older people are 'lost' in the past. Time is largely imagined in Western cultures as passing progressively in a 'linear, irreversible and uninterrupted flow' (Hendricks and Hendricks, 1976: 39), a normalised vision of temporality that we are socialised into. Those individuals whose experience falls outside such temporal norms are often perceived to be 'abnormal' or unwell (*ibid.*: 40). Owing to this normative vision of time as linear and evolutionary,

> the experience of discrete temporal moments echoes equally discrete moments in ontological experience: we are babies, then infants, children, adolescents, adults and, finally, old-aged. We see time cut up into regular, precisely measured and constantly applied units of greater and lesser duration and we see society segmented into a hierarchy of social levels and social beings of greater and lesser inclusivity. (Rapport and Overing, 2000b: 258)

'Old age' then is perceived as part of a neat progression from youth to middle age and beyond. Age categories are imagined as precisely delineated based on this segmentation of the passage of time and experience. Temporality, however, also reveals differences in social status, the hierarchies of which are unequal and disfavour the old (and the very young), holding them apart in a category of 'less than full adult'.

As I demonstrate in Chapter 4, people's lived experiences of 'old age' contradict this evolutionary model of ageing. 'Old age' is not experienced as a discrete identity and does not correspond to the same sort of linear progression as common-sense notions of the passage of time purports that it should. Indeed, Hazan argues that the main problem facing older people is not that of 'role relinquishment, functioning, being social strangers, or the stereotypes and cultural images in which they find themselves entrapped' (1996: 19) but rather that

> aged people exist in a world of disordered time, space and selfhood. It is a world shot through with paradox. The social construction of the aged as static and immobile stands in absolute contradiction to the personal experience and sensibility of the aged person, who is, in actual fact, undergoing rapid and massive changes. (1996: 19–20)

According to Hazan, it is this fundamental incongruity between social expectations and lived experience that alienates older people. What emerges from my fieldwork are patterns in older people's temporal structuring that are distinctive, which I consider in more detail in Chapter 3. I wish to challenge an assumption, common in the existing literature, of a normative, universally middle-aged self and point instead to the ways in which people's relationship with, and perceptions, of time and narrative can be distinctly different in older age than in youth or middle age.

Theorising time and people's relationships with time has attracted modest attention in anthropology including by, among others, Malinowski, Evans-Pritchard, Leach, Geertz, Gell (Hodges, 2008) and Hallowell. Time is 'pervasiv[e] as an inescapable dimension of all aspects of social experience and practice' (Munn, 1992: 93) and this pervasiveness is seemingly exacerbated in Western cultural settings, owing to the prominence of time reckoning technologies. And yet, despite the centrality of time in social life, the study of time has been described as 'often … [the]handmaiden to other anthropological frames and issues' without sufficient energies devoted to it as a basis of enquiry in its own right (Munn, 1992: 93).

However, since the 1970s and 1980s, influential social theorists including Bourdieu, Wolf and Giddens have incorporated time as an *implicit* constitutive element in their theories of social life (Hodges, 2008). Hodges argues that this temporalisation is tacit and unacknowledged in the processual and practice-theory approaches of such theorists, but it has, nonetheless, had a profound effect on anthropological thought. Hodges asserts that this unacknowledged temporal-isation has promoted an inherent, totalising, assumption in contemporary anthropological theory about the fluidity of time and of change as the driving force behind social life. He argues in turn for 'the need for reflexive knowledge of the temporal ontology of our theoretical models' (2008: 407). My work is as caught up in these issues as any other anthropologist influenced by these paradigm shifts. I do not pretend to resolve these dilemmas in this book. Indeed, the life course is a concept already bound up in a highly culturally coded under-standing of the supposed connection between time and social life, premised on simultaneous notions of change and the continuity of self. I make no apologies for this, but rather acknowledge them as framing considerations at work in both the ethnographic setting and for the analysis that follows. As Hodges himself writes, drawing from Munn (1992), temporality is 'embodied unconsciously in and through the subjective practices of daily existence' (Hodges, 2008: 406). I wish to examine in closer detail how these practices and experiences play out in older age for the people I worked with in Dodworth and offer an account of how and why temporality might matter differently at a specific part of the life course. Munn's theoretical perspective on time, centring on what she calls 'temporalisa-tion' and what I have been calling temporality, is one that guides me. Temporalisation emphasises the 'dimensions [of socio-cultural time that] are lived or apprehended concretely via the various meaningful connectivities among persons, objects and space continually being made in and through the everyday world' (1992: 116). Temporalisation, according to Munn, brings to the fore the symbolic, processual aspects of time and how these are produced via daily life and everyday practices.

These aspects of time should, however, not be mistaken as benign. Temporality is inextricably linked to power as 'control over time is not just a strategy of interaction: it is also a medium of hierarchic power and governance' (Munn, 1992: 109). While Adam, a sociologist, points to the ways in which time and power are linked via who controls whose time (1990: 120) and authors such as E. P. Thompson (1967) have addressed the control of time in the industrialised workplace via the clock, I wish instead to examine the implications of 'soft' power and time as control via *forms of temporality that are more socially valued than others*. Adam approximates this when she writes in her treatise on time and social theory how the 'structuring of social life should, however, not be thought of as a neutral fact. Once we ask who structures whose life, what rules are being adhered to and how these processes occur, then timed social life becomes fundamentally embedded in an understanding of the structural relations of power, normative structures and the negotiated interactions of social life' (1990: 109). The social relations of power and time are a backgrounding element of the material developed in this book and in my analysis of how living within different forms of temporality can at times be used against older people. As we shall also see, such as in the case of Ernest in Chapter 3, a different weighting of time can also be used by older people to assert authenticity and stake claims to socially valorised roles.

Finally, time is in and of itself a multifaceted entity that is difficult to get a hold of. For example, Adam calls attention to the multitude of different characteristics people refer to when talking about 'time': time as 'phenomena, things, processes, qualities, or a dimension, a category and a concept' (1990: 6). Gell (1992) for his part, in a rare book-length anthropological treatise on time itself, elaborates on differences between B-series time and A-series time identified by philosophers before him. B-series time is 'real' time, objective time, whereas A-series time is the subjective perception and experience of time. Clock time is thus only one aspect of time. Natural time (such as seasons and tides) and biological time (such as hibernation, cognitive development, digestion, sleep, gestation and ovulation) are highlighted by Adam as other integral elements of time that exceed social time and clock time (1990). But it is clock time that has had the most significant influence on Western assumptions about the unidirectionality and linearity of time: 'the abstract, spatial time of the clock has come to dominate the Western world to such an extent that it is related to as being time and as if there were no other times' (Adam, 1990: 67). Concepts of time that perceive it as measurable, universalist and linear (such as the 'life course') have thus become naturalised and have also shaped perceptions of human ageing whereby 'we inherit assumptions about our "movement through time" that restrict our options and often work against our interpretations of personal and social ageing' as 'in many situations universalist measures fail to reflect our subjective engagement with ourselves and with other people' (Coupland, 2009: 959–60). It is these processes and how they inflect the lived experience of older age that I examine in *Years in the making*.

## Temporality and older age: Hazan and Heikkinen

Two authors, Haim Hazan and Riitta-Liisa Heikkinen, have notably engaged with issues of temporality and older age. Their contributions deserve careful consideration here for points of convergence and divergence with my own approach. Hazan, exploring how ideologies of chronological time and decline were transformed into non-linear temporality by older people, engages with issues of temporality and selfhood of older people in a series of publications (1980, 1984, 1990, 1996). His primary fieldsite was a day-care centre for elderly Jewish people in a non-affluent part of London (Hackney), consisting of about 400 members, of whom about 150 attended daily and who ranged in age from their late 40s to their early 90s (1990). Hazan is interested in people's orientation to time in various shifting social contexts; he wishes to open up the theoretical angle that time is not 'a mere reflection of reality' but instead that 'time is an organising principle with its own dynamics' (1984: 575). Hazan draws attention to the ways in which older peoples' relationship with time is arguably configured in a different way from that of younger people. In Hazan's case, this is due to in part to the deeply negative social position older people come to occupy. He is concerned with the 'time universe' of the day-centre members whereby time was not 'a reflection of other social determinants' but instead 'something to be manipulated and reconstructed' (1980: 2). For Hazan, questions of temporality are framed in relation to competing tensions for older people between continuity and transformation. He posits that older people at the centre exist within two conflicting dimensions of time: 'social time' which condemns older people to stereotypes of static temporality and 'personal time' which involves 'the constant experience of change or disintegration and deterioration' (1980: 46, 88). It is this incongruity between social expectations and lived experience that motivates his work.

Hazan's fieldsite is a highly institutionalised setting. As older people in a day centre that was socially segregated from the outside world and who also were experiencing a significant disjuncture between stereotyped social assumptions of old age as a time of stagnation and their own experiences of personal time that were full of rapid change, Hazan says that centre members established their own alternative temporal reality. While talk of the past in the day centre was not entirely absent, Hazan describes it as being constrained, focused on creating a sense of egalitarianism which in turn served to position 'the revised past on a continuum with the present' (1984: 570) and make the past present-centred. For example, personal occupational histories and previous socio-economic distinctions were 'obliterated' and not discussed at the centre. He specifies a multitude of ways in which codes of behaviour by centre members created a present-based emphasis in daily life and which in effect create an 'arrest of change', 'a present-bound society' (1984: 571). This is a time perspective and framework that he has termed 'limbo time' (Hazan, 1980). Through its timelessness, limbo time provided a haven for his research participants, a way of resolving the incongruity between social and personal time. Hazan claims that within this temporal frame of limbo time, the day-centre members were able to reconfigure time so that the past and the future no longer mattered and that this in turn created a space that rejuvenated participants' selfhood and well-being (1980: 177). The principles of time as linear and irreversible are ones put forward as the 'problem of time' for all people and especially for older people, but Hazan's research shows how 'the Centre people not only did construct a new social reality, but by doing so also offered a solution to the problem of irreversibility [of time]' (1980: 179).

Since time is malleable and can be manipulated, it is thus a resource 'open to infinite possibilities of handling and management through people's attitudes and behaviour' (1980: 181). His work thus challenges taken for granted assumptions that past, present and future all need to be consecutive components of temporal framings in order to avoid disordered personhood (1980: 177), assumptions that older people are unable to effect change in the existential conditions they inhabit and assumptions that older people are statically inflexible (1980: 183). For Hazan, unidirectionality and linearity of time are disrupted by ageing and especially by older age. He argues that dominant models of time are thus particular to youth and middle age and not necessarily at all responsive to the experiences of older people, a point I return to in this chapter below. What I wish to explore is the ways in which temporality and selfhood are inextricably linked, whereby universal notions of selfhood also become problematic in light of these distinctive relationships with time.

For Hazan's group, atemporal responses to a negative and dangerous social context promoted 'limbo time'. In great contrast, the older people I worked with in Dodworth constantly dipped into the past to ground present experiences and future plans. Indeed, this cultural valorisation of the past is not only the domain of older people in Dodworth, but rather a common refrain in many parts of post-industrial Britain (see Edwards, 1998). This may well be due to the dynamics of Hazan's group who he knew via their institutional life and thus who were doubly socially marginalised: both as being older and via institutionalisation. However, Hazan's work is very valuable for the insights it provides into the possibilities of temporal difference as linked to ageing and the self. I develop some of his ideas in conversation with my material from Dodworth in Chapter 3.

A second social scientist who has explored temporality and experience with older people is Heikkinen. Over a series of three five-year intervals that commenced in 1990, Heikkinen explored themes of the ageing experience and being older via interviews with twenty Finnish people born in 1910 when they were aged 80 (2000, 2004). Using a phenomenological approach based on Heidegger, Husserl and Merleau-Ponty, Heikkinen pays particular attention to the shifts in these narrative accounts over time on the same themes. Her interviewees began at 85 to say that they had crossed the boundary into old age (something they had not said at age 80) and when both bodiliness and temporality emerge as key concepts. In regards to temporality, Heikkinen's findings are that the cohort at age 85 are living in a present-based temporal frame whereby the 'panoramic view of the future holds little promise ... it is the present rather than that-which-is-to-come that seems to be the home territoriality of their existence. For people of this age the most important dimension of time is the present of past things, the present of present things and the present of future things' (2000: 480). She continues, explaining that for the people she interviewed 'it seemed that ... time at the age of 85 had lost its dynamic, preservative meaning. In contrast, at the age of 80 most still looked ahead' (2000: 481).

Heikkinen states in a later article that her interviewees, aged 85, were 'developing an awareness of finitude. Many of them started to feel and think that their fatigue, their tiredness, the difficulties they were having with their memory, were all gradually leading them away. At the same time, though, this was something they took as natural, something that they would inevitably reach in due course' (2004: 575–6). By age 90, Heikkinen says that her interviewees began to seem 'timeless' and unconcerned with finitude; how time mattered had shifted from an engaged presence (age 80) and worries over time passing and eventually ending in a 'timelessness' at age 90 whereby her participants 'were in time as time itself ... settled in their temporality' rather than perceiving 'time in terms of a distance to something' as they had in their 80s (2004: 576). However, rather than this being a negative disengagement from life and society, Heikkinen is at pains to argue that these 90-year-olds had achieved full knowledge of what 'it means "to be me"' and 'no longer have to become anything', 'the (life-long) mission of living a life seemed to be completed ... these elderly narrators had reached their Dasein, their being-in-the-world, knowing and being aware of where they had arrived in their life' (2004: 579).

A final shift Heikkinen describes from age 85 to 90 concerns the self, consti-tuted in relation with others. Her findings are that the self increasingly becomes forged in relation to others both deceased and living, with a simultaneous collapse or softening of rigidity of temporal linearity becoming more manifest (2004: 577). She describes it thus: 'memories of childhood and youth begin to filter through into the narratives: it seems as if the 90-year-olds are returning to the field of presence to reopen it' (2004: 577–8) and the temporal field of relations loosen its insistence on a unilinear directionality of past, present and future, instead becoming nested together.

Emerging strongly from Heikkinen's analysis of her data is a sense of a trans-forming relationship with time of the ageing self that shifts incrementally from a future-oriented experience (age 80) to one organised around a present-facing reckoning of time (age 85), to finally a temporal insouciance and freedom from pressures of previous relationships with time (age 90). By 90, also evident was a dissipation of temporal linearity and softening of distinction between one's own biographical eras. This changing sense of time was imbricated with a shifting relationship with the physical body, all valuable insights into the shifting experi-ence of selfhood and time that I return to in Chapter 5. This is particularly instructive when juxtaposed with Munn's reflections on temporalisation and 'past-present-future' relations (1992: 115). Munn argues that 'inasmuch as people operate in a present that is always infused and which they are further infusing, with pasts and futures' (1992: 115), the relationship between past, present and future is critically important to temporalisation. Munn continues, 'ways of attending to the past also create modes of apprehending certain futures ... or of reconstructing a particular sense of the past in the present that informs the treatment of "the future in the present"' (1992: 115). What Munn and other social theorists of time have not taken due consideration of is how this reckoning of past-present-future can and does shift in emphasis, owing to an individual's changing circumstances, sense of self and bodily knowledge as Heikkinen's work and my own demonstrates, and as I elaborate on in Chapter 5 in my discussion of the 'remembered' self versus the 'inhabited' self.

What is not apparent from Heikkinen's work, however, is whether her cohort are embedded in overlapping social and familial networks, nor what this might add to the experience and knowledge of self, forged as it is in intersubjective relationships and, as emerges in Dodworth, in relationship to place that I explain in Chapter 3. Furthermore, while her research design is admirable for building in regular revisits at five-year intervals, a sense of scepticism lingers that is hard to shake. This is because, as presented by Heikkinen, these five-year shifts seemingly represent highly homogeneous incremental transformations in experience for the entire cohort. We do not learn about any other factors such as access to resources such as social and economic capital, recourse to family and friend networks, or the variability of physical and mental health and how they might all play differentially into such transformations. Instead, the shifts bind the subjectivity of ageing to a chronological calendar, as if pre-programmed.

Unlike Heikkinen's work, as I stated earlier, Dodworth is a place where it is not easy to be anonymous, owing to multiple intersecting and overlapping networks. The large majority of my research participants have lived in the Dodworth area their entire lives, a characteristic which has significant implications for the intersection of personal and collective memory as well as for the construction of a sense of self. 'Old Dodworthers', a term used often in Dodworth to demarcate people 'born and bred' in Dodworth or with nearly a lifetime's association with the village, can contextualise each other fairly intimately based on a lifetime of familiarity, although to greater and lesser degrees depending on the individuals concerned. Talking about these connections among themselves is a source of great pleasure for older people in Dodworth, but is also a way of reproducing and reinscribing the social order of which they speak onto an increasingly fragmented personal and collective reality. The epistemological and ontological issues of self and ageing in Dodworth are partially shaped by the persistent, constant local memory work done through talking about places, absences and relations by the older people involved in this research in a place that has changed significantly, in some respects, in a short period of time.

Memory talk was a dominant feature of my fieldwork experiences, a form of discourse that was about places, absences, and the web of relations that continually brought the past and present together. What emerged was a three-dimensionality of memory, an individual and collective way of placing oneself and others in relation to spatial aspects of the villagescape. Despite being erased, decayed, or passed on, remembered places and people in Dodworth still serve as points of orientation in the contemporary social landscape and feature heavily in local discourse. The power of social memory is not just in having memories of how the village used to be, but emerges through talking about these memories and using them to help navigate current social relations and circumstances. It is a form of social capital for those who can access it. The work of memory is also significant for how a sense of self and belonging is created through narrating individual and collective histories. Memory talk is produced, transmitted and reproduced among people who have known each other and about each others' lives (and each others' families' lives) for a very long time indeed. Memory talk involves a great deal of knowledge and a vocabulary of the area's social and individual histories. Owing to the relatively small size of Dodworth and immediately neighbouring villages, their geographical proximity and shared histories (particularly Dodworth, Silkstone, Silkstone Common and Higham), the stories about individuals and communities are deeply intertwined. The cohorts born in Dodworth between the beginning of the twentieth century and the Second World War went to school together, their parents often worked together, they lived next door or around the corner from each other, went to church school together and eventually came to work together themselves as well as courting and often marrying each other. The villages were by no means isolated or static, but of the 'old Dodworthers' that remain, there is a significant proportion who grew up and are growing older in either Dodworth or the immediate surrounding area.

However, the three-dimensionality of memory, by which I mean the intersection between place and memory, which creates a depth and texture to both social memories and to the places themselves, is not an impartial practice. The dialectical relationship between the personal and collective emerges from how people narrate memories of their lives, and narrating these stories is one way of commenting on shared history. It is also revealing of people's relationship with the present-day world. One of the most forceful themes to emerge from my research participants' narrative accounts was the transformations in the social and physical environments around them. In the face of a sense of moral decay and disorder, the work of memory becomes even more crucially important to help position and protect the ageing self in the present since talking about the past is a meaningful channel of social experience and interaction locally.

## Summary

This book is divided into seven chapters. Chapter 2 immerses the reader into the ethnographic setting, emphasising description and analysis of social transformation and post-industrial rupture in South Yorkshire and Dodworth more specifically. Based on the fundamental premise that experience and the self cannot be understood in a social vacuum, I seek in Chapter 2 to historicise the research locales and the lives of my research participants. I also introduce the reader to the specific research settings of public and private domains of everyday life and elaborate on the methodology used. Although for organisational purposes I have made a distinction between time spent in the public meeting places and time spent outside them, from the perspective of older people themselves, the boundary between the public meeting places and life outside is not always a sharply divided one. I do not wish to falsely dichotomise experience as interior and exterior to these social places, but instead demonstrate the multiple sites that inform older people's sense of self and the various vantage points for considering dynamic interactions that affords. Also, rather than simply describing social activity, I am interested in the subjective experience of older age from the perspective of the people I came to know in this particular historical moment and this particular socio-economic context. I begin delving into some of the issues prioritised in daily life and examine what are described as sources of pleasure as well as reasons for frustration. Not surprisingly, these feelings and experiences stem from a complicated mixture of factors. While some of these are attributed specifically to ageing and older age by my research participants, many others are not and arise instead from the experience of human life and are not at all specific to older age per se. The experience of 'old age' as a social label and category is not equivalent to the experience of daily life as an older person, and this underlying contradiction informs my writing.

Chapter 3 puts forward a two-fold argument about temporality: first, that experiences of time and the significance of time may shift as a person ages; second, that temporality becomes important in older age because of the uses it is put to against older people in conjunction with narrative – both in 'disrupted form' are used against older people to mark a supposed decline into a lesser form of adult selfhood. Temporality has a further level of significance that I explore in this chapter, namely how it is linked to place and to belonging via memory talk. In Chapter 4 I turn my attention to examining how the boundaries of 'old age' are delineated by older people intra-generationally among peers. Chapter 4 brings into focus a cultural account of the boundaries surrounding older age as both a social category and as a lived experience. It argues that 'old age' is not a frontier whose edges, once breached, are irreversible. Instead, using detailed and rich descriptions from the ethnographic data, it shows the subtle pressures that older people in this community put on themselves and on each other while they discriminate between 'normal' and 'real' old age. Of particular consideration are ideals of personal comportment, body talk and interpersonal monitoring for signs of 'real' old age. This material permits a closer consideration of the gap between pragmatics and epistemology in the way old age is conceptualised and experienced by older people. Chapter 5 turns to questions around the ageing self and the ways in which a normative middle-aged self does not accommodate experiences of body and of self in older age. For example, if 'doing' is an essential part of 'being' and of self, as my research participants continually told and showed me, what then transpires to being and self if what one can do shifts over time? Put another way, what are the connections between temporality, embodiment and subjectivity in older age? Chapter 5 considers what light the ageing self can shed on Western notions of self and subjectivity and considers what a theory of self might look like if it made room for lessons learned from older age, such as 'the remembered self' versus 'the inhabited self'.

Chapter 6 extends these reflections on selfhood to narrativity, a crucial element of the construction of self. This chapter examines how narrativity was used, interpreted and experienced in the daily lives of the older people with whom this research was conducted. This chapter furthers the analysis of Chapter 4 by demonstrating the distinctiveness of narrative styles at times employed by older people in comparison with younger adults. How such narrative activity and style are interpreted and responded to by their interlocutors forms a critical aspect of how oldness comes to be constructed and projected onto the older narrator, endangering the very work of building the self that narration seeks to accomplish. Chapter 7, the concluding chapter, ties the book's themes together and offers a series of reflections on the ethnographic method and older age.

My approach is one that brings multiple threads of meaning-making together.

Throughout this book I return time and again to the ways in which everyday experiences and interactions (as they are culturally framed and informed) forge the ageing self. These are not socially or culturally neutral practices. Instead, they have considerable implications for the day-to-day experiences of older people. Furthermore, such interactions and meaning-making are culturally constructed processes, embedded for any particular person in a historical moment and referring to a shared past. *Years in the making* demonstrates the merits of ethnography for grappling with these complicated processes and has allowed me to highlight the powerful roles of narrativity, temporality and social memory in the construction of the ageing self in Dodworth.

## Notes

1 I often use the expression 'older age' instead of the more conventional 'old age' to highlight the heterogeneity and variability of experience within this category as well as to distinguish it from stereotypical and negative concepts of 'old age', which I am seeking throughout this ethnography to problematise and better understand.

2 Although I use the term 'Western' throughout this book, I wish to signal here my discomfort with the unproblematic way it can be employed and the homogeneity it implies. While there are cultural similarities throughout the 'Western' world, blanket use of the term masks significant nuances among the component cultural groups, local levels of experience and class, gender and generational issues. On the other hand, the term serves as a useful shorthand to express certain shared tendencies, which background the questions I engage with here and so is difficult to dispense with altogether.

3 Research in 2003–4 was on a different topic ('Public understandings of genetically modified food', European Commission Fifth Framework Programme: Quality of Life and Management of Living Resources. Contract number: QLG7–CT-2001–01668, Jeanette Edwards, PI) but permitted me to take up new issues with some of the older people I had worked with previously.

4 Recent ethnographic monographs by anthropologists working on old age are few and far between. Some important exceptions include Oliver's (2007) work on the experience and concept of 'positive ageing' among older British migrants to Spain – investigating the identity paradoxes these migrants are confronted by – and therefore the ways in which the life course mediates migrant experiences. Cliggett (2005), based in Zambia, considers the gendered dimensions of what being 'old' means in the experience of older Gwemba Tonga people under severe conditions of drought and famine, treating ageing from an experiential perspective lodged in a period of socio-cultural change. Lamb (2000), based in India, explores indigenous notions of ageing, linked to social relations and selves and adds to theories of embodiment and gender.

5 Indeed, not only is this an implicit middle-aged universal, but as Kusserow (1999a) has pointed out in her work on the multiplicity of Western concepts of self, there is also a generic *middle-class* and *American* self often implicitly at work in references to 'the Western self'.

6 I often use the phrase 'my research participants' throughout this book to designate the people I came to know during my fieldwork. Although this phrase could be interpreted negatively as a use of the possessive case, this is not my intention. Instead, it signals an empathy with and sensitivity to the experiences of the research population I worked with as well as a proximity to their lives as lived. By no means do I intend by the use of

this phrase an ownership of their narrative accounts or their experiences. Rather, it is an indication of their participation in this research project by opening their daily lives to me and including me in it.

7 For discussions of the way the past is strategically used and how identity can be performed through memory and nostalgia, see Battaglia (1995b), Jameson (1989) and Stewart (1988); Battaglia (1993) also discusses the way forgetting can be used as a social strategy.

**2**

# Dodworth: people and place

## Introduction

Although most of South Yorkshire was heavily industrialised for nearly two centuries, many parts of the county are still extremely rural. Dodworth is a village in the county of South Yorkshire located two miles to the west of Barnsley, the nearest town, and Sheffield, the nearest city, is twenty miles south. The western side of Barnsley leads into the Pennine foothills, which are extensively agricultural and pastoral. Dodworth, like many other former pit villages, is a semi-rural setting. It is bracketed to the east by Barnsley and the M1 (a central national motorway running 200 miles from London to Leeds) and to the west by a scattering of small villages that are interspersed with farmland and woods (see Map 1). The landscape around Dodworth is particularly beautiful with undulating hills and valleys spotted with fields, livestock and villages, all trimmed by the distinctive dry-stone walls of the region. This same stone was used to build nearly every building in the area before the 1920s, many of which are still present.

Dodworth alone is home to four working farms with at least a dozen other farms in the immediate vicinity. The fields surrounding the village are criss-crossed by a substantial number of well-used footpaths to which the public has unfettered access. Nearly two hundred years of industrial activity has also left its mark on the region's landscape. 'Pit tops', the once prominent industrial complexes that supported the mining activities underground, have been partially eradicated. The substantial waste heaps – 120 feet high and with a footprint of 83 acres in the case of Dodworth – where mining refuse was tipped over centuries are still visible, although they are now covered in tree saplings and grasses. The pit buildings and winding wheels have been demolished and the deep shafts into the earth capped over. In some places, such as Dodworth, new light-industry factories have been built on top of where the mine used to be. Many other sites lay dormant with weeds sprouting up between the cracks in the concrete slabs that now cover the sprawling acres where generations of men went to work. With these changes, sites of significant economic, symbolic, social and cultural meaning in Dodworth and the surrounding area have been abruptly obliterated, although not forgotten.

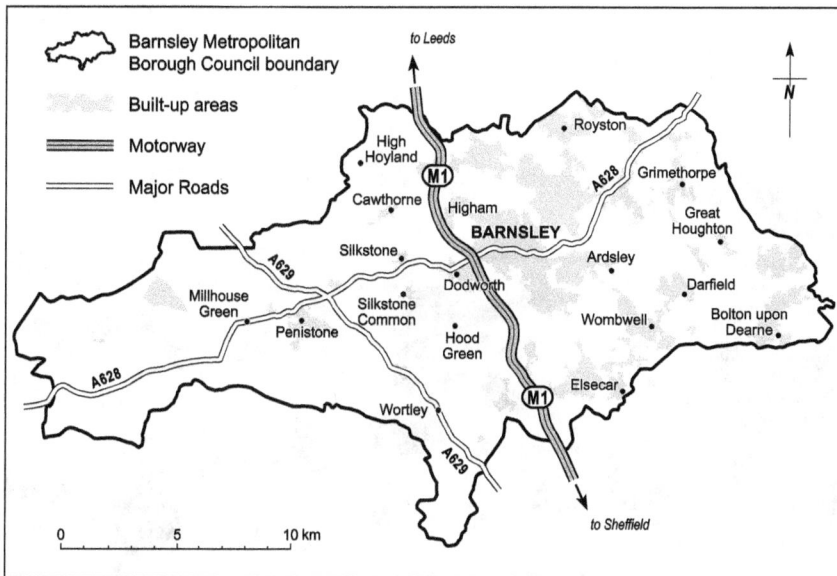

**Map 1** Selected villages in the greater Barnsley area.

Until 1974 when local government was reorganised throughout Britain, Dodworth had its own local council responsible for housing, planning, adminis-tration, public services and education. After 1974, Dodworth became part of the newly formed Barnsley Metropolitan Borough Council (BMBC), which assumed responsibility for what had previously been locally controlled affairs. The proximity of Barnsley to Dodworth, in conjunction with Barnsley being the seat of municipal affairs, means that the town plays a significant role in the everyday lives of most Dodworth residents, but Dodworth still retains a distinct identity as 'like but separate from' Barnsley. The population of Dodworth was 3,584 in 1991 and rose over the next decade to 5,742 by the time of the 2001 census (OPCS, 2001). This growth was largely due to the construction of a new housing estate during the mid-1990s in the crook of a valley in the village, a point I return to below.

Dodworth has three main streets running through it with about a dozen smaller branch roads. The village occupies just over one square mile (see Map 2). Dodworth residents distinguish a number of different areas and micro-locales within the village itself and one of the biggest distinctions is between Dodworth and Gilroyd, although these would appear contiguous to someone unfamiliar with the area. Other important micro-locales and place names include Tollbar, Crossroads, the Tanyard, the Green, Top of Dodworth, Dodworth Bottom, Intake, the Jabs, Gate, Snow Hill and Pilley Hill. Consequently, in a relatively small geographical area there is an abundance of names for various parts of the village. These names in turn are shorthand for village knowledge and navigation.

Dodworth has a small but well provisioned shopping area on High Street that

**Figure 1** The Crossroads, Dodworth High Street.

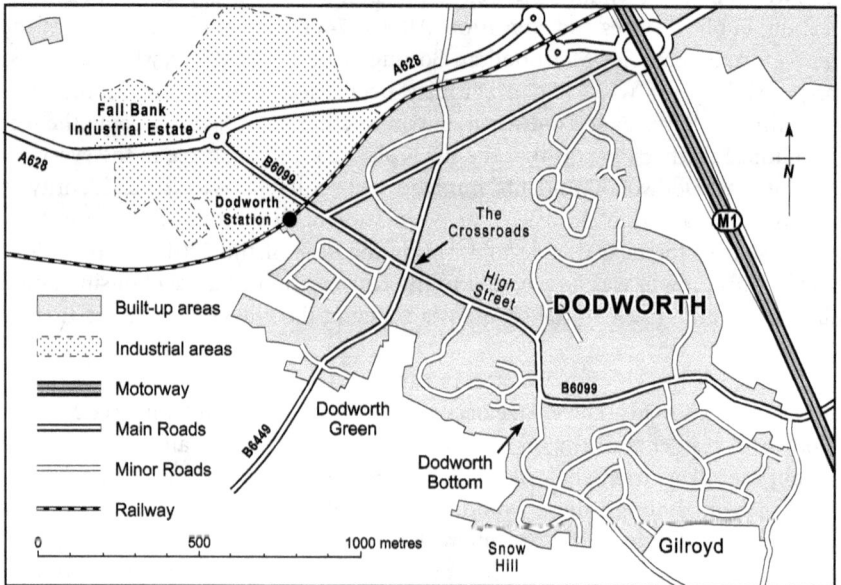

**Map 2** Dodworth and Gilroyd, edged by the M1 on the right. Barnsley is just to the east of the M1 and is largely out of view on this map.

houses a general store, the post office and pharmacy, the library, a doctor's surgery, a carpet store, a butcher, two hairdressers, a café, a small hardware store, a news-stand, two sandwich shops, a Chinese take-away and a florist. Nearby are two Indian restaurants, two fish and chip shops, a motel, an unmanned police station, an Anglican church, two Wesleyan Methodist chapels and a firm of architects. The village has a small railway station (local service only), two nursing homes, seven pubs and two social clubs. Dodworth also had three schools during my fieldwork, but the class of 2001 was the last to use the Church of England Infants' School, which then closed and merged with Dodworth Junior School. The infants' school opened originally in 1850 and many of my research participants attended lessons there in the 1920s and 1930s, making it an important memory site throughout my fieldwork.

A number of long-resident families live in Dodworth as do more recent arrivals. Local identity politics, highly attuned to issues of belonging and entitlement, demarcate 'Dodworthers' from outsiders on the basis of birth and prior family connection. Although discussions of the new 1990s estate present the incursion of outsiders as a relatively new phenomenon, oral history accounts attest otherwise. For example, Vivienne,[1] in her late eighties, as an explanation of why her neighbours (also in their eighties) do not mix socially told me 'But you see, they've only come to Dodworth ... they lived in Barnsley, but they've only come to Dodworth. They've been here ... since these houses were built and these houses are twenty-nine years old.' Her neighbours moved into Dodworth and a then new small estate of private bungalows at retirement. The increase in 'outsiders' moving into Dodworth is much commented upon by people of all generations who have grown up in the village and recent historical changes have promoted this. First, after amalgamation with Barnsley Metropolitan Borough Council in the 1970s, Dodworth council housing stock came under the control of Barnsley MBC and council houses that used to be open only to 'Dodworthers' became increasingly available to any council tenants in the Barnsley area, a trend that picked up momentum since the 1990s. This change is a sore point locally and appeared repeatedly during my fieldwork.

Second, since the mid-1990s and corresponding with the decline and erasure of coal mining, Dodworth in common with many parts of the north of England has experienced an explosion of private house building. Five hundred new houses were built in the village's largest housing development, in addition to clusters of other housing scattered around. This large housing estate in particular features 'executive homes' which are four to eight times as expensive as the older terrace houses or former council houses in the village. The residents of this new estate are understood as the symbolic other by long-time residents who 'all know each other and who in the end are all somehow related to each other' in comparison with these new residents who are said to 'keep themselves to themselves' and do not 'get involved' in the community. They also 'aren't friendly' and refuse to greet you on the street with a 'Hiya' or 'All right?' and are described by long-term residents as having radically altered the atmosphere of Dodworth.

Contemporary Dodworth thus in many ways is two communities. One, comprised largely of extended families that have been established in Dodworth and neighbouring villages for four or five generations, is based on, and reproduces, a deep sense of affiliation to place and local identity with low levels of anonymity. These individuals' and families' personal and shared histories are interwoven and 'known' to each other. These patterns are long-standing and can include as well as exclude: in 1940, one woman I became close friends with married a Dodworth man and moved to Dodworth from a village ten miles away. She was overwhelmed by what she described more than sixty years later to me as 'clannishness' among her Dodworth neighbours who made it very clear that she did not belong because she was not a Dodworther. Forty years after her in 1980, another woman I came to know in 2001 but then in her early twenties and from a neighbourhood in Barnsley three miles away, found herself in the same position when she began dating a Dodworth man. She described to me how heads turned and people stopped talking when she walked into the local pubs with him because she was not 'known'. Both women have now lived in the village for many years. While they still would not describe themselves as Dodworthers, they are now well known locally. Their stories demonstrate the extent to which the bonds that make up village life can also be alienating, as well as the strength those bonds had and can still have in parts of Dodworth. Issues of belonging, identity, localism and community are ones with long antecedents in the anthropology of Britain. Seminal works in this respect include that of Frankenberg in Glynceiriog (1957), Strathern in Elmdon (1981) and Cohen in Whalsay (1987); newer research includes, for example, Edwards in Bacup (2000) and Tyler in Leicestershire (2012). All attest to similar patterns of inclusion and exclusion in the working out of belonging and boundaries in Britain.

The second 'community' of Dodworth is the outsider or commuter families who for the most part live in the new estates, although an increasing number of 'outsiders' now live in the council properties and older housing stock. Unlike newcomers during other periods of great population growth in the late 1800s and the 1920s when the coal industry was booming, attracting many ancestors of the families who now consider themselves to be Dodworthers, these families on the new estates are divided from the longer-term residents by socio-economic and historical factors. They cannot be gradually incorporated through shared sites of employment or related sites of socialisation. Indeed, given the geographical location of the new estate, incorporation cannot even occur via neighbouring since the new estate is so physically separate from the rest of Dodworth. The description of one old Dodworther of the estate is that 'it's like a place on its own, cut off ... it's not part of the village'. Indeed, only one person I met in Dodworth during my fieldwork knew someone living there. A further layer of division between the two parts of Dodworth is age-related. The new estate is full of young families but does not attract older buyers. None of my research population lived there, nor was I ever directed there by the older people I came to know. It was as though the area did not exist. As such, my account of Dodworth is strongly biased away from the lives of the people living in this 'other' socio-temporal Dodworth as I, immersed in the life world of older

Dodworthers, followed the lead of my interlocutors and had no cause to go there.

## Dodworth: unpicking ideal types

Although identified today mainly for its recent coal-mining past, mining represents a small fraction of Dodworth's socio-economic history. First settled as an agricultural village in the Middle Ages and appearing in the Domesday Book of 1086, it is likely that the settlement had been in existence for a few hundred years before William conquered England and indeed probably before Norse invaders came to the area (Sykes, 1989). In addition to agriculture, small-scale smelting and tanning were important local industries in the seventeenth and eighteenth centuries (Hamby and Wyatt, 1997) as was the linen trade in the early nineteenth century (Threlkeld, 1989). Indeed, until the mid-1800s miners were a minority in the Barnsley area, far outnumbered by linen weavers (Threlkeld, 1989).

It is, however, mining that was of central importance for a century and a half in Dodworth and which still occupies a fundamental place in the local imaginary. Historical evidence of coal mining in South Yorkshire exists from medieval times, with mention of mines in Silkstone (early fourteenth century) and Barnsley (fifteenth century) (Gray, 1976: 31), but workings such as these were modest compared to the heavily industrialised pits of the nineteenth and twentieth centuries when technological advances permitted deeper mines to come into production, as well as the growth in canal and railway infrastructure to support the movement of vast amounts of coal (Threlkeld, 1989). Industrial-scale coal mining came to Dodworth in the 1850s in the form of deep shaft mines and drift mines, called 'day oils'[2] locally. Both were possible owing to the abundance of coal in the area. The coal seams in this region are so close to the surface in many places that a number of older residents recall coal picking from these exposed seams as children during the mining strike of 1926. Coal was the main household fuel. Normally their fathers would have received a coal allowance as part of their wages from the pit. During a strike, however, coal was always withheld by employers. In order to feed the coal fires in their homes for heating, washing and cooking, families would have to scavenge whatever coal they could from local outcrops during periods of industrial dispute.

The main pits in the Dodworth area from the mid-1860s through to the final pit closure in 1988 were Church Lane, Strafford, Wentworth-Silkstone (also called Levitt-Hagg), Redbrook, Rob Royd and Silkstone Fall. Owned and operated by a variety of different private companies and families before British coal mines came under control of the state in 1947, each of these pits has its own history of operations. Not all of them remained in operation through to the late 1980s, although Church Lane and Redbrook did; Levitt-Hagg closed in 1981 but the others closed earlier in the century. It is difficult to obtain data on employment patterns at these pits, but it is certain that by the lifetime of my research participants not all Dodworth miners worked at Dodworth mines. Men would commute by bus, by foot and by bike to other collieries in the region and come to work at Dodworth pits from other villages as well. It is probable that a sizeable proportion of the workforce at Church Lane Colliery and Wentworth-Silkstone were Dodworth men, but certainly the image of a village pit worked in by only local men is something that applied more to the 1800s than to the more recent past.

Mining work is notoriously dangerous. While working conditions gradually improved over the lifetime of my research cohort, mining continued to be an industry that exacted high tolls from its workforce through injury, disability and death. Some of these are felt long after retirement such as pneumoconiosis and vibration white finger, and the Barnsley area, like much of post-industrial Britain, has much higher than average disability rates. But mining is also more than just work. Mining has taken on powerful resonance in the local and national collective imagination, marking strong cultural ideas of community, masculinity and camaraderie. In many former mining areas there is palpable regret for a lost way of life that although onerous is also perceived by some as having been more ordered and meaningful. This vision of an ordered life (punctuated by the unpredictable dangers of mining work itself) centres around clear gender roles, a sense of community, nearby extended family and the centrality of the union. Despite the demise of coal mining, such nodes of reference still deeply inform the local imaginary. Stereotypical notions of what a pit village 'is' or 'was' are also produced and consumed on local and national registers through published local histories, in films, television documentaries and local conversation.

In a parallel fashion, the sociological literature on mining villages has also reified a model of the 'ideal-type' of mining community (Bulmer, 1975; Dennis, Henriques and Slaughter, 1956; Lockwood, 1966). According to this model, isolated mining communities or 'pit villages' are dominated by a single form of employment and are thought to be culturally and socially homogenous with high levels of social solidarity, strict division of labour and militant political activity. A strong sense of solidarity, glossed more and more frequently as 'community' in both the literature and the local discourse, is something that popular knowledge and social scientists alike attribute to the nature of pit work itself, rooted in the need of miners to be able to trust each other while underground to protect each others' safety and lives, a 'solidarity expressed in the pit [that] is continuous with that in social life' (Szurek, 1985: 147).

This model has been critiqued for blurring important local and regional differences in mining community life as well as masking a certain conservatism of some mining regions (Rees, 1993; Williamson, 1982; Winterton, 1993). My own fieldwork experiences presented me with a situation more complex than the traditional sociological model. In Dodworth, there are three important local considerations which depart from a 'traditional' study of a mining village.

First, Dodworth is no longer a place where men currently working as miners live. It is, however, for many of its residents, still understood to be a mining village. This is not a mere trifle of a label, but points to highly relevant social distinctiveness in regards to work, family, class and place-based networks, aspects that Strangleman has shown are ways in which 'in the absence of the [coal] industry ... the industry continues to shape people in the former coal districts' (Strangleman, 2001: 257). Second, Dodworth is not socially homogenous. While many men I met during my fieldwork had worked in the coal industry, there were also significant numbers who had worked in different industries such as railways, buses, gardening, steelworks and shopkeeping. I was at first frustrated by this, certain that I was missing something important and not 'discovering' the 'real' Dodworth. I was misled by my own expectations of what a 'real' pit village is and who would live there, based on the stereotypes outlined above.

Although such villages may have existed in parts of Britain, Dodworth was more diverse than the traditional models permit. Having said this, the older people I came to know in Dodworth are ageing in a place that, while never socially homogenous in regards to class, race or ethnicity, was also far less socially differentiated than might be the case in an urban setting, or a setting with more global immigrants. While there are many small micro-class divisions depending on factors such as education, occupation and housing, as well as bigger demarcations of class divides such as employee and employer, over the majority of the lifetimes of the people I worked with, Dodworth has tended to be composed of a largely white, working-class population.

Third, unlike the stereotyped image of pit villages consisting of male bread-winners and female housewives, Dodworth women did a remarkable amount of work besides their own housework to keep the family finances afloat, both in the generation of women that formed my research population and also their mothers before them. It is generally accepted that the rise in industrialisation in the 1800s meant an increasing differentiation between men's and women's roles in the home. When the workplace shifted to the factory or the mine, 'paid labour became separated from unpaid housework' and men became the main earners rather than the whole family contributing to the family income (Liddington and Norris, 1978: 50). The most intense division of roles is purported to have been in areas such as the mining regions, where women's and men's work was entirely segregated and women usually worked only at home (Thompson, 1992a: 64).

However, economic pressures meant that many married women in Dodworth *did* seek work. Before marriage, all the women I came to know in Dodworth had worked, including in the tin factory, the shirt factory, the rug mill, in shops, as nurses and as domestic servants. Once married, most women gave up these full-time jobs, but not all. Others gave up their jobs after marriage but then worked part-time to help ends meet. Census figures mask the amount of casual part-time work that went unreported but which significantly bridged household finances. Such work included women 'going round collecting' weekly payments for hire-purchase plans, cleaning the church hall or the local school, working as domestic cleaners for wealthier families, decorating other people's houses and washing laundry for other families. A great deal of entrepreneurial skill was required to make ends meet and work like this often made the difference to straightened family finances. For example, Vivienne recounted to me how when she was a school girl in the late 1920s she and her mother would work together. Vivienne had lived in Dodworth since the Second World War when she married a

Dodworth man. She worked in the offices at the Co-op and later at a local colliery accounting office; after her husband returned from the war they worked together running their own business in a corner shop (where Vivienne was responsible for all the book-keeping) that they lived above with their two children, retiring to a bungalow in the early 1980s.

Vivienne's mother, widowed by an accident that had killed Vivienne's father in the pit and left the family in difficult circumstances, baked teacakes by the dozen and Vivienne delivered them to their regular circuit of customers when she still lived at home before marriage. They also used to boil gallons of peas together in the washing copper, which people would come to buy from their back door. Thus, while the transformation of female labour and women's entry into the workplace has been well documented in Britain since the 1980s, the paid work done by married women who were also full-time housewives in the generations before them has remained largely unremarked upon. In sum, these elements of historical and contemporary life in Dodworth are important reminders of the limitations of 'ideal type' models of mining communities, but also help clarify the research setting in which I found myself.

## The 'acrid fog of anxiety' of the past as tool of reflection

The coal, iron, steel, cotton manufacturing and shipbuilding industries of the north of England enjoyed immense success over many decades in the 1800s and early 1900s. However, between the two world wars, this stupendous economic success suffered devastating decline. The unemployment rate peaked in the coalfields in 1931 and 1932 with a third of coal miners out of work and with workers in other industries even more negatively affected, including steelworkers (48 per cent out of work) (Hobsbawm, 1968: 175).

The regional consequences for people living in the north of England, Dodworth among them, were terrible. In early twentieth-century Britain, as today, there was a 'gradient of poverty' running from the South to the North, 'a geographical distribution of inequality' (Thompson, 1992a: 22). For my primary research cohort whose birth years range from 1911 to 1930, such detail is not incidental. Even in subsequent times of economic recovery and full employment, such as in the 1970s, the unequal distribution of poverty in the North compared to the South was a topic of public discussion (Taylor et al., 1996: 164). In 1979 the three north of England census regions (Yorkshire and Humberside, the Northwest and the North-east), after almost thirty-five years of attempted post-war social and economic regeneration, were again living with markedly higher rates of poverty than any other region in Britain (Taylor et al., 1996: 164).[3]

In Dodworth, the 1931 census data shows a male unemployment rate of more than ten per cent (OPCS, 1934). Personal experiences of the depression were a recurring theme in the narrative accounts of the older people in Dodworth. For example, Stanley, in his early eighties, told me that like the majority of his peers, he left school at the age of 14. This was in October 1936 and although he applied straight away for work, he could not get a job until January 1937 when he took a place at the pit 'and was happy to *get* the work'. Memories like these are a tool which helps people reflect, a process which in turn creates positionality. Tommy, in his mid-eighties, told me how he got work with a greengrocer at age 14, but 'he sacked me when I turned sixteen because he didn't want to have to pay national insurance stamps'. Through family connections, Tommy ended up selling Sheffield-made cutlery door to door with a peddler's licence and vividly remembers one of his regulars asking him one day 'Are you one of those who can't get a job?', a shameful state for a young man in a working-class area where steady employment was a mark of good character and reliability. Between the age of 14, which marked the start of his working life and age 21, he worked at six different very low-paying jobs and was on and off the dole. These circumstances irrevocably marked his young life, but also gave him a perspective on the 'poor young fellas' of today who are chronically unemployed in South Yorkshire, owing to the mine closures. Tommy, like many of his peers, uses his recollections of the past to read the present set of circumstances faced by a younger generation and to comment on it by linking himself with them through a shared sort of experience, namely the painful realities of un- and under-employment. Echoing Tommy is Hobsbawm, writing about the way this post-First World War depression marked a generation of British women and men:

> The years of slump followed those of world war and everybody lived in the shadow of these cataclysms ... a job lost meant more than a period of uncertainty or poverty. It might mean a family of lives destroyed. This acrid fog of anxiety was the atmosphere which men and women breathed during a generation. Its effect cannot be statistically measured, but equally, it cannot be left out of any account of these years. (Hobsbawm, 1968: 176)

This 'acrid fog of anxiety' has perhaps ebbed in the years since my research participants were adolescents and young adults, but such experiences undoubtedly inform their subjectivity still today and their accounts of their younger lives. These difficult economic times were grinding for many Dodworth families. Indeed, when trying to explain these times to me, accounts often return to being 'brought up with little'. Poverty is remembered as touching on all aspects of life: modes of transportation, work, technology, communication, clothing one's children, economic circumstances and housework. A profound sense of change comparing current prosperity to poverty in the past permeates the narratives of my research participants, as demonstrated in this excerpt from an interview with Mary (mid-seventies):

> This house [we lived in], it were one double bedroom and a half a bedroom ... you'd have a double bed for me parents and a double bed for us three girls to sleep in, now that's how we were brought up. And you used to have a little coal fire in bedroom and you used to have to keep gas light on all night because there were cockroaches running all over the place. Horrible! I mean, we'd die now ... everybody had nits, all kids and them that say that they hadn't, well! [chortles with laughter], they'd be lying ... I mean, that's why I can't understand why people of my age get airs and graces because everyone were more or less on same

> level, it were very rare that anybody had any money ... Me dad lost an eye at pit and I think, I think he got about 100 pounds compensation at the time and he used to have to spend about six weeks in the dark ... With his money, he bought a horse and cart, me dad, and he'd go round selling firewood and collecting scrap iron, anything, anything and then selling it on.

Many of the themes in Mary's narrative weave throughout the discourse in Dodworth of older people, about the world they lived in when they were younger. This vision of the past centres primarily around people being poor but equal ('everyone were more or less on same level, it were very rare that anybody had any money') and how people had to get by with less ('you see, there weren't stuff what there is now'). This was still the era before nationalised health care or state pensions and the economic demands on working-class families were high even in times of full employment. Stories of widespread poverty in Dodworth form a prominent element of collective memory and individual histories.

Given the relative poverty and poor housing conditions of this area over many decades, it might be surprising to learn that there are also a number of large properties in the immediate area which were home to wealthy land-owning families, both aristocratic and industrialist. The majority of these still stand, silent witnesses to a different social order of the past. They include Noblethorpe Hall, Wentworth Castle and Dodworth Grange. The presence of these houses does not go unnoticed and the connection between their existence and the labour of the working classes in the area was commented on by more than one person during my fieldwork. A former coal mine electrician, Steve, in his late seventies told me that 'all the big houses round here ... they were built on slave labour and on child labour'; a second retired miner, Tom, in his eighties said that 'all the big houses around here were built out of coal'. The sentiments expressed here reflect the knowing perceptions of men whose working lives have been spent labouring in a dangerous and exploitative industry. Their reflections on social inequality are mirrored by the accounts of older women who, when younger, worked 'in service' in some of the same houses for the wealthy resident families.

## The closure of the coalfields

As stated previously, not everyone in Dodworth worked in the coal industry and not everyone in my research population was directly affected by the demise of mining. However, the closure of the pits signals a central moment in the village's history. The disappearance of this major source of employment and identity has transformed Dodworth on both experiential and practical levels. Within a decade, the area had gone from being modestly prosperous to being labelled one of the 'most deprived' areas of Europe (*Barnsley Chronicle*, 12 April 2002). Post-war prosperity kept unemployment low nationally throughout the 1950s (Hobsbawm, 1968), but in the greater Barnsley area the exhaustion of coal reserves and a subsequent closure programme throughout the area in the 1960s (Threlkeld, 1989: 108) signalled new change. However, the skyrocketing price of oil in the 1970s made coal again a cheaper source of energy in high demand. This era also saw the rise of union militancy in the Yorkshire coalfield, which had not been present to the same extent since the 1926 strike (Threlkeld, 1989: 103). During the oil crisis, the National Union of Mineworkers (NUM) went on strike twice: in 1972 and in 1974. After both strikes, the miners won wage increases and their standard of living rose. The successful strikes in the 1970s were abhorrent to the Conservatives who, in 1979, came to power again under Margaret Thatcher. Slowly, the scene was being set for the Miners' Strike of 1984–85. In 1976, 21,000 men living in the Barnsley area worked in mining, representing 47 per cent of male employment and in 1977–78, the Barnsley coalfield produced 25 per cent of the Yorkshire coalfield's output (Threlkeld, 1989: 207). In 1920, 1,200 men worked at Church Lane pit in Dodworth (Lloyd and Swallow, 1924: 18) and in December 1981, 1,255 men were still employed there, although it cannot be determined from these numbers how many of these men also lived in Dodworth (personal communication, Philip Thompson, NUM, 17 May 2000).

By 1981 the number of Barnsley men working as miners had fallen to 14,834 and although the National Coal Board was still the single largest employer in Barnsley (Threlkeld, 1989: 147; 1993: 143), the 1984–85 Miners' Strike was just over the horizon. This strike symbolises for many people the final demise of coal mining in Britain, when most mining families were again 'reduced to subsistence living' (Szurek, 1985: 6) from their more comfortable circumstances of ten years previously. Throughout Yorkshire, 55,000 miners were on strike (Threlkeld, 1993: 125) and many thousands more family members were directly affected, as were small businesses that depended on mining incomes for their own. The strike was not successful. Four months after it ended, Barnsley pits lost 3,000 jobs and another 4,000 were lost by 1987. Church Lane pit in Dodworth was closed in 1986 and the remaining workforce transferred to Redbrook, which was itself closed in 1988. By May 1993 the only two mines that remained open in Barnsley (Houghton Main and Grimethorpe) had also closed, ending two centuries of intensive coal mining in the Barnsley region and 140 years of mining in Dodworth.

Long-time Dodworth residents lament the shifts brought about by the deindustrialisation of the area. Whether miners or not, there is a palpable sense of a world turned upside down in people's narrative accounts. While the disappearance of work in coal mining is a central factor in this, so are other frequent comparisons between today and the past. Today is perceived as a transformed world and one in which a fundamental and profound moral slippage has occurred. Such feelings are particularly evident in comparisons made by my research participants between their experiences as young people and today's youth. One man summed this up by describing his fond memories of the Mechanics Institute in Dodworth. This was a large, multilevel multifunctional community hall and education centre with a reading room, billiards tables, whist drives and mother and baby clinic, which was torn down in the late 1980s. It also had a substantial dance floor and was for many decades used by local teenagers and young adults as a popular venue. Mack, 83 years old, a cornet player and keen musician in his youth, remembers fondly many dances he played at there. He compares these memories with the circumstances of today's teenagers: 'there's nothing for them now, just boozing, just a lot content to sit back and watch telly'. Talk like this represents some older people's perception of a new way of being which does not resonate with their own lived experience, despite the sympathies that some like Tommy might express for younger generations going through similar experiences that they themselves did.

While this general sense of deep change in ways of being permeates older people's narratives, there are also more specific transformations that are strongly felt and spoken of. Individually, these may be small changes, but taken together they add up to a heavy burden of erasure. Some of these old patterns changed throughout Britain, such as the shift from 'old money' to 'new money' in 1971 when decimal coinage was introduced, but others were unique to the Barnsley area. Part of the life experiences of my research population for many decades, they now simply no longer exist. These include holidays (such as Whitsuntide, May Day dances, Empire Day, Barnsley Feast Week and Dodworth Feast); food which is no longer available or which no longer has the richness of flavour that it used to (such as certain cuts of beef which were banned because of the BSE crisis in Britain, but also vegetables which now come from foreign markets or are grown out of season); Barnsley market (which although still in existence is viewed as a mere shadow of its former self); technical knowledge that is no longer relevant (both in the home and in the workplace) nor understood by younger generations; houses and buildings in the village that have been torn down; fields that no longer exist; the dwindling number of people attending community events; and open coal fires in homes that have been nearly all replaced by coal substitutes or gas, said to be less warming and less pleasing than a real coal fire.

Tropes such as these that evoke a romanticised past, what Williams called 'the well-known habit of using the past, the "good old days", as a stick to beat the present' (Williams, 1975: 21, quoted in Crow, 1994: 40), have been widely commented on and are not only at work in Dodworth. The idea that people (and not just older people) perceive the past as a golden age which has given way to social anomie and moral decay has been termed 'respectable fears' by Pearson (1983). But yet, in Dodworth, as much as my research participants may feel alienated from some aspects of today's social order, many also feel as though they grew up in what they perceive as a more morally cohesive world. As Eileen, a woman in her early seventies put it:

> Memories always stay with you and make you who you are. Our memories are going to be richer than young ones now because of all that we've lived through and that's made us tough. We didn't have much, but we looked after each other. All my grandkids know today is the telly and computer games. They don't play the way we used to.

Having experienced marked economic deprivation in their youth underlies a world view that contrasts poverty of the past with prosperity of the present in two ways. The first is a morally laden perspective that perceives poverty as character building and implying, conversely, a sense of moral decay and disorder in the more prosperous present day. Second, the contrast between past and present circulates in discourse among older Dodworth residents as a symbol of profound transformation in ways of being, a transformation that people lament. The status of Dodworth as part of an industrial centre that has disintegrated thus has wide ranging implications for multiple levels of everyday life.

## The self and ageing in Dodworth

In parallel with this socio-economic upheaval, the social markers relevant to the construction of people's senses of self have also shifted dramatically. Taken-for-granted connections between identity, economic productivity and contribution to community and family life are no longer as straightforward as they once were. In the face of such a shifting environment, not just economically or socially, but in the sense that a place has, how do people as individuals and as a collectivity define the anchoring points in their lives? For the older residents of Dodworth, this question comes to be particularly at stake as they approach the end of their lives under conditions largely alien to the balance of their lifetimes of experience.

While, of course, sharing broader British and Western notions of self as highly autonomous and individualistic as discussed in Chapter 1, there are certain aspects of life in Dodworth that form an important background to the self, framing my discussion of the ageing self to come. The first of these are markers of local identity such as having a Barnsley accent or being a 'Dodworther' through virtue of being born and raised in Dodworth. These signifiers provide a special social anchorage in the locality, fostering a source and sense of belonging. The way identity is made manifest through a Barnsley accent is particularly striking and featured strongly in my research experiences. A Barnsley accent is one variation of a Yorkshire accent but it is also said to be one of the most distinctive. Having a 'broad Barnsley accent' signals deep class, belonging and identity affili-ations. It was a topic that people never tired of bringing to my attention. During my very first evening at one of the centres that I describe below, I was teased by Art that 'we'll teach you to speak proper Yorkshire' after trying (and succeeding) to stump me with phrases such as 'put wood in t'door oil'[4] and 'tripping over t'cozzie edge'.[5] During the same evening, Hilda asked me in a concerned way 'do you understand what they're saying?' and clarifying what I could not understand in Ida and Ruth's rapid-fire joking. Ida and Ruth had been chuckling about the prospect of hitching their husbands' prams together and letting them look after themselves while Ida and Ruth went off and found two fancy men. Hilda explained to me that 'fancy men' were younger lovers and that 'pram' was being used ironically instead of 'wheelchair'.

A week later, while in line at the post office and engaged in polite conversation with two strangers in the queue (who wanted to know where I was from), I was asked how I liked living Yorkshire and whether or not I was able to understand the accent of 'people round here'. Similarly, while visiting with one of the centre organisers to gain permission to attend her centre, I was asked by her and her husband about my Master's fieldwork in an Innu community in Labrador. I told them how I spent months not understanding the background conversation around me because everyone spoke *Innuaimun* unless they were speaking to me, when they spoke in English. The organiser's husband, a Dodworther, said 'Oh, aye, I'll bet it's like that here, too!' with a chuckle. As these examples show, a broad Barnsley accent is asserted as *different* (and usually proudly so). It is also assumed that outsiders (British and non-British alike) will have difficulty understanding what is said by native speakers since they do not possess the same local knowledge and adeptness with the accent.

A Barnsley accent is also widely assumed among my research contacts, both young and old, to represent shared regional identity characteristics. Frankness, speaking one's mind and a sharp joking wit are all held up as idealised key attributes of a Yorkshire person. Explaining to me why one of the regulars at a local Dodworth pub is nicknamed 'Anteater' (due to his long nose and squinting eyes), a middle-aged son of one of my research participants laughingly ended the brief story with 'That's Yorkshire for you! We tell it as we find it!'.[6] Similarly, at a centre meeting which had seen an unpleasant run-in between my two companions Len and Vivienne and a third person, Len turned to me afterwards and said that:

> Broad Yorkshire doesn't waste time saying the *long* way what you can say the *short* way, like: 'Damn and bugger what they think!', instead of going on about how [voice changes into a sing-song rhythm] other people have their own opinions which should be respected and everyone's opinion counts and such like ... [voice returns to normal] Pah! What a load of rubbish!

Importantly, especially given the transformations in so many other aspects of daily life that I discuss in this chapter, accent and regional identity were the two characteristics of everyday living that were discussed frequently by my research population, but which were never described as changing, unlike nearly everything else. Speaking broad Barnsley and ideas of 'Yorkshireness' are two of the few anchoring points that still feel constant to the people I talked to in the face of profound social transformation.

A second contextualising feature of the ageing self in Dodworth is the local social dynamics. Dodworth is for many residents a close-knit village with long-standing and complicated family connections as well as low levels of anonymity and powerful social currents of gossip. Many people's extended family members live in close proximity and many of my research participants are long-term village residents. These individuals and families have gone to school and to work together, socialised together and share similar memories of the village history. These bonds are not always positive ones and can at times be as alienating for lifelong residents as for relative newcomers. Whether sources of strength or alienation, they deeply inform the way of being in the world that underlies constructions of the self. I turn my attention now to the public sites of social interaction for older people in Dodworth, key considerations for some of the forums in which the ageing self gets worked out and performed.

## Public spaces for older people: the centres and the luncheon club

Two public meeting places for older people in Dodworth are community centres and luncheon clubs. Attendance at these groups is not something that all older village residents took part in nor did all my research participants attend all groups. However, for the people who do choose to and are able to attend them, they form a central element of weekly schedules and social life. They were also a vital initial site for my fieldwork. What follows is a brief introduction to both settings and my position in each.

### The centres

Dodworth has seven community centres. Each community centre has an associated cluster of between twenty and forty immediately adjacent council-owned bungalows, built by Dodworth council in the 1960s and 1970s. Each cluster has a person on call, called a warden, to help in cases of emergency. Wardens are always women. The warden also visits each bungalow and house on her rounds every morning, except Sunday, for a couple of minutes to make sure each resident is well. These are not isolated complexes for older people but were purpose-built by the local authority and are interspersed within Dodworth's housing stock. Each bungalow cluster and affiliated centre is named after local sites. While confusing for the purposes of writing about them, 'the centres' in local usage refer both to the physical buildings and to the weekly activities run there for older people. I will describe the physical aspects of the centres here but, from then on, when I refer to 'the centres' or 'a centre', I mean the group meetings that occur there and not the buildings themselves.

Along with many other transformed aspects of community life, changes in the centres are another source of regret that mark discourse about the social transformations in Dodworth. The centres have been active social meeting places since they were opened, but numbers of people participating have dropped significantly. The members at Strafford Centre, for instance, say how even as little as three years previously, in 1998, there were thirty regular members, a number which hovered during my fieldwork at about twenty. Ten years ago, circa 1990, there would have been at least six whist tables on a centre whist night whereas now it is usually two and sometimes three. Rob Royd Centre is estimated to have had seventy active members in the 1980s and Cooper used to have fifty, but both have since declined to between twenty and thirty.

The frequency of centre activities has also changed. For example, Rob Royd Centre used to have four days of activities. Mrs Ryder, a member who has been attending since the early 1980s and who is in her late eighties, remembers it as follows:

> Monday there was tea and bingo in the afternoon; Tuesday there was a coffee morning, Thursday there was bingo and tea between 7.00 and 8.30 p.m. and Friday there was a whist drive that started at 7.00 p.m.

At that time, she used to go up for a whist drive there which attracted over twenty regular players. Today, Rob Royd Centre no longer sponsors whist at all and there is only one weekly tea and bingo session. Similarly, the range of services offered at the centres has also altered. For example, there used to be a television in Strafford Centre which also used to be open all day. Men would watch the horse races on the centre television. The centre also used to subscribe to three daily papers, which people would come to read. This was before Dodworth was amalgamated with Barnsley council and instead had its own local authority, a time when, as Anne (in her mid-eighties) told me repeatedly, 'we knew who we were voting for on council'. This era is evoked as a golden age when the centres were packed, the village lively and 'Dodworth was for Dodworthers'. Barnsley Metropolitan Borough Council amalgamated in 1974, at a time when most of the centre members I knew would have been in their late fifties. Since that time, enormous unforeseen rupture has occurred on the macro-level with the closure of the mines and the subsequent re-ordering of social life in the village. The restructuring of local governance is coincidental to this transformation, but has deep symbolic implications in the local imagination where it figures as further evidence of the shift in landmarks of meaning and order.

The centres have also changed in terms of who uses them, having originally been used by a wider generational slice of the community. While older village residents have always been encouraged to attend, the centres also used to attract more pre-retirement members and younger village residents. This involvement centred in particular around whist drives and bus trips to holiday destinations. Pictures I have seen of group bus trips departing from Dodworth centres dating from the late 1960s and early 1970s show attendance ranging from thirty to fifty members.[7] As the category of old age is forged in part through social interactions, this shift in attendance has interesting and important implications for the construction of old age in the centres. It signals a greater degree of segregation of the generations in Dodworth than in the recent past, with a consequently smaller range in the sorts of social interactions that can occur. Similarly, the former presence of televisions and newspapers symbolically represent a greater openness to the world outside the centres in the past. While the centres used to receive national, daily newspapers, now only one of them that I attended had any newspapers present, and this was the weekly local paper, the *Barnsley Chronicle*. The mere presence of even this paper sparked a great deal of discussion and debate about local issues (especially as they related to the recent history of Dodworth people and places), marking the atmosphere of this one centre as slightly more vocal and with more exchange of information than the others. Taken together, the shifts in who uses the centres and to what extent they offer conduits to outside information mark an increasingly self-referential dynamic within the centres compared to the recent past.

Of the seven centres in Dodworth, I attended four over the course of my fieldwork and of these, three intensively. The centres were recommended to me by the elected municipal representative (local councillor) as a good place to begin my research. With her support, I gained permission from the centre organisers to attend their weekly meetings. Each centre I visited is a single-storey building with at least one large carpeted room. The centres also have laundries (used in rota by some bungalow residents) and kitchenettes. The kitchenettes are equipped with a sink, stove and oven, counter space, dishes and cutlery. All of the centres have large windows and, consequently, lots of natural light during the summer months. They are modest yet comfortable spaces to be in. Many of the wardens (who are also responsible for cleaning them) have added homely touches such as crocheted headrest covers, framed pictures on the walls, collections of porcelain figurines, silk flower arrangements and coloured glass pieces which dot the rooms. The main room is where the weekly social activities take place. Lining the edges of the centres are an eclectic variety of armchairs, coffee tables, sofas and larger tables. The furniture is clean and well looked after, but by no means new. Each centre also has a few pieces of furniture ranging from armchairs to side-boards, which have either been donated by members of the community or left to the centre upon the death of a centre member. The centres' interiors thus tended to be an eclectic mixture of old and new, but the overall atmosphere is that of large, slightly impersonal, communal living rooms.

Like the physical layout, the format of each centre and what happens there at each meeting is slightly different, but there are also many similarities. In each centre at some point during the appointed day, either the warden or the committee members prepare the centre for the upcoming weekly social by putting out the tea cups, milk jugs and biscuits, turning the heating on, boiling the enormous water kettle and putting out the bingo cards. Centre members then will start arriving about twenty minutes before everything is due to start, trickling into the room in ones and twos, greeting each other, getting settled in their chairs, sometimes moving around to chat with each other and other times staying seated. Seating plans, although not written down, are fixed, with each member having her or his regular place. When I first started attending the centres, these first few minutes were an absolutely crucial period of time during the afternoon's or evening's activities as I would have a chance to circulate and chat, one to one, with the various members, gradually building up a rapport. As time went on, this slice of time continued to be one of my favourite parts of the gatherings. I could move about easily, talking to people, follow up on previous conversations, catch up on current events and maintain regular contact with people. By the appointed hour, everyone who is coming has arrived and the previously chatty buzz dies away as either the bingo or whist begins. The next two to three hours, depending on the centre, is structured around playing bingo or whist, with a break for tea, biscuits and a chat in the middle. After the event is over, people make their way home without lingering.

## The luncheon club

Another main public meeting place for older people that I attended was a luncheon club in one of the neighbouring villages. Held in a large, sunny, carpeted hall with a kitchen attached to a local chapel, this weekly event is run by a dedicated volunteer and subsidised with funds from a national charity, Age

Concern. The luncheon club rents the space from the chapel and members pay £2.50 for a large hot meal, served weekly at 12.30 p.m. The food is cooked by a local training school and delivered to the hall. Although member numbers fluctuate, there were between twenty and twenty-five regular members during my fieldwork and a rota of about sixteen volunteers who came to serve the meal once a month. Some members would come a bit early and sit together in the cold foyer room, making small talk and waiting for the previous meeting (a mums and toddlers group) to leave. Then, as more people arrived, those who are able help set up the tables and chairs, lay the tablecloths, silverware and glasses. While this goes on, there is a gentle hum of chatting among the members. Some people know each other quite well and, as in the centres, have long-standing associations with one another. Others recognise each other by their faces and a few more recent newcomers are familiar at first only to the people whose table they share. New members to the luncheon club are integrated quickly, however, and the atmosphere is relaxed and welcoming.

People line up to pay for their meal and to buy raffle tickets (25 pence for five numbers) and the members also donate items such as tinned food and bottles of soap to the raffle on an ad hoc basis. It is considered good form for raffle winners to donate a prize to be raffled off at a later date. Some members have been coming since the club started in 1986, although a total of fifteen members only started attending just before I began, or during my fieldwork. Even more than at the centres, there was much fluctuation in membership with some members moving away or dying, or no longer being able to travel to the club. The luncheon club is completely run by women, but out of the twenty-five members that I knew over the course of a year, five were men.

Ironically, although I came to feel quite attached to the luncheon club and extremely comfortable there, initially my visits were fraught with tension. These tensions, upon reflection and with hindsight, are particularly interesting in terms of how oldness is constructed and performed by the members themselves. I first attended the luncheon club by invitation from one of the women I had met in Dodworth in her mid-eighties and with whom I had developed a close friendship. As she said, since I was interested in 'what old folk get up to', she thought I should come to the luncheon club with her and get a good meal in the process. After ensuring that I had permission from the organiser (herself a woman in her early eighties) and that it was clear that I was a student conducting research on old age, I went to one luncheon and was made welcome as a guest. I asked if I could come again and received permission. My friend however was taken aside and told that the dinners were for 'old age pensioners'. If I wanted to continue coming that was fine, but I would have to help out in the kitchen. I was all too happy to oblige, as long as I could still participate in the socialising and talking that happened during the meals and not have to spend all of my time in the kitchen. This was mutually agreed upon. What I did not initially realise, however, was that unlike the centres, the club involves a significant symbolic divide between the members and the 'helpers', that is, the volunteers that make sure the tables are set up, serve the meals, collect dirty dishes, serve tea and coffee and wash the dishes. Although four of the members do a great deal of work both in terms of organising and serving the meals, they attend every week and are not categorised as 'helpers'. The helpers are on a monthly rota system and only two of them come out of the kitchen to eat with the members, so my desire to sit with the members each week and eat with them was not completely unheard of, but it was generally not done and I certainly was the only helper who sat with the members *every* week. The matter was complicated further by the respective chronological ages of the helpers versus the members: in a couple of instances, the helpers were the same age as some of the members, but they preferred to remain apart from the members, making it clear that they were there to serve rather than be served.

Although I did not realise it, as a (1) visibly younger person, who was (2) asking to attend regularly and not monthly, and (3) serve as well as eat, I was trespassing on implicit rules, which produced a fairly awkward situation. I could sense the tension among the organisers and helpers towards me, but at the time did not understand what was wrong. I had asked permission to carry on as I was and been told yes, but I was oblivious to the rules (ones which I had not experienced at the centres, so had not anticipated at the luncheon club), which could not be articulated to me. Essentially, unlike other 'non-old age pensioners' who volunteer as helpers, I had not arrived at the luncheon club in the guise of a volunteer, but rather from the position of a de facto elderly member. Thus, the understanding of what membership signifies – which is tied so closely in this instance to the construction of old age and oldness – and my ignorance of it, combined explosively. There are passages in my fieldnotes about how alienated and discouraged I felt at the luncheon club because I could sense the tension but could not understand it. Normally, I would have backed away, but since the signals coming from the organiser were the only ambiguous ones I received and the members themselves enjoyed having me there, I plodded along. Eventually, when it became obvious that I was reliably going to attend each week and that the organiser could rely on me, that the members liked me being there because I was chatty and friendly and that I had made myself indispensable in the kitchen, the tension began to evaporate.

Arguably, the polarised social categories of 'old' versus 'young' had also been at stake. Although I doubt anyone in my fieldsite would consciously redefine my social place as closer to 'old' than 'young', unconsciously people extended their experience to mine. This was done with comments such as 'do you remember ...' being directed specifically to me, despite being about events from decades before I was born. This was often retracted with a joke, but indicates the way in which seemingly impermeable social categories based on age can become momentarily irrelevant, but then spring back into place. The contradiction between my role as server and my chronological age versus my desire to behave in all other respects as a member was still present, but the terms in which I was placed had shifted.

## Defining 'old age'?: methodological reflections

Data for this research were gathered over fourteen months of fieldwork which began in December 1999, supplemented by a second period of fieldwork in 2003–4, continued residence in Dodworth until 2005 and ongoing connections since that time. I based my collection of data on three intersecting activities: participant observation, in-depth interviews and archival research on local and regional social histories. Because of the difficulties that I discuss more fully in Chapter 4 in marking precisely at what chronological age 'old age' begins, I did not want to delineate my study group in the conventional sense. Instead, because 'being old' is a perception that is constructed in different contexts and between different social actors, a significant component of my research was to explore what the markers of old age are and how they vary. Attending to how these markers were negotiated and used became an important part of my fieldwork. As I anticipated, usage varied from individual to individual (due in part to such characteristics as gender differences, social class, educational backgrounds and work histories), as well as varying according to the context of social interaction for a specific individual (for example, group settings versus one-on-one interactions; with me as a researcher versus with close family members; with children versus grandchildren). How the boundaries of old age were signalled and in what sort of terms provided me with important insights into conceptions of self and the transformations of ageing, as in the example from the luncheon club above.

Although I did not want to limit myself to a traditional definition of older age, I expected that the chronological ages of my research participants would range anywhere from the sixties through the nineties and possibly into the hundreds. Instead, what I experienced was only two women in their late sixties self-identifying as 'old' (by their participation in activities and settings deemed to be for 'old 'uns'). The vast majority of people in my research pool, however, were in their mid-seventies to mid-eighties, with some people in their early seventies, three women in their early nineties and two women who were both one hundred years old.[8] This means that the very oldest research participants were born in 1908 and the youngest was born in 1930. As such, the people I spent time with and interviewed represent multiple age cohorts. Some were only in their early teens when the Second World War started, but others were already parents with two or three children and had been working full time for nearly fifteen years.

Further general demographic details include three-quarters of the people I came to know having either been directly involved in mining or having a father, husband or brother who was. Eighteen men connected with this study worked in the mining industry at some point during their lives, although three of these men entered into other professions later on; another six men never worked in coal mining, with three of these working in the steel industry. Other male occupations of my research participants include bus driving, nursing, shopkeeping, sales, glassworks and gardening. More than two-thirds of the women participating in this project worked outside the home before marriage. Nearly half of the women worked full or part time after they were married. The large majority of my research population left school at 14, although one won a scholarship to attend a regional high school from age 11 to 16 and left with commercial arithmetic training. No one in my research population attended university. All but two couples had children and all had been married, although many were widowed by the time I met them.

Recognising variations in experience between and within age cohorts was something I was attentive to, but I found more often than not that these differences were not easy to discern. One distinction that was more apparent was that women at the younger end of the cohorts tended to have worked full time outside the home more than their slightly older contemporaries. Unsurprisingly, gender and perceptions of variations in class were two other factors which played into my research. As stated in Chapter 1, I attend to gender and class wherever possible in my analysis, but these were not the main objectives of my work and as such they tend to emerge, recede and then emerge again in the text rather than fundamentally structuring my analysis.

Four other main differentiating factors emerged in my research population: some people were members of former mining families but not themselves miners (women and men), some were former miners (men) and some had no personal or familial involvement in the mining industry (both women and men). The fourth broad category that was subjectively significant was whether or not the individual (women and men) came from Dodworth and self-identified as 'old Dodworthers'. Of the people I interviewed formally or informally, a high percentage of people I worked with were born in Dodworth (58 per cent). A further 9 per cent were born in immediately neighbouring villages; 26 per cent were born in the greater Barnsley area (particularly Barnsley itself); 2 per cent were born in Yorkshire but outside the Barnsley area and only 5 per cent were born outside Yorkshire. Given the dominance of Barnsley as the local town only two miles away where Dodworth people would travel to for shopping, work and socialising, this means that 93 per cent of the people I worked with had lived most of their lives within a ten-mile radius of Dodworth, if not immediately in the village itself, which the majority had. This, in turn, meant that many, but not all, of the people in my research population had extensive, long-standing, multifaceted knowledge of each other over many decades. This stemmed from overlapping and intersecting experiences of going to school together, working life, neighbouring, church or chapel and place of residence in the micro-neighbourhoods of the village. Dodworth is thus a densely networked place. Three other important but secondary categories of people I sought out were the younger family members of my research participants (including children and grandchildren), bungalow wardens and long-term middle-aged community residents.

## Not an anthropologist 'at home'

My choice of fieldsite made many people curious. One senior anthropology professor at McGill University in Montreal where I was a doctoral student encouraged me to think about doing work in France instead of Britain, as it was a 'more exotic' setting and would improve my chances of getting a job after earning my doctorate. Some of my peers ridiculed fieldwork in an English-speaking locale as 'easy' although, it must be said, this was a minority opinion. British friends not resident in the Barnsley area could not understand why I would want to live in an area they derided as ugly, boring, poverty-stricken, or dangerous, or all of these. Some people resident in Dodworth found it strange that I had come 'all the way from Canada' to be in Dodworth.

On the other hand, no one questioned my desire to study ageing and old age. This included the older people I came to know who seemed to think that studying old age via themselves was not objectionable, even if they themselves did not self-perceive as 'old'. Fellow academics did not object to me studying ageing, either. Ironically then, old age is deemed worthy of study by both the general public and the academy in a way that Dodworth and Barnsley are not.

But from my perspective, I have always felt that conducting research in Dodworth was as relevant and as challenging as any other fieldsite an anthropologist might choose. While not conducting anthropology at home, I was also not carrying out fieldwork in a setting that was completely unfamiliar. This opened up some interesting ironies in my fieldwork experiences. Despite the many cultural similarities between North America where I grew up and Britain, there were a number of times I was caught off guard by significant cultural divergences and patterns of behaviour that were uncomfortably unfamiliar or unknown to me. I incorporate these experiences into the chapters to come as another level of reflection and analysis, both on ageing as well as on local cultural patterns, such as when I discuss Ella in Chapter 4 and Olive in Chapter 6. The disjuncture between my expectations for comportment and the actual experiences I had was of course not a constant experience, but rather a pattern that was repeated many times throughout my fieldwork. Indeed, it was so marked that I came to call experiences like these in my fieldnotes 'the cringe factor' as a shorthand for my discomfort. By this I mean that my own everyday parameters of 'normal' social discourse were being disrupted in a way that they usually were not. I decided that such involuntary responses on my part were a signal that the situation called for closer attention as fieldwork material – what was it about the interaction that was provoking discomfort on my part? While conducting fieldwork, I always tried to attend to my own reactions as another potential source of cultural knowledge since my responses were so deeply embedded in cultural patterns. In this fashion, I am using the dissonance created in certain contexts as an additional research tool to attempt to reveal more of the ways in which old age is constructed in interaction between generations and between individuals. In using myself explicitly as an analytical device, I seek to complicate boundaries of difference and similarity between self and other.

Relatively few North American anthropologists have carried out fieldwork in Britain, and this work has often been in Scotland and Wales rather than in England (Rapport, 2002: 4). On the other hand, a long-standing indigenous social anthropological tradition of conducting fieldwork in Britain does exist and extends throughout Britain (Edwards, 2000: 9; Rapport, 2002: 17–18). This has prompted reflection within British social anthropology on the implications and challenges of anthropology at home (see, for example, Jackson, 1987; Okely, 1996). Rapport draws our attention to both what 'British' is and what 'home' is and how they are concepts that remain fluid and relational. What brings these concepts together in methodological terms and fieldwork practice is 'a fluency in the forms of interaction in use in those British socio-cultural milieux which are the focus of the research' (2002: 18). Rapport further argues on behalf of this fluency that:

> An anthropologist thoroughly at home in linguistic denotation, and familiar with behavioural form, is more able to appreciate the connotative: to pick up on those niceties of interaction and ambivalences and ambiguities of exchange, where the most intricate (and interesting) aspects of sociocultural worlds are constructed, negotiated, contested and disseminated ... By way of linguistic expertise (verbal and non-verbal) and extra-linguistic adroitness, the field-worker at home in the milieu being studied is well placed to identify those vital differences and diversities ... which provide the dynamo of cultural practice and social process. (Rapport, 2002: 7)

While by no means wishing to detract from the richness and subtleties of anthropology conducted in less familiar sites, I concur with Rapport's point. In particular, I believe that the sort of research questions I came to Dodworth with are especially well suited to working in a 'home' site. This is because the perspective I adopted in my fieldwork into the ageing self, subjectivity, and experience relies so much on paying careful attention to the niceties, ambivalences, ambiguities, negotiation, contestation and dissemination inherent in social life as evoked by Rapport.

### Beginning fieldwork

It was ultimately serendipity that brought me to Dodworth. Certain that I wanted to conduct research in the Barnsley area because of its recent socio-economic history, I could have carried out fieldwork in any number of area villages. Scarce availability of rental accommodation became a crucial determining factor, though, with several fraught weeks searching in vain for a flat in villages I had initially identified. I turned to local contacts at BBC Radio Sheffield for advice as well as a local author in her seventies, whom I had previously met. Both suggested Dodworth and I was also introduced to one of the local Dodworth councillors who was enthusiastic about my project. Fortuitously, I was able to secure a flat above a shop on Dodworth High Street and moved there in December 1999 when I had just turned 27 years old. However, December was also a tricky time to begin fieldwork. The first two weeks were good ones for initiating contacts, but soon the Christmas holidays began taking centre stage and being in touch with people was more difficult. So I turned instead to the archive and local studies section of the Barnsley library, immersing myself in everything I could find on Dodworth and the local area. This period of research proved extremely useful when trying to understand the local social histories I was about to encounter.

Once life returned to normal after Christmas and the Millennium, foundational ethnographic work occupied all of my time. After introducing myself to three of the seven wardens and meeting with them to discuss my research, I started attending weekly events in three different centres, including bingo, whist and teas. Most of these occurred in the evenings, although one was a regular afternoon meeting. All lasted between two and three hours. Each centre's social event is open for anyone who wants to attend. Generally speaking, these are Dodworth residents over retirement age and include both people living in council bungalows and those who lived in their own homes. Out of the forty-three regular members who attended the three main centres I was based in, twenty of them lived in their own homes and not in council bungalows. Over the next couple of months, and in conjunction with the luncheon club, attending these meetings became an invaluable way to meet people and to become a familiar face myself. I spent time learning about the village structure and about life at the centres and club, observing the social and symbolic interactions of older people and what they experienced there. This work was most intensive for the first three months of my fieldwork, but continued throughout as I kept attending the centres' and club activities.

Significantly to the development of my research, after living in Dodworth for a few months I bought a small terraced house with my boyfriend, a British man I had moved to Dodworth with, and who had been my partner for a number of years. Although entirely unwitting on my part, buying the house was to prove hugely significant. Unlike the anonymous flat in the High Street, the house on Holdroyd's Yard that we purchased was firmly entrenched in the social history of many Dodworth families I came to know. A rental property itself for many years until the 1960s, the house and others on Holdroyd's Yard had been home to a surprising number of old Dodworthers. Many stories about the characters who had lived there and how they were connected to other people in the village, alive and dead, began emerging as people came to link me with the Yard. Over the course of my fieldwork, I met people and family members for each decade of the 1900s from 1910 on who had lived or been born in that particular house. Buying this house undoubtedly shaped my fieldwork experiences in multiple ways: it cemented my fascination with the oral histories of Dodworth and in the ways in which local people and places were bound together in those narrative accounts. It was also interpreted, rightly, as a gesture of my committing to Dodworth, something that in a fieldsite where localness and place are so integral to identity and belonging, resonated positively. It appears that living on Holdroyd's Yard gave people the skein required to begin weaving me into the web of stories, lives and related places that predated my arrival and that had already shaped the contours of their own experiences. This is a way of relating to the world, to place and to others that informs subjectivity in powerful ways in Dodworth and one that I shall return to in more depth in Chapter 3.

Via connections made in the centres, I started asking, and being invited, to visit individuals in their homes to speak with them in more depth. Because I would usually do this during the day while continuing to attend centres primarily in the evenings, in many cases I would see people several times a week in a variety of settings. This afforded me a multiple perspective on a number of situations with a number of individuals. In turn, I had the chance to observe and reflect on how the ageing self was constructed in social interactions over time and also to ask people themselves for their own perceptions of these behaviours and interactions. There were some individuals that I was never able to visit in their own homes owing to factors such as illness, regular babysitting duties and mourning, but nearly everyone I asked if I could visit accepted. Significantly, given the traditional divides in the community between male and female spheres, the only person to refuse an interview – and someone I came to know quite well – was a man in his seventies who said that talking about his life and himself 'isn't for me'. This was in turn interpreted by some of my women friends in the village as gender-appropriate behaviour.

The public meeting places were invaluable spaces for informal, relaxed interaction and participation. On the other hand, they also attracted a self-selecting group of older people, those who like 'mixing', playing bingo or whist or attending luncheon club. Another important consideration was the extent to which the centres were dominated by women and by playing bingo. In any older population, it is highly probable that there will be more women than men owing to demographic pressures, but the centres and luncheon club were all run by women (with a few key men at one centre). Many of the men I met over the year who did not attend centres said this was because they did not like bingo and besides, the centres were 'a women's get together', in the words of one. Indeed, of the forty-three regular centre participants, only eight were men.

My challenge then became to move beyond this sphere and meet non-centre participants as well as more men. The people who proved most difficult to meet were of course the ones who did not attend the public meeting places (both men and women) or any of the other activities I attended with key informants. Obviously, I wanted to access these people because they might offer interesting counter-voices on experiences of older age, but even by mobilising all my contacts, this was difficult to achieve. In addressing this problem, I started by meeting spouses of centre members who did not themselves attend the centre. The next step was to spend time in male-dominated spaces such as the Tap Hole, a bar in the former Working Men's Club – renamed, not insignificantly, as the Dodworth Social Club. With the help of friends in the village and over time, I did build up these male contacts and contacts with people who did not publicly socialise. To my surprise, I found that the snowball method was sluggish at best and not very effective in Dodworth. I think this is because although people were happy for me to spend time with them, 'going visiting' was not something they themselves did. Informal discussions with other researchers confirm this and also indicate that entertaining typically was not something British working-class families did, preferring instead to meet in more public spaces such as clubs and pubs. As such, I could not tag along when people went to visit friends (because they generally did not) and people were reticent to refer me on for fear of imposing on others.[9] It is also likely that people wanted to protect themselves from the accusation of meddling in their neighbours' affairs and that meeting peers in public places helped protect the integrity of private spaces. There were important individual exceptions to this which helped me enormously, but generally speaking this was the pattern.

In the case of the men, I think that some of the difficulties I experienced were compounded by the powerful gender divisions in the village, which are still present. I was not initially aware of this and, still in the first flush of fieldwork, it took me a while to realise how segregated by gender spaces are in Dodworth for older people. Going into a pub or drinking alcohol are not activities most women in their seventies and eighties pursued while younger nor in the present day. On the other hand, they were, and continue to be for some, critical aspects of men's social worlds, being also an extension of their work world when younger. As a woman, it was viewed as perfectly acceptable that I participate in the strongly female-dominated centres and visit women in their homes. However, the male meeting spaces, particularly at the pub and Dodworth Social Club were not seen as appropriate places for me to be by either gender. I was also warned about the dangers of visiting men alone in their homes, partly out of concern for my reputation. Indeed, the fear of being talked about was so strong for some widowed men and women that they would worry about sitting together in public places or visiting each other in their homes, practices that were usually assiduously avoided.

Furthermore, I was enmeshed in the destabilising experience of conducting research in an unfamiliar Western setting. Because I was white, English-speaking and had a British partner, I was expected to know the social rules that governed everything from gender relations to funeral etiquette to linguistic nuance even though many local practices and understandings were unfamiliar to me as I had never before lived in Britain. I had previously always lived in the United States and Canada and thus ironically, while I did share enough basic cultural principles with my British interlocutors to sense these unspoken assumptions and adjust my behaviour accordingly, I did not always recognise the need to question these practices immediately as one might do in a less familiar cultural setting. This is one of the problematic aspects of conducting fieldwork in a Western setting as a foreign westerner. On the other hand, the cultural practices were also at times familiar enough that I could ask and process complicated ideas about self and experience with a richness that might have suffered from a deeper language barrier or cultural gulf.

Perhaps unsurprisingly, given the deep gender divisions of a mining community which persist for the generation I was engaging with, I internalised two social messages. The first was that as a woman, the tap room was not a suitable place for me. Second, I internalised the feeling that the seat of 'real culture' was that of the *men* of Dodworth who could tell me about mining life, the graft, the danger, the camaraderie. Instead, what I learned more about are the intersecting worlds of the home where the spheres of men and women do overlap (especially once retired), the public spaces where women dominate and the private domains of both women and men. This is not to say that I only spent time with women and that I never entered 'male' spaces. To the best of my ability, I tried to balance both of these intersecting spheres and to be attuned to the differences between them as well as to the similarities. I also learned a great deal about the heterogeneity of Dodworth which I discussed earlier in this chapter in terms of male and female employment from the late 1920s through the 1980s and indeed, today. This underlines the extent to which this was an ethnographic study, engaged with the today of people's lives, but simultaneously (because of the interests of the people I studied), it is also deeply attuned to tracing the social history and oral history of the older residents of Dodworth.

## Deepening the contacts: in-depth interviews

The following stage of research was much more in depth, conducted with a significantly smaller group of people. As the experience of old age is constituted intersubjectively, it was key that I trace the nature of the everyday relationships, activities and practices that the older people I worked with engaged in. As stated in Chapter 1, this included occasions such as shopping, visits from family and friends, attending hospital appointments, attending social events, taking cake decorating classes, visiting hospitalised spouses or friends, attending social clubs, going to funerals and reception teas afterwards, visiting friends in residential homes, dealing with insurance brokers, handling government forms, going to the post office, cooking, cleaning, chatting with neighbours, gardening, watching crown green bowls matches, visiting the mobile library, watching television and going on walks. A great deal of time was spent simply sitting at home and talking, as well. My closest friends came to be three widowed women (two of whom have themselves been friends since the 1930s) and two married couples. Sadly, just at the end of my fieldwork one of these men died and the other married couple moved two hours to the west of Dodworth to live in a residential home. Sharing hours, week after week with these and other people provided insight into a number of the key aspects of daily life analysed in this book, including narrativity, social history, memory work, village knowledge, concepts of old age, intergenerational relations, temporality and the positioning of self. Whenever possible, I tried also to balance my observation of and participation in these activities by asking people for their reflections on, and perceptions of, what transpired.

During research I was alert to the resources (in terms of social and symbolic capital) individuals drew on to mediate the experience of 'being old' in the context of social change. When I first arrived, I believed that one of these would be the symbolic capital of the recent industrial coal-mining past that former miners and members of mining communities would hold. What I found instead was a much more complicated context where the demise of mining was one part of a larger, fundamental transformation in the order of things. Additionally, as much as the industrial past was at times glorified, it was also recognised as damaging and dangerous. In many cases, having children and grandchildren in well-paying, professional careers and not working as manual labourers in heavy industry was a more significant source of social capital than having family members who had been in the coal mining industry.

Personal narratives were crucial in order to elicit notions of self and, in turn, to be able to situate these narratives within local history. In interviews, I paid particular attention to people's sense of self in the present; their sense of self in relation to the past and their sense of self in interactive settings with other people and with social institutions. I was also interested by how older people reconstruct the past and how they place themselves within it. What events, historical and individual, marked their lives and senses of self most deeply? These events often emerged over the course of many interactions rather than suddenly in an interview, but once I became familiar with individual life stories I was able to ask more specific questions towards this end. The social power of memory became evident during fieldwork and I became increasingly interested in it. How people narrate memories of their lives and their surroundings is one way of commenting on history, but also revealing of their relationship with the present world. Frequent comparisons between today and the past revealed attitudes about the relative fragmentation of social life, about the changing social environment (work patterns, family fabric), about the shifting social roles of older people and about their worlds of reference (this includes, to varying degrees, Dodworth, Yorkshire, Britain, Europe and the Commonwealth).

In addition to participant observation and interviewing, the third component of my research was archival. Using local studies collections in the Sheffield, Leeds and Barnsley public libraries, the Goodchild Wakefield Archive Collection and the University of Birmingham Library, I spent six weeks over the course of fieldwork conducting archival and census research. I was interested in two inter-secting topics: local and regional histories (especially the social history of Dodworth and South Yorkshire mining communities) and creating a picture of the transformations that had occurred in the area via census returns (in terms of housing, migration patterns and employment). Incorporating this informa-tion into my research helped me understand the locale better as well as to familiarise myself with events and ways of life to which the older people I worked with referred. It also permitted me another perspective on historical events, which helped me better comprehend how older people were positioning them-selves in respect to the remembered past.

## Notes

1 I use pseudonyms in this book for all people and centres to protect anonymity. Dodworth, however, is not a pseudonym. This is in keeping with local pride in the identity and specificity of Dodworth as Dodworth that its residents strongly assert. To attempt to mask its identity via a pseudonym would fly in the face of this link between people and place that local residents are deeply invested in.

2 Meaning 'day holes'; the 'h' is often silent in the Barnsley version of the Yorkshire accent.

3 Although note that between the two world wars, some parts of the North benefited from growth in new industries such as electronics and motor car manufacturing (Taylor, A. J. P. 1965: 305).

4 'Shut the door'.

5 'Tripping over the curb'.
6 For a rich analysis of nicknames and joking in nearby Royston, see Cave (2001).
7 These holiday trips, often day-trips, to destinations like seaside resorts were very popular and sponsored by community groups. This was due in part to the low car-ownership rates and the high cost of travel abroad, trends which have changed radically since the 1980s.
8 This study population is composed of ninety-six people that I came to know over the course of fieldwork and had repeated informal conversations and interactions with. Of this group, I conducted in-depth, taped interviews with twenty-seven people and had multiple interviews over the course of fieldwork with ten of these individuals.
9 The fear of imposing or 'putting on people' is a leitmotif that played out throughout my fieldwork; I return to it in Chapter 4.

# 3

# Endings, pasts and futures: temporal complexities and memory talk

## Introduction

Relationships with time came to preoccupy me in Dodworth. On the one hand, I was aware of social stereotypes that posit older people are 'lost in the past', but this was emphatically not the case for the people I came to know in Dodworth. On the other hand, Dodworth is a place where the past matters a great deal, namely through 'memory talk' whereby the past is highly valorised locally across generations and intersects with claims of belonging. Considerations of temporal relations and their meaning are thus rendered more complex in light of this cultural dynamic. As such, in this chapter I pay detailed critical attention to two distinctive aspects of temporality – experience of and through time – that emerged in Dodworth. The first of these are the ways in which, despite not being 'lost in the past', temporality can be said to be distinctive for older people. The second is the ways in which the past and talking about the past helps configure a sense of self as an 'old Dodworther' or not. A consideration of both aspects permits me to begin fleshing out with ethnographic detail the connections between the ageing self, subjectivity and temporality that I sketched in Chapters 1 and 2.

In Chapter 1, I outlined key parameters for an approach to the ageing self that takes temporality more fully into account. There I argued that narrativity and temporality figure powerfully in the creation of self, that both are bound up in the ontology of everyday life and in processes of social interaction through which people make meaning and make sense of the world. I drew attention to the possibility that as one's subjective position in the world shifts, owing to physical, social and cultural factors, one's relationship with time and narrative accounts of experience may also be transformed. I also considered the work of Hazan and Heikkinen to help me further consider distinctive forms of temporality and selfhood in older age. For his part, Hazan considers how the people he worked with were caught between competing temporal tensions of fixity and change: he argues that social stereotypes assume a static time universe for older people but that this is in great contrast to their own experiences of constant change. He finds that in response, day centre members reconfigured temporal frames into a present-facing limbo time. Rather than creating a sense of fractured personhood, Hazan argues that this instead was restorative to members' sense of well-being. By contrast, Heikkinen documents shifts over a fifteen-year period in temporality and subjectivity for a cohort of older Finns. A changing sense of time from future-oriented to present-facing and then finally to a freeing form of temporal detachment in her research cohort attests to the different possibilities the ageing self is attuned to.

Drawing on my ethnographic fieldwork, in this chapter I develop Hazan and Heikkinen's insights on temporal dynamics and ageing by contrasting them with my findings based on older people's experiences of everyday life as lived in non-institutional settings. First, I consider the distinctive aspects of temporality that repeatedly emerged as my fieldwork progressed and I became increasingly incorporated into the daily lives of older individuals. Time came to feel differently weighted, a sensation that accrued over multiple encounters with various individuals. By this, I mean that there were different temporal inflections placed on elements of daily life than I was previously accustomed to. This included a sense of urgency and anxiety over timeliness, intergenerational and interpersonal tensions over relationships to the past and to time, the importance of fixed schedules in contrast with 'empty' time, the salience of temporal markers such as silver and golden wedding anniversaries and expectations for the future.

Second, I became intensely aware of the acute significance of the past to the people I was working with: Dodworth is a place where memories of the past matter. The past, an elastic historical period in which multiple decades of the twentieth century are brought into focus at various conversational and rhetorical junctures, is commonly woven into everyday discussions of the present day. 'The past' in this sense is a supremely fluid moment. It encompasses a wide slice of time, ranging from the childhood (and sometimes before) of the speaker to more recent moments. Memory talk is bound up in discussion of transformed local landscapes, in iconic village figures, in memories of everyday folk and in places, sites and houses that may no longer be physically present but which still determinedly occupy social space. Knowledge of Dodworth's past and a facility in evoking these created a sense of belonging for many village residents, but also excluded others. In this sense, the accumulative experiences of change through time deeply informed identity and subjectivity of a number of people I worked with. This dynamic is not limited to the older cohorts I know best, but is instead evident intergenerationally in Dodworth. Thus, how temporality is linked to place and helps shore up a sense of belonging is one central consideration of this chapter. I explore the work of memory in Dodworth and its complex interactions with place, absence, social relations and social rupture.

Ultimately, in this chapter I explore the ways in which older age can challenge normative models of temporal experience. I seek to examine the consequences of shifting temporal relations for subjectivity not aligning with these norms. I wish to resist the commonplace assumptions that older people become self-evidently past-facing and that they do not engage meaningfully with ideas about the future

– ideas which stem from the assumed alignment of older age with the end of life and thus the end of time. As I stated in Chapter 1, the assumption that the proximity of death is a dominant element informing the constitution of the ageing self is one I challenge. In so doing, I call attention to the distinctive relationship with time that emerges for many older people, but which is flattened, sterilised and stigmatised by negative social stereotypes. To begin, I turn first to aspects of temporal structuring.

## Temporal structuring of daily life

The daily and weekly schedules of my research participants were an important consideration for how their everyday time was organised. Nearly all the older people I came to know have highly structured weekly schedules and would often recite them by rote. In Chapter 2, I discussed the centres and one reason people gave for attending them is that it helps structure their time. Indeed, my research participants who attended the centres would often describe their weekly schedule around centre meetings. Mrs Ryder's description was typical in this respect:

> Monday and Tuesday I stay in and Monday I do my washing. Wednesday I go to Mitchelson centre, Thursday I go to Stonecliffe centre and Friday I go to Hemsworth centre.[1] Saturday I stay in. Sunday I go with either Keith or Peter and they pick me up, take me to church and then we have our dinner. If I'm at Keith's, then we go to the Club after dinner and if I'm at Peter's he brings me home before my tea and I have my tea here.

For Mrs Ryder, attending the centres forms a significant element of her schedule, how time is 'passed' and how the passage of time is marked. So too does the weekly household cleaning. Another key consideration is the role of her sons, Keith and Peter, in helping facilitate her travel and opportunities for socialising with family, at church and in the working men's club. Mrs Ryder, who I met at two of the centres she attends, was nearly ninety and although born in Huddersfield, had moved to next-door Silkstone Common as a very young child and then to Dodworth upon marriage to a Dodworth man. He had predeceased her, but they had four children together and her children still lived in the area. After leaving school, she worked in the rug mill and then was 'in service' for a well-to-do family in the Leeds area. Both her husband and her father worked in the Levitt-Hagg pit and one of her sons also worked as a miner. She is well known in the centres and a regular attender.

While the centres help organise the weekly schedules of people who attend them, the centres also observe and mark the cycle of seasonal events, such as Christmas, Easter, Bonfire Night, the birthdays of members and the running of the Grand National horse race. Thus, the very act of attending the centres helps reinscribe certain temporal rhythms onto days and weeks that might otherwise lack them. The recitation by rote of one's weekly schedule was such a regular narrative form, however, that I was also struck by the way in which maintaining a full and regular schedule was in, and of, itself a source of pleasure. This calls to mind what Adam (2010) terms 'ontological security' and which I examine in closer detail later in this chapter. Such specific and regular use of time and of place is extremely commonplace among my research population and was not limited to centre members. On particular days and at particular times the same people can be seen walking their established routes on the way to particular errands or tasks such as collecting pension payments, going to the mobile library van, attending centres or the club, or waiting to catch a certain bus in order to go shopping in Barnsley.

Daily structuring in relation to cleaning, for women, is also an important link with past practices, which mirrors and maintains the patterns of a lifetime, while simultaneously navigating change, as evident in this interview segment with Emma. In her early eighties when I first met her, Emma and her husband, Ernest, lived in a council bungalow in Dodworth and attended one of the centres. Emma was born in Dodworth and Ernest in neighbouring Silkstone; they had lived in both villages after marrying in 1941 and returned to Dodworth after Ernest retired from the Mines Rescue service where he had worked up to a senior position. He, like Emma's father and brother and his own brothers, worked in the coal industry and had worked for many years as a miner while Emma's mother had worked in service for a wealthy local landowner until she married. Emma finished school aged 14 and went to work at the Barnsley Canister tin factory in the mid-1930s, giving up work on marriage to start a family and look after the home. She is now a grandmother and a great-grandmother, with some of her grandchildren and great-grandchildren living locally and others abroad. I asked Emma if she used to do different housecleaning tasks on different days and she replied:

EMMA:  I still do! Wash on a Monday, bedrooms on a Tuesday and then through
            here [the living room] on a Friday.
CATHRINE: And Wednesday you have off!
EMMA:  And Wednesday I go out and Thursday we go up there [to the centre].
CATHRINE: How about on the weekend?
EMMA:  Well, we don't go nowhere much love … you see, when you can't walk,
            you … and he [Emma's husband] gave car up when he were seventy, he
            says I'm not driving no more after seventy.

Cleaning is particularly spoken of by many of the women in my research group as a source of activity, 'something to do'. Thus, while cleaning is emphasised as a way of 'filling time' on an explicit level of discourse, its salience can also be understood as a symbolic way of introducing rhythm and structure into days and weeks, as well as being a way of maintaining continuity of social roles across a lifetime in this highly gender divided sphere of domestic work. Cleaning intersects with personal time (scheduling in the present day as well as ordering throughout one's lifetime) and historical time (continuity with the past when these activities were done for a family and in the face of former environmental pressures from the local coal industry which produced a never-ending source of oily particulate that needed removing from houses, people and clothes).

Cleaning, however, was not the only way people spoke of passing the time. Like cleaning, most ways of passing time followed strong gender divides, with gardening, visits from family members and watching the television being an exception and something that both women and men enjoyed. Dog walking (at specific times in the day), listening to music (big band, brass band, male voice choirs, opera), going to the club or pub and watching local sporting matches, such as crown green bowls, were predominantly men's activities to pass the time. For women (in addition to cleaning and housekeeping), knitting, volunteer work, reading, embroidery, baking, shopping and seeing friends were common ways to pass the time.

Attention to fixed schedules, precise structuring and having pastimes contrasted sharply with the spans of 'empty' time that people also express. This empty time or motionless waiting can feel heavy and strangulating. Many times I would arrive at someone's home unexpectedly and be greeted with 'Oh, I'm glad you've come – I was getting so fed up with myself', indicating my visit as a welcome relief from boredom. For some, this stems from the inability to move about easily or for sustained periods of time. Indeed, the extent to which someone gets out and can do things for themselves are protectively maintained for as long as possible for fear of 'giving in' to old age. However, impaired mobility can restrict people to the house for long periods of time and also reflects for some the shrinking social world that impaired mobility can bring. Changed corporeality can come to interfere with everyday expectations and abilities to 'do', which in turn can prompt shifts in one's perception and experiences of time. I explain this in more detail in Chapter 5.

But of course, chronological ageing does not map simply on to corporeal experiences. People's physical abilities vary greatly from individual to individual. Ivy, for instance, in her eighties, goes on long hikes each Friday with her walking group, followed by whist and bingo every Friday evening. Vivienne, finding it increasingly difficult to walk the quarter mile from her home to the High Street shops, GP surgery or library in Dodworth, had the financial means to purchase a motorised scooter which she now relies on. But even for people who have found ways around increasing physical impairment, days can still feel very long: Vivienne, a dedicated luncheon club member, recounted to me how in the mornings she gets up 'very often around 7 o'clock in the morning, I make a cup of tea, then go back and try to sleep or read a bit and get up at quarter to nine, which shortens the day'. Her account contrasts strongly with Ivy above but also Anne (in her eighties) who related to me one day in conversation that some of her family members worry that she gets bored living on her own to which she laughed and replied 'Bored? Not likely! I don't have *time* to be bored!'. Anne, born and raised in Dodworth, has a large family spanning three generations with many of them living nearby. Her father, brother and nephew were miners but her husband, whom she met one night at a dance (as many of her contemporaries also did), worked as a labourer on the railways but had died a number of years before I met her. Anne, like many other women I came to know, worked part time at various jobs after her children started school, including a window washing round. Anne's comments about not being bored fit neatly with her sense of self as independent, able to go on her own to Barnsley, to run errands and actively keeping in touch with her friends and family.

Despite these individual differences, as a cohort, the people I worked with spoke of the activities and tasks they carried out to 'pass the time' whereas I was often quizzed by them on how I was 'spending' my time. This linguistic nuance is a revealing inflection that hinges on ideas of time as a commodity for some but not all. Younger adults, enmeshed in the ebb and flow of demands made by the workplace, educational institutions, or young family life have time to spare, spend, waste and lose, but seemingly have precious little time to pass. Older people, no longer bound by these considerations in the same ways, have a surfeit of time which cannot be spent and instead must be passed. However, at times this feels like a burden that cannot be lifted rather than a useful resource. Adam has written how unlike the value of money which is always in positive relation to higher quantities (the more the better), in regards to time, more is only better if one 'has *not* got any ... having time decreases its value ... time abundance is accorded a low social value and scarcity a high one ... Time is like currency. Its value fluctuates with supply and demand' (1990: 114). To illustrate her point, Adam invites us to consider those with too much time on their hands, such as the incarcerated and the unemployed.

In an instructive contrast, consider Craig Jeffrey's recent work on 'timepass' among young middle-class Indian men in Uttar Pradesh. Highly educated but chronically unemployed, this generational cohort are waiting for opportunity to knock but macro-level processes mean that it may never do so. And yet, rather than an excess of time engendering simply a feeling of hopelessness and emptiness for these young men, Jeffrey argues that waiting may instead also offer a rich source of positive collaborative energy to work for social change (2008). Such possibilities for young men in north India compared with the relative absence of similar ones for older people in Dodworth speaks, I believe, to a very different set of social expectations and aspirations because of their different position in relation to time and to the assumption that older people, if anything, are simultaneously running out of time. They have both too much time and not enough, a temporal conundrum that inflects their subjectivity.

## Key wedding anniversaries as temporal markers

While daily and weekly patterns were important temporal markers, wedding anniversaries were interesting markers of a different sort. Silver (twenty-five years of marriage), ruby (forty years), golden (fifty years) and diamond (sixty years) wedding anniversaries are of particular importance to demarcate in conversation. For example, Hilda told me how she first married, aged 18, in 1948 and was married for seventeen years before her husband died. She then underlined this for me by saying 'I would have had my golden wedding anniversary with him if he was still alive', but that since she remarried in 1968, she and her second husband celebrated their silver wedding anniversary in 1993. On another occasion, Violet was telling me about how she married her first husband when she was aged 23 in 1944. They had been married for twenty-four years when he was killed in an accident at work. She later remarried and was married for twenty-one years when her second husband died of a heart attack. Recounting these events made Violet cry and through her tears she summed up these forty-five years of bifurcated marriage with 'and I've never had a silver wedding'.

Troubled by similar thoughts in the months building up to August 2001, Emma repeatedly told me how it would have been her and Ernest's diamond wedding anniversary if he had lived. She also repeatedly told me the story over a period of months about how she kept teasing Ernest that she was going to make a speech at the anniversary party that they had been planning for years. She said she was going to get up and say how 'we've had some stormy passages, but we weathered it!', but she never had the chance because he died nine months before their anniversary. She mentioned this frequently and the month of what would have been their anniversary celebration was an emotionally difficult time for her. Similarly, Vivienne was profoundly upset in the summer of 2001 around her anniversary date, which would have been her golden wedding celebration, although her husband had died more than fifteen years ago.

These special anniversaries condense and concentrate meaning and time in a powerful way, holding a great deal of symbolic weight, which is more than just about the longevity of a couple's married life. This pattern of anniversaries serves as a general social marker that moves towards the more personal. Paralleling Leach's observation about Western time being paradoxically irreversible and repetitive (1961: 125), wedding anniversaries illustrate a linear time organised around key symbolic moments, but they also occur repeatedly within time (i.e. annually or clusters of years), which introduces a sort of rhythmic structure. Temporality is, in these cases, condensed and thus experienced differently from a simple linear movement from year to year. There is a blurring of time that is no longer measured by years, but by clusters of years which add up to a silver, a golden or a diamond wedding anniversary. In this way a certain play with time and temporal experience occurs, made possible by the depth of temporal experience.

Furthermore, wedding anniversaries demonstrate how expected markers of social time are embedded in the subjective experience of the individual, marking out a predictable future, independent of (or transcending) the singularities of trajectories as actually experienced. This is why Hilda, Violet, Emma and Vivienne seem to feel cheated out of their key anniversary celebrations owing to the deaths of their spouses. They grieve for a possible or anticipated future which will never arrive. In a complicated temporal turn, the anticipated markers of anniversaries that can never come to be are behind them (and have become the future anterior in this sense), but despite them being in the past, the anticipation of them still maintains an organising power at the symbolic level. The symbolic power of these anniversaries remains as a temporal punctuation even though the moment is no longer ever going to be realised at the individual level because the spouse has died. Also, since the anniversaries that do happen are a positive occasion for reinscribing social relations (occasions which do not arise as often as they used to), they are losses to be mourned when the occasion does not arise because to the death of a spouse. This then becomes a double loss: both of the spouse, but also of a socially reaffirming moment which in the spouse's absence is not possible to celebrate. Notices are sometimes placed in the *Barnsley Chronicle* memorial page when one of the spouses is absent, but more often than not it is silent, passing unmarked apart from brief mentions by the living spouse as in the examples above.

## Haste and urgency

A third distinctive temporal reference point among my research participants is a sense of urgency about time that was repeatedly transmitted to me during my fieldwork. For example, I called Margaret in the morning to see if we were still going to attend the Women's Institute[2] meeting together that evening. We agreed to meet at her house with her warning me to 'be prompt!' for 6:30 p.m. because the seats at the meetings go quickly and she wanted to be there as early as possible. She can see the front door of the community centre where the meetings are held from her kitchen window; it is no more than a minute's walk from her house to the centre. I suggested I would come at 6:20 p.m. instead and she agreed that would be better. When I arrived at her house, she already had her coat and shoes on and was ready to go. She had been standing behind her net curtains in the kitchen keeping an eye out on the centre to see if we could go over, but the lights were not turned on yet. After a few nervous minutes, she decided it was time to go anyway and so off we went. Apart from the committee members who were moving about in the centre without many lights on, we were the first ones there. Margaret saved four chairs together, two for us and one each for Elsie and Mavis.

At a very different, less formal setting, Anne and Evelyn were worrying about the seating at the Stafford centre dinner. I arrived ten minutes early and they were just going in to claim their seats. We stopped for a chat on the way into the main room. No one else had arrived yet apart from them, the warden and me. Despite this, Anne told Evelyn to hurry up and sit down at the table so no one took her seat, an urgency that to me seemed misplaced and unnecessary. To Anne, it was perfectly reasonable and indeed it would have been foolish to have been more blasé about. Anxiety over timeliness was a reoccurring pattern in my fieldwork experiences. Being on time or even early was an absolute and yet unspoken requirement of membership for the centre groups. I learned this through personal experience, arriving just after 6 p.m. only once for whist and never doing it again for fear of being asked not to come at all.

This recurring pattern of time anxiety and time urgency perplexed me. Before beginning fieldwork, I anticipated that with fewer demands on their time, older people's daily schedules would be highly flexible and carefree. I found instead the very opposite with the maintenance of regularity and timeliness instead highly valorised. The perception of the passage of time and how time moves also seemed distinctly different for my research population than for younger people. For example, anniversaries condense time. There is an urgency in getting to places early and being ready on time. This translated for me into an awareness of the critical importance of being on time (which I soon internalised because of my research participants' expectations) but also a certain amount of frustration and irritation on my part with their punctuality. No matter how early or ready to go I was, the people I was meeting were earlier and had been waiting longer in advance. This urgency about time and perception of how time moves is in part a management skill to handle the demands that reduced bodily mobility create, but it was also explained to me as being due to the pleasurable anticipation of getting out and doing things rather than staying at home wondering how to 'pass' or 'fill' one's time. It also could reflect a certain anxiety about not being excluded in the face of a wider social marginalisation, which colours most older people's daily experience.

### Older age as embodied transformation in temporal patterns and priorities

Like most older people I knew in Dodworth, Ernest, in his mid-eighties and retired from coal-mining work since the age of 65, does not think of himself as 'old':

> ERNEST: As far as I'm concerned, I've never really felt old, I've known I've been getting old, but I've never really felt it ... it isn't until these last two years that I've realised I've been getting older ... I've been pretty healthy ... at work I had a medical examination every year ... it didn't really hit me until I started with this head-do, you see, twelve months ago ... and I'm eighty-four now and eighty-five next January, so uh, up 'til eighty-four, I never really, felt any different ...
>
> EMMA (Ernest's wife): You've slowed down a bit.
>
> ERNEST: Oh, I've slowed down, but apart from slowing down.
>
> EMMA: You used to run about.
>
> ERNEST: The slowing, the slowing down comes gradual, so very gradual ... that you haven't realised it, the slowing down process.
>
> CATHRINE: What is slowing down? What does that refer to? Do you mean everyday things?
>
> ERNEST: The physical, physically ... I wouldn't say mental because uh, uh, I mean even now, we [referring to him and Emma] both have our wits about us, you know!

While not feeling old, Ernest nevertheless recognises changes in his body, a slowing down which is due to ageing. Linked to these changes is a phrase which I heard him use on many occasions which demonstrates some of what 'old age' signified to him. One late spring evening, we were walking together on the way to the club from his home. As we approached a steep hill that was between us and a pint of beer, Ernest said to me: 'No rushing any more! ... My rushing days are done.'

This turn of phrase was his way of pre-emptively letting me know that he (and consequently I) was going to take his time getting up the hill and to walk up it slowly but steadily. His health at the time was stable, but he'd 'get puffed'[3] and light-headed with too much heavy physical exertion. On paper, the phrase 'my rushing days are done' sounds maudlin, as if Ernest is mourning a loss of busy days and dejectedly accepting the onset of old age. However, the way he would say it and what it connotes conveyed a sense of paced moderation, a recognition of a release from the demands of work and raising a family, which meant that there was no need to feel pressed for time or to try and get everything done at all at once. While he certainly did not mean that he was no longer active, Ernest's expectations about being older included a reorganisation of his temporal patterns and priorities to accommodate the physical changes of his body and to make the most of the new possibilities brought about by shifts in his social position. Physical change is thus a marker that indicates an alteration in the relationship with the self and time.

A second level of significance to Ernest getting 'puffed' and not wanting to rush is made clearer by Andrew Cave's work in a nearby village called Royston, only a few miles away from Dodworth (2001). Cave's work is a study of how regional and socio-occupational language varieties (that of coal mining) work as markers of social identity. In his fieldwork experiences, he began noticing how greetings between male friends were 'sometimes quickly followed by references to the fact that some coalminers have difficulty breathing because they are suffering from industrial diseases such as pneumoconiosis', expressions such as 'let him get his breath' (2001: 190). Pneumoconiosis is a serious condition brought on by years of exposure underground to fine particles of coal dust. These particles settle in the lungs and can severely restrict normal breathing and many men eventually die from the condition. Not all miners have developed pneumoconiosis, but many have and there has been a protracted debate about compensation due to these men by the government. Few men have received payments, a point of great public indignation in the coalfields. Cave draws our attention to how 'when a coal miner requests time to "get his breath" or when his colleague demands it on his behalf, those present recognise it as a necessary pause, an integral part of the greeting process' (2001: 193). He explains that this pause can be read on a variety of levels: a physical need to ease breathlessness, but also as a

> symbolic pause which pays respect … (one which draws) attention to one's poor state of health due to industrial disease, but in an acceptable mode, without seeming to demand unnecessary attention. Against a wider cultural context these linguistic routines operate as clear acts of identity, acknowledgements that during their working lives some men have swallowed a lot of dust and importantly, most of them are 'not getting owt for it'.[4] (2001: 193)

Ernest, a miner from the age of 14 until his retirement at age 65, never spoke of 'dust on the chest' in terms of himself and to my knowledge he was not diagnosed with pneumoconiosis. However, he was well spoken of and well regarded in Dodworth as a lifelong mining man. It is highly possible that the linguistic routine Cave documents and explains in Royston is one that Ernest was borrowing to evoke his own breathing problems in this culturally acceptable mode, one that is specifically tied to the industrial history of the area. Ernest employs it in reference to ageing, but also perhaps as part of his wider identity as a coal miner and his four decades of experience underground, breathing dust. In relationship to time, Ernest uses it to stake a claim to a different pace, one not premised on the moral valorisation of speed, but one necessitated by his transformed corporeality brought on not just by age but also by particular socio-economic conditions and experiences.

## A simultaneous disavowal of and engagement with the future

In Chapter 1 I quote Luckmann on the production of self being about retrospection (referring to the past) and projection (looking towards the future) (1991:163). In a similar vein, Charles Taylor writes that:

> As I project my life forward and endorse the existing direction or give it a new one, I project a future story, not just a state of the momentary future but a bent for my life to come. This sense of *my life as having a direction towards what I am not yet* is what Alasdair MacIntyre captures in his notion quoted above that life is seen as a 'quest'. (1989: 48; emphasis added)

While anticipation and desire for the unfolding of future events plays a significant role in the creation of self, my research participants had a specific relationship with this aspect of temporality which calls the linearity of the above into question. Occasionally, when I asked in interviews how they felt about the future, people would respond positively, such as here with Mary:

> CATHRINE: Do you have dreams for the future? Things you want to do?
> MARY: Yeah, definitely, yes definitely. Um . . . as I say we're hoping to do this, this cruise in March or April. And what we'll do is book and we'll have a cheap holiday so that us money builds up, or go on us cruise and then have a few cheap holidays after.

Mary and her husband Tom are, without a doubt, one of the best travelled couples I met and one of the most active pairs among my research population. Mary, born and bred in Dodworth, was in her mid-seventies when I met her, as was her husband Tom. Mary's father and two brothers had worked as miners, as had Tom until he broke his back in a pit accident and then retrained as a nursing home caretaker. Mary worked before marriage in two different mills and then a factory part time after marriage, retraining as a nurse in her forties while raising a family with Tom, and earlier had worked in munitions for the war effort. When I knew them, they seemed (largely driven by Mary) to be in the middle of an extended period of travelling, both abroad and in Britain and would talk with great pleasure and anticipation about when they were next going away. Their desire and physical ability to travel seemed in many ways to mirror their openness on to the world and their gusto for doing everything that they could while they still had the chance, both in a matter of fact anticipation of ageing, but also as a way of postponing its onset.

Despite Mary's optimism, a more typical response to my questions about the future to the older people I worked with would be people asserting that they do not *have* a future. They would also assert a sense of 'living on borrowed time'. Consider this excerpt from my fieldnotes after two separate visits with Vivienne:

> Just as I was leaving Vivienne's house after spending a couple of hours together she said that she'd told Mrs Parkin at the luncheon club during the last dinner there how one of the questions I had asked her in an interview was how she thought of or felt about the future because she wanted to hear what someone else had to say because she herself does not feel she *has* future. I asked what Mrs Parkin had said and Vivienne said that she'd agreed with her and that they'd 'sort of had a good laugh over it'.

> I went to visit with Vivienne to wish her an early happy birthday since I will be away on the actual day and we chatted for an hour and a half about past and present events, particularly about her 'first true love' from when she was fifteen to twenty-two. She says that they never had a sexual relationship but that when they were seeing each other she couldn't wait to get down into the woods for kisses and cuddles together and that 'it was lovely'. Then, when I was leaving, she told me how one of her daughters on the weekend had told her to 'stop living in the past!' because Vivienne had been reminiscing about when she and her husband used to take trips together and had had a new blossoming of romance after they retired and before he died. Vivienne told me, 'Well, I mean, what have I got to look forward to except the cemetery?!' as a way of explaining why she likes to talk about past events. When I asked her if she really meant it, she said yes she did and that life was so empty now compared to what it used to be.

While Vivienne's narrative accounts tend to be particularly vivid and reflexive, there is a shared sense of rupture that backgrounds all of my respondents' ways of talking about their pasts and futures, which highlight intergenerational tensions and perspectives on time. Ageing selves are positioned differently in relationship with the future, compared with people at other points in life. Reflections such as these are only possible from a unique temporal position that permits a long perspective when looking backwards and a certain insouciance when looking forward. Experience of, and through, time is differently structured for older people, a 'time universe' which is not necessarily linear (paralleling narrative structures, as discussed in Chapter 6) and which does not necessarily anticipate a future. As Anne told me when I was upset about the imminent death of a close, older friend, 'once you get past eighty, it's borrowed time anyway'. Taylor's assertions about selfhood, quests and the creative potentiality of the what-is-yet-to-come takes on a different hue in light of an experience of time in which the future is foreshortened.

However, feeling as though one does not have a future does not mean that one is lost in the past. Despite this, older people are often accused of living in the past, as does Vivienne's daughter. This phrase, 'living in the past', connotes an unconcern with or irrelevance of the present on the part of older people. Such a disassociation with the present is not the case in the lives of my research participants where a number of present-day concerns play out on a daily basis. Talking about the past is not bifurcated from current events but rather is often enmeshed with them. The relationship between past and present is, however, different for my research participants than from their younger family members, immersed as it is in a temporal depth of experience. So too is the future conceptualised in distinctive ways between generations. This varies from the planning and travelling for Mary and Tom to Anne's insouciance, and to Vivienne's feelings that she does not have a future. All three positions have significant implications for subjectivity and sense of self of the speakers and also reveal a much more complicated series of temporal relationships than older people are usually credited with, not a mere 'living in the past'.

However, while the older people I knew were highly likely to deny having a future to look forward to, this is also in contrast to how many of them had planned their funerals and knew exactly where they would be interred. Consider for example this segment of another interview with Mary:

> CATHRINE: Do you ever imagine ten years in the future when you may not be able
> to get around as fast?
> MARY: Yeah, well, what we do after we've been to Canada, we are now hoping at
> Christmas to book a cruise to the States because I've said a few more years
> and then we will have had it with travelling and what have you. Yeah. In
> fact, I've arranged my own funeral.
> CATHRINE: You haven't!!
> MARY: I've paid for it and everything.
> CATHRINE: Mary! (startled laughter from me)
> MARY: Ah, she thinks it's horrible! (laughing at my reaction)

Of particular note is how Mary enters the topic, with no segue whatsoever between travelling, travelling plans and planning her funeral, as if they were all of a similar nature. In a way they are since they are all important future events. A similarly overt discussion about planning one's future after death comes from an interview with Emma, Ernest's wife, when Ernest was still alive. While Mary envisages her funeral, Emma and Ernest envisage their graves:

> Now, I'm wanting to let us both [Emma and Ernest] be cremated and ashes go
> [in my family's plot], cause there'd be room for two, but, no, he [Ernest] don't
> want that neither, he wants to go under that tree, down below you know, against
> church, all them that's ashes, they're put down there and I think it's a far nicer
> place [up in the rest of the cemetery], but anyway, I shall have to do as he says.[5]

This intergenerational dynamic is not limited to my own fieldwork experiences, as an exchange on the BBC Radio Four's *Today* programme aptly demonstrates. The story being covered was about research on a stress hormones study that claims to be able to predict if a couple will stay married. For a bit of fun, the programme found two couples who agreed to be interviewed on the show and to have a blood sample taken to test for the stress hormones. One couple had been married for forty-nine years; the second couple had known each other for three years and were getting married in the summer. After the perfunctory admiration for the couple who had been together for forty-nine years and the congratulations for the couple with the upcoming wedding, the following transpired:

> JAMES NAUGHTIE (presenter): And we'll find out if you have another forty-nine years together.
> HUSBAND: (interjects) We're going in the same graveyard.
> JAMES NAUGHTIE: (splutter/nervous laugh) Ah! Yes! Well! I'm sure you won't have to worry about that for a while!

Naughtie's discomfort sparked by the husband's matter-of-fact anticipation of death and the husband's overt planning and envisioning of being buried with his wife immediately caught my attention. Not only did the exchange mirror how I had reacted many times when death was mentioned during my fieldwork, it also illustrates the difference in temporal positioning between generations. The husband's response to Naughtie's pleasantry was not meant to be morbid, but rather as a vision of where he and his wife will be sometime in the next forty-nine years. Naughtie, an experienced and adept interviewer who rarely loses his composure, is completely thrown by the breach of inappropriate taboo topics (death and burial applied to the self) and grasps at an embarrassed reassurance: 'I'm sure you won't have to worry about that for a while!' In contrast, it is evident that this is a topic that the couple have discussed and which is centrally important to them (or, at the very least, to the husband) for imagining their future circumstances: an eternal togetherness in a grave that reflects the long married life that preceded it. A radically different temporal realm from the one Naughtie occupies is revealed as is the briefest of glimmers into what is at stake in coming to terms with one's own mortality, a future that is imagined as unfolding for the subject in its partial absence. This is a 'future story' and 'life having direction towards what I am not yet' that at the same time acknowledges a future without the living, animated self, but a form of self nonetheless. Similarly, Mary's matter-of-factness contrasts with my shock, which is in and of itself telling about the different temporal space inhabited by younger and old in regards to futurity.

Adam states that everyday relationships to the future are 'lived and enacted with reference to *repetition, finitude* and *change*' (2010: 8; emphasis in original) and that each of these features assist in structuring life so that the future can be engaged with and made. Repetition, she says, plays out on multiple levels, from the rhythms in the physical environments around us (solar, lunar) to the internal bio-rhythms of our bodies, to socio-cultural cycles and rhythms. Such repetition provides a certain amount of predictability, routine and 'ontological security'; the loss of repetition due to transition or life phases destabilises the possibility of anticipating the future; furthermore, 'anchorage in rhythmic structures is neither fixed nor stable but changes with context and over the life course' (2010: 9). Adam also draws on Heidegger's perspective of 'life ... lived unto death' and that 'this lived futurity is what marks us as humans and characterizes our projects' but that over the course of a life, one's location to finitude shifts: 'with advancing years ... the future takes on a very different, possibly threatening, meaning. When looming finitude turns the personal future into fact, the less discomfiting focus on the past may substitute the future orientation with memories of younger years' (2010: 10). Adam here argues for a differential relationship with time as one ages, positing that the past and one's youth may be more comfortable reference points than impending death. By contrast, while the older people I came to know in Dodworth expressed a growing ambivalence about the future, it did not always follow that the past became their focus. Even for Vivienne, who is censured by her daughter for talking too much about the past, talking about the past was never divorced from current events and present living. The perspective of time, and how it binds past and present, thus becomes an antidote to the 'discomfit' Adam focuses on. Furthermore, in the case of some couples I knew, future orientation had not disappeared as Mary, Ernest and Emma all imagine futures that extend well beyond their deaths and yet also acknowledge that this is a future in which they will no longer be active subjects in the conventional sense.

## Putting the past to work

The material I have so far presented highlights the ways in which time can said to be differently weighted for older people than for those younger. I have argued that past, present and future sit together in different ways, given the depth of experience and a sense of a foreshortened future. I wish now to complicate this argument by turning my attention to the ways in which talk of the past is put to work in Dodworth. As stated in the introduction to this chapter, Dodworth is a place where talk of the past, what I call 'memory talk', forms an important resource in social discourse. Such a cultural valorisation of memory talk and its emphasis on past and present could obfuscate the relations with the future of older people that I describe above, if taken only by itself. It is thus important that both are read together in order to appreciate the richness of temporal experience for the older people I worked with. I wish to consider here the salience of the past and how memory talk, for those able to engage in it, shores up the social position of individuals in the present and helps establish some as 'old Dodworthers'– an important element of self-understanding. This should not, however, be miscon-strued as being only concerned with the past, for memory talk takes meaning in light of current events.

Memory talks occurs at the level of everyday practices of chatting and village gossip. Recounting, sharing and contesting memories of the village and its inhab-itants is active, processual and performative, embedded in everyday social practices in Dodworth. This is not social memory in a ritual, sacred sense, but rather woven into the fabric of daily talk and gossip in all its variety, contradic-tion and everydayness. Crucially, this is also a form of remembering that is remarkably spatialised within deeply localised parameters. I now elucidate with an ethnographic vignette that contextualises the practice of memory talk.

## The death of an 'old Dodworther'

Percy Ingham, an 'old Dodworther' by virtue of having been born and raised in Dodworth, died in October 2000. As with most deaths that affected the village, I came to know about Percy's death through the grapevine. The first person to tell me about it was Anne, when I was visiting her at home. She was eager to share the news, unhindered by the fact that I did not know Percy and had not heard his name before, since he was now living outside the village. Despite this, I recognised his surname as a local one. Anne and Percy were not related, but as she explained to me, she 'knew him and his sisters' from when they were young, all growing up together in a part of Dodworth called Church Hill. She had learned of his death during her trip to Barnsley when she ran into one of his family members on the bus. Without hesitation, Anne then rattled off the names of Percy's brothers and sisters: there was Percy, Norris, Sarah, Ada, Stanley, Annie and Florence. Then, trying to help me place him, Anne told me that one of the women I know in the village is Stanley's (Percy's brother) daughter. Swept up in remembering about Church Hill, a cluster of houses near Dodworth Church that has now largely but not completely been demolished, where she had known him and his family, Anne started to tell me about a shop, owned by the Breezes that used to be nearby on Bower Row, near to Lambert Fold which used to be behind Traveller's Inn, which itself used to be called 'Johnny Hep's' because it was Johnny who had it and where Alfie Breeze, still alive today, lives in Dodworth.

Continuing, she said that on the same row, on the end nearest to the pub, lived a family called Harrison, adding that Doris Harrison used to work for the council. I asked Anne which other families used to live on that row. More details came quickly: The Pashleys (that's the same family as Norman Pashley and his sister Hilda, who lives in Gilroyd); the Woodcocks (most of them died in a car crash, but his son is a CID[6] man); and Kenworthy had the shop to start off with, although the Breezes took it over; Arthur Lodge who we used to call 'Doctor' because he used to try and concoct things. Then there was Frank Hill, another row of houses nearby, named after Frank Ownsworth who was the landlord. On that row there was Amy Hollins, in the first house; her brother Donald now lives on Station Road and her other brother lives on Mitchelson Avenue. Then there was Muriel Tordiff who lived in the second house but later moved; the Robinsons who used to have a farm at Hood Green; Then the Greens, but their Marjorie has just died. Next to them were the Newtons, and Sally Newton lived there; her husband was related to Laurie Newton. Then, in that big house that stands on its own, that was the Herrings' house; then the Hodgsons, the Inghams, the Nichols and the Houghs … Our conversation moved on, but this flood of information about people and places, some still present and many others now absent or deceased, washed over me in a familiar fashion since it had happened to me so many times during my fieldwork with so many different people.

As I listened, I thought of how this way of remembering and reciting details about the villagescape made the physical geography of the village come alive with both the social relations of the people who lived there and the local histories of events that had transpired there. Later that week, at a centre's whist drive, the subject of Percy's death came up again. This time information about his death was discussed among a group of about ten whist players. Many of them remembered him and shared a certain set of knowledge and memories about both Percy and his extended family. Although they did not go into as much detail as Anne had when I asked her about Church Hill, similar themes were discussed to those that Anne had initially brought up in our conversation – where Percy was living when he died, who he was related to in the village (both living and dead), if he had been at the same school as the speaker and elaborate discussions about specifically where in Dodworth he used to live in his youth. This in particular was used as a way of identifying exactly who he was and which Ingham family he was a member of, for those whist players who needed help placing him.

Although this example of memory talk happened in the context of Mr Ingham's death, memory talk is by no means restricted to this sort of event and occurs in multiple contexts. What is constant in memory talk, however, is a calling back and forth between past and present. The use of memories about the past in terms of the present operates between speakers as mnemonic tools to help them situate and place people, such as when the whist players were describing which Ingham family Percy was a member of. People in Dodworth endlessly place each other by shared memories of where what had been and by what events they had experienced together. Part of figuring out who is who in the village necessitates a referencing back in time to activities, relationships and places of habitation occupied by the person in question previously.

What is also striking in memory talk is how *place* operates within this shuttling back and forth between past and present. Both places and people are named explicitly in this discourse and are explicitly linked. Often describing an absent third party or explaining who someone was hinged critically on where they had lived in the village; similarly, describing places and buildings in the village is nearly always a backgrounding characteristic of memory talk. This is partly why my move to Holdroyd's Yard proved so significant as the Yard was a prominent site of memories for many in Dodworth.

A second salient aspect of memory talk is the web of relations contained in them and how these in turn relate to village places. By the web of relations, I mean who is and was related to whom in Dodworth and neighbouring villages. Just as in *Village on the Border* (1957) where Frankenberg describes the multiple and intersecting informal ties of experience (including work, recreation, shared schooling) and of kinship that constitute relations in Glynceiriog, many people in Dodworth are embedded in complex sets of relationships that have built up over a lifetime of local residence. These relationships are often, in turn, reflected in local places, particularly by where people used to (and sometimes still do) live. By listening to and partaking in everyday conversation, which is laden with these shared memories, I learned an enormous amount about different familial and historical connections in Dodworth.

Furthermore, the webs of relations in Dodworth are part of the public domain and part of the local social memory. That is to say that not only would people recite their own webs of relations in the village and in the history of the village, but they would also talk about other people's webs of relations, as part of everyday conversation. In this way, my material mirrors that of Rowles (1983) who, drawing on ethnographic fieldwork in Appalachia, was a pioneering author in the systematic exploration of the role of place attachment in the maintenance of a sense of identity and belonging in older age. He develops the concept of 'autobiographical insideness' to capture the temporal depth of place attachment for the older people he worked with. Autobiographical insideness is an accumulated 'reservoir of memorable and self defining incidents' that have been experienced over time in a particular locale (1983: 310). Rowles argues that place attachment and autobiographical insideness work together to sustain personal identity when the temporal depth of association with a locale has accumulated over a sustained period of time. Similarly, Dodworth is a textured social milieu where the living and the dead, individuals, families, relatives and neighbours are closely related by a myriad of present and remembered links. Memory talk helps establish and reproduce a sense of belonging for those who can partake in it.

However, while in Dodworth place and people are recurrent themes in memory talk, the extent to which the memories are personal and individual or collectively shared varies a great deal. For example, as evidenced at the whist drive, not everyone has equal access to all aspects of shared village memories since not everyone could remember Percy. What is remembered and discussed is not a fixed, rigid thing but rather is a process that is often fragmentary and sometimes contentious. As such, remembering is not a homogenous process, but operates instead on different levels and in different forums. Despite these different levels, memory talk is inherently framed by shared memories, shared experiences and place. In addition to the way memories of places and people are used as landmarks, talking about memories of places *erased* and people *deceased* is equally important in this form of discourse. Bower Row and Lambert Fold, for example, no longer exist and while Church Hill and Frank Hill are still there, all but a few of the houses that stood there for the thirty years when Anne lived there, between the 1920s and 1950s, are gone. Despite their absence, both still operate as landmarks in the webs of relations and in memory talk in the village. This intersecting use of place, people and absence are characteristics of memory talk in Dodworth.

## Remembering in '3-D'

As my fieldwork progressed, I became increasingly aware of the spatial aspect of the repertoires of memories I was hearing and being taught. For example, walking down different streets in Dodworth, I could visualise the homes that had been there and recite the names of the people who had lived there, although I had never seen or met them: George Henry Hart, the local bookie; the cottages linked to the pub where Ida's family used to live before they were torn down and where to look in the stone wall for traces of the two old sets of stairs that had led to the front doors (see figure 2); where Emma's dad used to keep pigs and where her

**Figure 2** Where Ida's house used to be.

mother used to stand calling to them until they would come running for scraps; the path home that Evelyn used to walk down in the dark after dancing all night with her girlfriends during the war; the impossibly steep hill that they used to take bets on Mr Hamby being able to cycle to the top of without stopping; Dr Leischman's house, before he committed suicide; the driveway where Jack used to haul cartload after cartload of coal uphill to his coal store after working a seven-hour shift at the pit. Within only a few months of starting fieldwork, I had already been well schooled in various landmarks of my research participants' lives, landmarks that had been repeated to me many times already (paralleling the narrative practices that I detail in Chapter 6) and which were to continue to figure powerfully in my fieldwork experiences.

Aware that I was learning these memories and their spatial referents and aware that knowing them made me able to participate in a discourse that has significant local identity implications, I was at a loss as to how to explain or conceptualise memory in this way. I began to think of it and shorthand it in my fieldnotes as a 'three-dimensionality of memory'. By this, I meant Dodworth and the way it is 'seen' and described by village residents, as well as trying to capture the richness and perspective of place and social relationships that are embedded in social memory practices in Dodworth. The forms of collective memory I was already conversant in seemed two-dimensional in comparison with what I was being taught in Dodworth in that they did not hold associations with local places or webs of relations. In this sense, space constitutes a first dimension, time a second and relationality (both to people and to places) a third. Rather than being a flat viewing of the village as it was in 2000, I could read onto the physical villagescape not only shops and homes that have since been destroyed, but also multiple layers of meaning, including social relations that had played out in these places and how they mapped on to contemporary webs of relations in Dodworth. As Anne reminded me when describing who Percy Ingham was, explaining who Percy the individual was meant not only explaining and locating his family, but also a social fabric which included people who were not his family members, village places and village stories.

However, it is entirely possible that I was so powerfully struck by the three-dimensionality of remembering in Dodworth because of my own relative shortness of association with any one locale over my lifetime. That is to say, in contrast with the majority of my research participants, I have not and probably never will be as long-term a resident of any one place as they have been. Perhaps this is why learning how to see is a common experience of both anthropologists and travellers. In a similar example, Rodman describes her experiences in Vanuatu and how:

> As I mapped the village, a grandmother told me about the birth sites of her children. One birth house had been over here, another time she had given birth in a menstruation hut over there, realizing she would not make it to the hospital eight miles away in time. Although I put an *X* on my map in the locations she pointed out, they were marked by nothing I could see in the landscape. Yet for the old woman these memories were etched as clearly in the landscape as if they bore commemorative plaques. (1992: 650)

Ryden has called this kind of knowledge the 'invisible landscape', a form of knowledge and set of meanings that comes with a sense of place, 'an unseen layer of usage [that] ... to passing observers ... will remain invisible unless it is somehow called to their attention' (Ryden, 1993: 40). As with Ryden and Rodman, I was also seeing the invisible landscape, having finally accrued enough local insight to perceive the strongly relational dimension of memory talk which works the relations between people into village places (both present and erased) and vice versa.

Another point this material raises is the concept of layering, as in Ryden's description of 'an unseen layer'. Ingold signals a subtle distinction of this word with important implications when it is used to describe how meaning becomes read onto the physical environment. Ingold's dwelling perspective highlights how the stories people tell about the world around them 'is not like weaving a tapestry to *cover up* the world, it is rather a way of guiding the attention of listeners or readers *into* it' (1993: 153, emphasis original). In other words, people do not 'layer' meaning onto the otherwise unchanging physical forms of the environment. Rather, they construct relationships with place. Likewise, the three-dimensionality of memory in Dodworth cannot simply be described as a form of layering meaning onto places, but rather needs to be understood as a simultaneously individual and collective way of placing oneself and webs of relations within contours of meaning in the villagescape. Indeed, as evidenced in the beginning of this chapter, people in Dodworth talk about village residents and places that are long gone, yet which are made still tangible through the ways in which memory talk hinges on local knowledge, such as who owned which shop where, who lived next door, the locations of farms, shops, pits, bus stops, paths and people's homes.

Importantly, this talk and these memories have a critical social role in present-day discourse. They are used both to place other people and to place oneself in the history of the village. Adeptness in this way of talking and remembering is a way of staking a claim to belonging through demonstrating a temporally rich knowledge of Dodworth. Skill in using this local knowledge also garners social capital, maintains identity and marks some people out as 'old Dodworthers'. As in Glynceiriog, 'knowledge of one another's background and lives and the past and present sharing of mutual experiences' (Frankenberg, 1957: 22) forge connections between Dodworthers and creates identity *as* Dodworthers. Furthermore, the power of these memories is not just in having them, but comes through recounting them, exchanging them and using them to help navigate current social relations. It is in this way that I argue that memory is put to work in Dodworth, constituting local identity as an 'old Dodworther': as belonging to and constitutive of, the village. Having and using a three-dimensional form of memory also operates as a form of social and cultural distinction within the village. Not everyone in Dodworth can (or wants to) participate in memory talk. The most obvious example of this is non-Dodworthers who have moved into the village later in life and who described to me the feeling that one 'needs a passport to live in Dodworth'. People who have not lived in Dodworth for an extended period of time do not have the same level of access to, nor perhaps the same interest in, the memory talk as I describe it here. They are also cut off from some local channels of social engagement for the same reason.

## Conclusions

Issues of temporality and identity for older people are not simply academic ones, but are rooted in day-to-day experience. Harvey reminds us of Bourdieu's (1977) point that 'symbolic orderings of space and time provide a framework for experience through which we learn who or what we are in society' (Harvey, 1989: 214). For older people, this symbolic ordering takes on particular salience. Older people in Britain, as in many other parts of the Western world, are subject to a number of stereotypes about living in the past, about being removed from the flow of time. Fabian's (1983) observations on how time in anthropological practice defines and constructs the Other is strongly evocative in this respect. Fabian says that time and temporal frameworks are used in anthropology to distance the observer from the observed by denying the observed coevalness, placing the observed in a different temporal flow from that of the observer (1983: ix–35). Hazan similarly observes that older people are:

> deemed disoriented, maladjusted and incoherent, unless proven otherwise. Consequently, any information produced by an old person about herself or himself and the world, unless congruous with the construction of reality of the

non-old, is liable to be discredited. Hence, repetitious locutions uttered by elderly persons, adherence to maxims and aphorisms, a-chronological accounts of life histories, inconsistent speech acts, profuse recourse to reminiscences, or, alternatively, dead silence – all serve as testimonies to 'garbled talk', 'disorientation' and 'senility'. (1996: 25 emphasis added)

Hazan's observation is eerily reminiscent of ethnocentrism and how others are often construed in mainstream culture as unintelligible, unintelligent and far less knowledgeable than the Western observer who Fabian calls to our attention. It is my contention that one of the ways in which older people are rendered into the Other is via a belief-system that assumes older people do not inhabit the present (or that they only inhabit the present) and that they do not engage meaningfully with ideas about the future. Such beliefs contribute to the otherisation of older people in Western society by denying coevalness and, consequently, full adult personhood to those with a different relationship with time from the younger middle-aged norm as attributions of less-than-full-adulthood are made when individuals whose experience and expression falls outside the temporal norms of linearity and irreversibility are perceived as deviant (Hendricks and Hendricks, 1976). This position of otherness is then reinforced and reproduced by dominant media images and messages that stigmatise older people as a social problem.[7]

It could be assumed that one way of combating such stereotypes of older people is to reinsert older people in the same normative temporal framework as middle-aged adults. Paradoxically, however, this risks imposing a normalising perspective on to older people who might, at a certain point in their lives, be positioning themselves differently with respect to temporality. They might be reflectively detaching themselves from things that seem less important in their lives and focusing on other moments in time which seem more meaningful. As Hendricks and Hendricks point out, 'time is not a thing ... instead it permeates the knower ... [People] need this presupposed temporal framework in order to know, act, think and relate to the world' (1976: 26) and if this relation is put under new pressures, either by growing older, through larger macro-scale changes, or both, then the way people 'know, act, think and relate to the world' will also shift, creating distinctive forms of temporality. Older people are at once perceived as removed from the flow of time by stereotypes and yet also seem too saturated with it. The 'disrupted' temporal relations of which older people are accused (assumptions of their inability to remember current events accurately, assumed difficulty of configuring memories and events chronologically), effectively exclude older people from normative temporal frames of reference which, crucially, are used to adjudicate on full personhood. Somewhat mediating this, however, in Dodworth is the social valorisation of memory talk for those who are able to perform it, owing to a lifetime of knowledge and experience of the locale. Not only is it a source of pleasure, it is also a way to anchor one's identity and sense of self in the local area and the webs of relationships of people and place.

## Notes

1 These centre names are again pseudonyms.
2 The Women's Institute is a national organisation for women with local chapters that meet monthly.
3 'Short of breath'.
4 'Not getting anything for it'; alludes to not receiving compensation for lung damage over many years of workplace exposure.
5 Dodworth Church yard has two portions of its cemetery: the more traditional burial plots and a smaller and more contemporary section near the tree that Emma refers to, which is for cremated remains only.
6 'Criminal Investigation Division'.
7 Although there is quite a strong political movement of elderly activist groups that counter these stereotypes and also a small body of literature that explores how such constructs are manipulated and used by elderly people as resistance (Dawson, 1990; Hockey and James, 1993; Vesperi, 1985).

**4**

---

# Monitoring the boundaries of age: intra-generational perspectives on 'old age'

## Introduction

As compared to other parts of the life course, the social category of 'old age' is a remarkably broad term. While childhood alone can contain the stages of 'preemies', 'infants', 'toddlers', 'terrible-twos' and 'pre-school', there is a relative absence of distinction within the social category of old age hood (Hockey and James, 1993) and the category is left to cover a wide range of heterogeneous experiences and changes without distinguishing among them. Since so few terms exist in everyday English to evoke the wide range of experiences encapsulated in the category of old age, social scientists researching ageing have had to stumble their way through, denoting differences which are believed to exist but whose boundaries are contested and blurred. This uncertainty is reflected in the difficult task faced by researchers delineating the segment of the ageing population they are working with. Some attempts to distinguish different categories of oldness include the 'old old' versus the 'young old' (Myerhoff, 1984: 307); the 'disabled elderly' (Ikels, 1997); 'the third age ... [which is] ... the adolescence of old age' (Hazan, 1996: 33); 'deep old age' (Featherstone and Hepworth, 1989); 'advanced old age' (Heikkinen, 2004); the 'frail elderly' (Kayser-Jones, 1981: ix); 'the oldest old – persons over eighty five years of age' (Suzman *et al.*, 1992); 'the "young old" and the "old old" ... contemporarily used to distinguish between those who are over and under 75' (Hockey and James, 1993: 87); 'the very old – those in their eighties' (Cumming and Henry, 1961: 201); and 'the very old ... 85 years and older' (Clark and Anderson, 1967: 33). Emerging from these examples is the persistent problem of who can be said to be old and how to describe the heterogeneity of older age. Furthermore, even once terms that seek to do this come into regular use by specialists, there seems to be little consensus as to what these categories encode either objectively or subjectively.

The problems inherent in distinguishing these different categories of ageing are also evident in the terms that such definitions at times resort to. Many of the examples mentioned above circle implicitly around the same basic question: Is chronological age a clearer indicator of the difference in categories of old age ('over eighty five years of age') or is physical ability ('frail') a more reliable frame of reference? A further complication facing attempts to delineate what old age is and who is old comes from ethnographic record. Generally, people designated as elderly by the wider society do not self-identify as old (Hunt, 1978: 9; see also Itzin, 1990; Kaufman, 1986; Matthews, 1979: 30; Thompson, 1992b; Thompson, Itzin and Abendstern, 1990; although see Heikkinen, 2004 for a qualifying position). This body of literature has built up important insights into older people's self-perceptions of the meaning of old age; examined the strategies older people employ in a continuing 'search for meaning and fulfilment in later life' (Thompson, 1992b: 28); and studied negative and limiting stereotypes which do not match lived experiences of growing older. Indeed, it is this incongruence between personal experiences and negative social stereotypes which mean that few people self-identify as old (Itzin, 1990).

Emerging from the literature then is an intriguing disjuncture between, on the one hand, the cultural assertion or knowledge that old age exists as a category and, on the other hand, how the category is applied in actual practice to oneself and to others. One aspect of this dynamic that has not been examined is the ways in which what old 'means' and how it is measured is not just constructed by younger people and laid like a blanket onto older people, but is indeed also constructed by older people themselves. This is an important distinction, as the former perpetuates a troubling vision of older people as agentless victims, no longer fully adult human beings. I propose instead that what old age is and who is old is also constructed in a myriad of small, everyday moments and interactions that include those among older people themselves. I investigate in this chapter how intra-generational relationships play a part in the making of old age as a social category and distinctions between 'real' and 'normal' old age.

While it is not my desire to pin down once and for all categories and definitions of older age, I seek instead to examine their implications for everyday experience in the lives of older people that they represent. As such, this chapter explores the gap between epistemological categories of old age and oldness ('knowing' that old age exists) and the pragmatics of implementing these same categories (discerning when and in what contexts the label of oldness should, culturally speaking, be applied to which individuals, including the self). I demonstrate how this gap between epistemological categories and pragmatics reveals the extent to which oldness is a relational concept rather than one that can be measured by physical or chronological markers. Influenced by Foucault's work on discipline and power (1979), I develop a theory of monitoring to explain how mental acuity and social comportment are used as markers of oldness among peers in Dodworth. I examine the ways in which oldness is constructed intra-generationally and how older people themselves strategically negotiate the discourse of oldness in everyday interactions and experience.

## Categories of old age and oldness in everyday experiences of older people

In refocusing attention on old age as a category, it may at first appear that I am taking a retrograde step. Authors such as Maria Vesperi have challenged social scientists to break away from traditional assumptions of old age as a category. Vesperi argues:

> That the old form a discrete social category – identified by custom – is an assumption social scientists share with the rest of American society. It is my belief, however, that attention must be shifted from the category 'old age' to the context of aging and that old age itself is not a discrete social or even physical caste. The cultural construction of old age is a process; it is the concretization of abstract, unexamined assumptions within the context of everyday interaction. (Vesperi, 1985: 24)

Vesperi alludes here to the difficulty that social scientific research on ageing has had in identifying how the cultural construction of old age is forged and in turn how older age is experienced by older people themselves. Remedying this is an interest that she and I share. While I agree with her that the category of old age is a cultural construction that needs to be problematised, I am also interested in how the disjuncture between the epistemological and pragmatic categories of old age itself informs the lived experience and subjectivity of older people. That is to say I believe that there is not an even mapping between the epistemology of the category of old age – the socially accepted and agreed knowledge that 'old age exists' – with the pragmatics of actually acting on this knowledge in everyday life – knowing what counts as 'old age' and who counts as 'old'. Asking questions about this gap is relevant because it permits a reinsertion of the category of old age into a theoretical framework which queries the contexts of ageing within everyday life experiences and the subjectivity of older people themselves. It also permits a closer examination of how old age is made intra-generationally and not just between members of different generations. This chapter examines how the social category of old age is built, used, perceived, negotiated and experienced by older people themselves, both as individuals and as members of groups. In particular, I first pay close attention to the distinction that the people I worked with made between *acting* and *looking* one's age for what this reveals about expectations of comportment and the boundaries surrounding old age as both a social category and as a lived experience. I then turn my attention to the experiences of two women at one of the centres, Ella and Mrs Atherton. Through a series of events that occurred there, I explore how oldness can be seen as a relational concept and the extremely complex ways in which people negotiate the discourse of oldness in the centres and outside of them.

## 'Looking' and 'acting' your age: ideals of personal comportment

Walking through the village on my way to the bus stop one morning, I ran into Iris, a friend in her early eighties who was going the same way as me. She started telling me about her husband, Sam and how he had gone to the hospital yesterday for a routine check-up but had been kept in unexpectedly because they had discovered blood clots in one of his legs. Iris continued, telling me about how she herself has to go on Monday for a test on her intestine, that she is having trouble during our conversation concentrating and that she is feeling increasingly anxious since the last time we saw each other. She finished by telling me that there is 'nowt in getting old'[1] but that at least I am getting to see both sides of life through my fieldwork. At least now, she said, I will know the importance of having children and a family to help me in *my* old age unlike her, whose children are spread out and grandchildren are even further away.

In order to take her mind off these troubles, I took out a small picture album that I happened to have with me in my bag. The album was full of pictures from my wedding, which had taken place not long before in the midst of my fieldwork, and which I had not yet had a chance to share with her. In attendance at the wedding were two older women from Dodworth who I had become close to and whom she knew. Iris admired the photos, but her two overarching comments were:

> Look at Mrs Taylor with her shopping bags in the photo! That's what old age does to you – you forget how to dress, how to behave; you lose concentration over what you are doing.

This was not a particularly kind commentary, but it was a revealing one on the part of Iris. The shopping bags Iris was referring to are square nylon carrying bags that Mrs Taylor used to carry her camera and confetti in on the wedding day and which she is holding in her hand in the photo I showed Iris. The presence or absence of the bag had never entered my consciousness, but was the first thing Iris picked up on in her scrutiny of the photo. Such bags are often carried into Barnsley on shopping trips by older people. Iris's assessment of Mrs Taylor's oldness as evidenced by the shopping bag in the photo needs also to be contextualised within Iris's own current state of mind in which she is frustrated by not being able to watch movies or read books any more because, as she tells me, she can no longer concentrate on them long enough to enjoy them – something she attributes to old age. Iris is in a sense bringing mental acuity ('you forget how to') back to comportment and saying that old age starts to make you *act* in a way you would never do otherwise. Old age, according to Iris, is a force that subverts one's own autonomy over mind *and* body. Put another way, prompting a threat to the integrity of self, some aspects of ageing can be intercepted but others are not controllable.

Our bus never showed up, so Iris invited me back to her place for a cup of tea to warm up instead. I gratefully accepted. After we had sat down with our tea in her living room, she popped into another room for a second and returned with her own wedding photo. It was a single studio shot. Pointing to her mother in the shot she said: 'That's how Mrs Taylor should have looked'. Iris's mother was wearing a small hat, a dark woollen coat which was buttoned up over a dress, was holding a purse and had dress shoes on her feet. Conspicuously absent, however, were any shopping bags.

This vignette serves as a springboard into thinking through several intersecting issues and through a gendered lens. I am concerned here with the implications of everyday language, norms of personal comportment, monitoring *of* and being monitored *by* peers for the ways in which the boundaries of old age are experienced and described by older people I came to know. In particular, what is at stake in older people's own descriptions of 'acting' and 'looking' one's age? What gendered dimensions might there be to these? A particular focus here is the ways in which the boundaries of 'old age' are patrolled by older people themselves in everyday life. One such way that this is accomplished is by the paying of close attention to one's own comportment and that of peers (such as Mrs Taylor's shopping bags) and the use in everyday language of terms such as 'looking' and 'acting' one's age. It also demonstrates some of what counts as 'real' old age for the older people involved in this research, as opposed to ageing which is described as 'normal'. Briefly stated, the older people I came to know perceived looking one's age as a negative attribute, while acting one's age was more ambivalent and context dependent. However, what is expected of and possible for men and for women in this regard can be different. Also, what 'age' codifies in each phrase is different and it is these differences which are so revealing about aspects of what 'oldness' is taken to mean by older people themselves.

In the case of looking one's age, 'age' is a negative attribute. If someone is said to be looking their age, it is a comment on a presence which individuals normally seek to render absent, or unremarkable, but which has become visible and revealed, although this may only be temporary. As such, 'looking one's age' usually means that someone looks tired, worn out, not well. It is a euphemism for saying that someone looks old.

In the case of acting one's age, age connotes a sense of respectability which centres around two opposing forces that an older individual is expected to balance, but which older people are often also censured for if perceived to overstep, namely 'keeping active'. On the one hand, peers expect each other to manage and control their oldness by avoiding 'putting on' other people and striving to help themselves – acting and keeping active as fully capable and independent adults. On the other hand, older people are also expected to respect the limits of their ageing body and not to attempt too much. An example of this comes from an argument between two lifelong friends in their eighties, Anne and Evelyn, about how much strenuous housework is too much. Anne we have met already in Chapter 3 and I have mentioned Evelyn in passing previously here. The two women have been friends since school days and grew up together in Dodworth. Evelyn's mother was born in Gilroyd and her father in Rotherham but when Evelyn's grandfather died, his uncle who was the manager at Strafford Pit brought her grandmother and children to live in Dodworth. Her father grew up to be a miner; Evelyn herself worked in service as a young woman and then married a man who was killed during the war. She eventually married again, living away from her mid-fifties to her early sixties and returning again to Dodworth after that. Since Evelyn's return to Dodworth and once they had both become widowed, the two women had renewed their friendship and saw a good deal of each other. One Tuesday while the three of us were visiting together, this disagreement bubbled to the surface.

Anne had been painting the rooms in her bungalow. She had been working bit by bit on the green walls in the bathroom, painting them white and on Sunday had climbed up on a chair to reach the section above the window. Suddenly, she lost her balance and fell off, bruising her upper right thigh on the hard porcelain of the sink. She had not told any of her children or grandchildren because 'they'd play pop with me'[2] and also because doing this work on her own is crucial to her sense of self and all about, as she put it, 'having some independence'. Evelyn was outraged and aghast at hearing this story. She chastised her friend, saying that Anne was being thoughtless and that she would 'be a burden on (her) family if something serious should happen!' According to Evelyn, if Anne had injured herself badly, she would be 'putting on' her family, something that she, Evelyn, avoids at all costs. This did not go down well with Anne who saw painting her own home as doing exactly that: avoiding 'putting on' her family and that if something went wrong, 'I shouldn't be having *my* kids looking after me, I'd go in hospital; that's what it's there for!' Evelyn was still unconvinced, saying that no matter where Anne was, her children would still be worried about her because of her injuries and that she would de facto be putting on them anyway. Simply put, Evelyn felt that Anne was trying to do too much and was taking on tasks now beyond her ability.

This is an excellent example of the everyday experiences of juggling entailed by balancing expectations for personal comportment that simultaneously demand that people stay active in order to ward off old age while also not attempting too much. Indeed, as discussed in Chapter 5, staying active is generally perceived positively and friends would often recount to me with relish what tasks they had accomplished that particular day when I went to visit them. As evidenced in the example above, however, these forces play out in individual people's lives according to personality and to priorities which are situationally dependent.

From a gendered perspective, it is not an accident that staying active gets played out for women in terms of housework more often than men. This is linked historically and culturally to expectations whereby 'cleaning, or not ... was a publicly available indicator of the moral worth of each household and women were, and still are, the moral guardians of the house and its relationships' (Edwards, 2000: 5). While older women might tell me what jobs they had done 'around the house', housework would give way to other sorts of activities in the accounts I would receive from male contacts. In Mack's case, an 86-year-old widower, he would instead make mention of whether or not he had been able to tend his garden that day or make his regular trip to the Gilroyd social club for a drink with friends, or for Jim, in his early nineties, whether or not he managed to take his beloved dog on walks through the fields bordering the village. There are thus implications for the ways in which public and private spaces are accessed, inhabited and experienced in terms of ageing that are gendered and historically contingent but that also have an impact on how channels for challenging and experiencing labels of 'oldness' can be felt or evaded.

This is one side of the balancing act. 'Acting' one's age on the other hand *does* offer the opportunity for agency as it is conceived of by my research participants. People can make choices, it is argued. Exercising agency in practice is another matter, however. To illustrate, consider Margery. Formerly a member of one of the regular bingo and whist nights that met every week in the village hall, but no longer attending, her name came up one evening at whist because her sister's school photograph was in the *Barnsley Chronicle* that day, sparking group members to engage deeply in memory talk, swapping stories of both Margaret and her sister.

I asked why she had stopped attending and inadvertently touched a nerve. Members there were still aghast at what had transpired and relished relating the details to me. One evening a few years ago, as the story goes, Margery caught her coat on a door handle as she was getting ready to go home which made her fall over, 'screaming and hollering and blaming everyone else for what she'd done to her own self'. Now, according to the group, all she does is sit at home. Ivy, whom we first met in Chapter 3, and will see again in more detail in Chapter 5, piped up that 'Margery's forever telling me "I'm eighty-one and that's why I sit all day", and I says to her, "*I'm* eighty-one and I get out and it doesn't stop *me*"', to nods of agreement from members sitting around her.

The final blow which sealed consensus, however, was that not only has Margery given up and does not do things any more, but that 'she puts on people – she's one of those sorts, she'll not try to help herself', particularly as she's got her daughter (note to gendered self) looking after her. According to the group, she will not try to walk or even to dress herself. Giving up (and not helping herself), is the ultimate condemnation of a person's character and personifies Margery in the group's opinion as 'oldness' incarnate, *acting* her age in the most negative way possible. Importantly however, she is attributed with the choice of whether or not to 'act' her age. Embracing autonomy and activity would redeem her, but she persists in helplessness.

I wondered if such an attitude was specific to the dynamics of centre members who by definition 'keep going' by attending social gatherings like the centres. Perhaps their judgement of Margery was particularly severe because of this. I found, however, that similar feelings were expressed by a wide variety of people whether or not they were centre members, such as Albert, a man in his eighties who has never been a centre member and who now rarely leaves his house. Despite this, helping himself is extremely important as evidenced through his description to me of some other people who 'like to act old':

ALBERT: I will tell you that now. There is some people that likes to act old and I
        never did  ...
CATHRINE: And how do they act when they act old?

ALBERT: Well, uh, wanting their family to carry them about, wanting people to, you know, say 'Hello, how ar' you goin' [said by Albert in wavery, weary way] that sort of thing, you know, that got me ... I mean, same as last night, the phone rang and I picked it up and a voice said: 'Is that so and so?' [said by Albert in pitiful, weak, warbly voice] I says 'No', I says, 'I think you've got a wrong number', I says, 'This is Barnsley 279345'... 'uhhhh' (is the noise the person made on the other end of the line) ... Really, really, old, moaning, you know and I've never, moaned, never ... now a lot of people, a lot of people same as I am with all these complaints that I've got you know what they say [in small whispery voice] 'Oh I'm fed up of this.' They're really miserable people.

Here, Albert imagines into his narrative an 'old person', the sort of person he describes himself in contrast to. He evokes this old person by mimicking stereotypical vocal and behavioural characteristics (thin, wavery voice, needy, complaining) and is adamant that helplessness and 'moaning' about one's problems (signs of oldness and giving in) are not the way he approaches his life, despite a number of physical ailments he has, including diabetes and the loss of one leg. Albert, born and raised in Pogmoor, less than two miles to the east of Dodworth, has lived in Dodworth for many decades after marrying a Dodworth woman in 1939. He worked in the steel industry and so was exempted from serving in the army during the war but lost his leg in a motorcycle accident in his late twenties. Despite this, he went on to be promoted at work to operating a high-level crane, a stoicism that is reflected in his comments above.

However, despite Albert's assertions, the subjective experience of how ageing changes one's behaviour can be very unsettling. Sally, who we hear more from in Chapter 5, searching for a way to describe the transformations that she was experiencing, told me: 'As you get older, you don't have the same grip on yourself.' This statement insinuates that the mental and physical norms of comportment that one takes for granted in youth and middle age become more elusive and demand more conscious attention as one ages in order to maintain them and her comments converge with the judgemental remarks from Iris that I begin this section with.

While Albert and others abhor people who 'act their age' and 'won't help themselves', I have also heard individuals being censured by their peers for trying too hard to avoid the physical changes of ageing. People who are still driving when they are perceived as too weak or too ill to be driving properly are gossiped about; people who insist on a weekly walk to fetch their pension from the post office even though they are obviously suffering to get there are talked about by other centre members as looking 'terrible, exhausted', even though they themselves say that the walk does them good and 'keeps them going'. People evaluate their peers' physical conditions among themselves in conversation and make judgements on whether they are trying to do more than they are able to, or if as in the example of Margery, not enough. People's behaviour is also censured at the centres if they 'act' more their age than need be, with hearing loss in particular being a sore spot during bingo. For example, at a centre bingo night one evening,

Doris asked a couple times throughout the evening what number had just been called. Gladys, irate over the interruption to both the bingo and her own concentration snapped to the woman sitting beside her about Doris: 'She has a hearing aid but she'll not wear it!', loudly enough for me on the other side of the room to hear her. No one reacted to what Gladys had said, but many undoubtedly also heard her. This outburst demonstrates that although it is fine to be 'normally' old, one is supposed to do as much as possible to put off the ill effects of age. Individuals are expected to prevent disabilities (like hearing loss) from getting in everyone else's way. The markers of old age need to be clamped down on and controlled or managed in some way.[3] If someone is perceived as not doing anything about them, then they run the risk of censure.

My consideration of 'acting' and 'looking' one's age in part means thinking about the affective component of the tension between subjective experiences of the self and social stereotypes of behaviour in old age. Essentially, while people were monitored for signs of decline, they were also censured if perceived to be overstepping the bounds of acceptable behaviour for 'someone her age'. I return to this issue in the section on monitoring, below, but first I would like to consider in more ethnographic detail the ways in which oldness is a relational and situational concept. To do so, I turn now to an extended ethnographic vignette based over a period of time and multiple interactions both inside and outside one of the Dodworth centres.

## Ella and Mrs Atherton: the situational construction of old age

Ella, Anne, Evelyn and I often sat together during weekly bingo and tea at one of the centres. Ella had missed the past two centre meetings because of a trip to respite care and on this particular afternoon, her first one back, she was telling us about some randy 'Casanova' who had been pestering her and propositioning her during her stay at the respite centre. Evelyn and Anne were listening to her with a sort of bemused 'Yes, dear' indulgence to her stories, but as always, they gave off signals that distanced themselves from Ella. These included tones of disbelief in their murmured responses, occasional rolling of eyes when Ella was not looking and collusive smiles to me and to each other about Ella's stories. Although sounding malicious, such gestures were not meant in a mean way, but rather had become part of the collective way members interacted with Ella at the centre. This is in part due to how her stories and narrative style are often partial or fragmented. Although she speaks sensibly, the listener has to work to situate what she is saying. In other words, the listener has to write in or bridge tiny gaps in her narrative that speakers usually include in order to contextualise what they are saying, but which she does not (see Chapter 6 where I discuss narrative style more directly). Most of the time, however, Anne and Evelyn do not attempt to bridge these gaps. They instead will listen for only so long before changing the topic, often before it is conventionally polite to do so.

Ella's linguistic behaviour is interpreted by members as a sign that she 'isn't all there', an interpretation that is unfortunately reinforced by a second, physical characteristic. Owing to Parkinson's disease, Ella also experiences involuntary trembling. This ailment causes her hands to shake uncontrollably – highly visible tremors that make even drinking tea or putting sugar and milk into her tea cup difficult. Although she is one of the youngest centre members chronologically speaking, since Ella manifests both markedly negative linguistic and physical behaviours, she has become marginalised by the group. Indeed, before this particular afternoon, while I had been aware of the gaps in Ella's stories and confused by them, I had also been taking my social cues from Anne, Evelyn and the other members in my assessment of Ella. I came to realise that until that afternoon, three months into my fieldwork, Ella had barely registered on my social radar as someone I should take seriously and pay attention to despite seeing her every week at the centre. This was because she is ever so slightly, and yet markedly, treated differently from other members, signals that I had inter-nalised before reflecting on. These signals were largely that Ella was mentally confused. They were signals that I readily accepted, unconsciously unwilling to alienate other members by overly associating with a marginal member. As I became more aware of this dynamic and also more established as a member in my own right, I was increasingly able to extract myself from this pattern and interact with her in a more balanced fashion. The prevailing attitude to Ella is not voiced and was only ever implicit but the vagueness in her narrative patterns in conjunction with the highly visible impairment of her motor skill functions are interpreted by other members as markers of oldness, overt characteristics which make other members uncomfortable. On the other hand, while she is kept at arm's length by some members, she is not completely marginalised because in all other respects such as appearance, comportment, manners, alertness and timeli-ness she meets the group's expectations.

One series of events two months later was particularly revealing about Ella's own relative oldness. All was transpiring as usual that day at the centre. Tea had been served and finished and bingo recommenced. Then, with only two houses of bingo left, something extraordinary began to happen. There was a bit of a commotion at the entrance to the centre and then a woman in a wheelchair made her way into the room. She was visibly disgruntled and Karen, the warden in her late forties who helped run the centre, called out to her: 'What're you doing?', implying that the woman should not be out and about. The woman, whom I had never seen before during five months of fieldwork, began saying how no one had come to get her and that she'd never before missed the beginning of bingo at the centre and she wouldn't have missed it today, either, except that no one had come to fetch her from her house. She continued, saying that it was a good thing she had made it here before the end of the first house of bingo. Karen simultaneously scoffed at this, pointing out to the rest of us how we were well beyond the first house of the afternoon, while also helping the newly arrived woman get set up with a bingo card and marker. Once the new arrival was settled, the bingo caller tried to recommence, but the new woman was loudly annoyed because the bingo marker would not mark properly. This was because she was holding it upside down, although she did not realise it. One of the members seated near me called out to her to turn it around, whereupon it began working and bingo started again.

It was a complete mystery to me what was transpiring. I thought perhaps that the woman was Karen's auntie or mother. At the end of bingo, Karen asked me if I would push the woman, called Mrs Atherton, home in her wheelchair. She lived nearby and was not a relative of Karen's but a local resident. In order to get to the centre, she had wheeled herself out, pushing the wheelchair with her walking sticks, using them like barge poles. Ella had at this point gone over to chat with Mrs Atherton, one of the few members to do so. After Karen explained to Mrs Atherton who I was and that I was going to take her home, I sat and waited for Ella and Mrs Atherton to finish their chat. Loudly, disrupting this moment of calm, one of the members raised the alarm of 'Where are her keys?' and that we must find them before I could bring her home. This was directed at Mrs Atherton but said in the third person. Four members (all women) at once descended upon Mrs Atherton, going through her purse, her lap and her coat pockets, fumbling, prying, looking for the missing keys. It was maddening for me to watch as it seemed so invasive. Yet at the same time, these actions were businesslike and no-nonsense on the part of the members involved, giving the sense that this had all happened before on previous occasions. While her possessions being rifled, Mrs Atherton continuously proclaimed that she did not know where her keys were, but she thought 'they might be in my pocket?' The keys were nowhere to be found. One woman twice whispered to me 'confidentially' but within everyone's hearing how Mrs Atherton's door was probably unlocked anyway because she is 'always leaving it unlocked'. I got the clear impression from these few minutes that Mrs Atherton was well known by the members but was not perceived as an equal.

Despite no one being able to find the keys, we set off anyway. Ella decided to come along, still chatting to Mrs Atherton. While waiting for Ella to get her coat on, Mrs Atherton asked me three times in as many minutes what day it was and again insisted that she always comes to the centre and is never late. As we left the centre and Ella and Mrs Atherton continued their conversation, I realised that a profound transformation in Ella had taken place since she had begun talking to Mrs Atherton and was continuing while we walked. Ella's art of conversation and her social composure had entirely returned. It seemed that faced with someone who was even more marginalised than herself, even more clearly otherised, Ella's own grasp of social linguistic narrative norms clicked back into place. This momentum of her repossession of self continued as she gave Mrs Atherton a kiss goodbye and said, 'It's Ella Norris, do you remember me?' as we were leaving. Mrs Atherton said yes and then also complimented Ella on her pleated skirt and the way it hung and the way it moved, which pleased Ella enormously. Ella replied using normal conversational conventions, something I had never seen her do so effortlessly and seamlessly before in the five months I had known her.

Mrs Atherton also demonstrated her own moments of perfect clarity when we arrived at her door. After I tried it and found it was indeed locked, she produced the 'missing' keys in seconds. Despite the best efforts of four people clucking over her in the centre looking for her keys, she had been holding them in her hands inside her mittens where no one had been able to check. Whether or not this was intentional on her part was not clear, but at the very least it demonstrates that she is far more capable of looking after herself than her peers gave her credit for. Her front door was locked while she was out of the house, she had not lost her keys and she was perfectly capable of re-entering her home with or without my presence.

From the shift in Ella's comportment, to the group descent upon Mrs Atherton to locate her keys, to her having them in her hands all along, the entire thirty minutes had been an extraordinary series of revelations about these two women who are treated by their peers as little more than children. On the one hand, free to interact outside of the centre context with someone she knew and had previously been neighbours with, Ella transformed from a socially marginalised person who acted and was treated as old to a social equal who was just as capable of holding a conversation and maintaining social norms. In addition to already knowing Mrs Atherton and being outside the centre context with its ingrained patterns of interaction and collective assumptions about Ella's state of being, a further potential contributing factor to Ella's transformation could be the relative degrees of marginalisation these two women lived with. In comparison to Ella's partial marginalisation, Mrs Atherton (as I explain below) was resoundingly marginalised by the other members for the attributes of oldness that she manifested. Ella, as part of the group, would be aware of these social messages. It is possible that in this small example Ella became temporarily liberated from the label of 'old woman' in contrast with someone manifesting more extreme and less socially accepted markers of old age than she herself does, namely Mrs Atherton. Thus while 'old' is a powerfully stigmatising label, it is also a contextually dependent one that can at times ebb and flow with the attribution of oldness shifting in relation to others.

## Building social consensus

In spite of Mrs Atherton's moments of clarity, such as protecting her keys, the group consensus at the centre about her was resoundingly negative. In the following months, the topic of Mrs Atherton arose on more than one occasion in her absence at the centre and she was always referred to as 'old', language seldom used about anyone else involved with the centre.[4] A prime example of this came during a tea break at the centre two months later when a group discussion began about Mrs Atherton. Such communal discussions are rare in the centres and this one highlighted the strength of people's feeling on the topic. Members were recounting how she had made an appearance again in the middle of bingo the previous week when I had not been present. Apparently, the episode had started when Mrs Atherton wheeled herself to the centre door but was not able to open it so instead pounded on the door with her walking sticks to attract assistance. However, as one of the members said, 'We just ignored her'. Her disruptive behaviour was attributed in a variety of terms, with Edna starting the conversation by saying how Mrs Atherton 'is old'. Evelyn said instead that, 'It's her age' which makes her act like this, while Karen said that, 'It's an illness, she's ill'. Unlike definitions of old age which have emerged from other research that privileges chronology or ability as markers of oldness, being old in this context had much more to do with what is deemed to be proper social comportment, conventions that Mrs Atherton was not respecting.

Not only had Mrs Atherton come late to bingo, this time once she finally gained entrance she was angry, with members reporting that she was again saying that no one came for her to bring her to the centre and declaring that she never misses a centre meeting. According to the members who had been there, Mrs Atherton had been irritated in particular with Edna, her neighbour and was blaming her for being forgotten, although according to Edna, no arrangement existed between them. Then Edna said that she knows that Mrs Atherton is lonely, but that:

> We all know what it's like to be lonely [addressing the other centre members in the room], but she's not like us, she can't get out to go to [into town] or go visiting like we can and to be honest, I think she'd be better off in a home because at least she'd have some company there.

During this conversation, a group catharsis of discomfort about Mrs Atherton occurred. Feelings about how she disturbs centre patterns as well as individual members' sense of well-being were aired. Through this process and ones earlier, both between individuals and as a group, consensus is reaffirmed about Mrs Atherton, who is stigmatised as a marginal figure, worthy of ostracisation ('We just ignored her') due to her unacceptably high levels of oldness.

Importantly though, this ostracisation is not attributed to her personality, such as mean-spiritedness or being a troublemaker, but is rather perceived and discussed by the group as being due specifically to old age. Unlike the other members, Mrs Atherton is perceived as old because she is disruptive, because she is temporally confused (about which day it is, about how often she attends bingo, about what time the bingo starts), because she 'can't get out', because 'she's not like us', because she repeats herself and because she forgets answers she has been given to questions, and asks them again. Members elaborate on her oldness by talking about Mrs Atherton in terms of how 'her mind is starting to go' and that 'she forgets herself sometimes'. Consequently, Mrs Atherton is now perceived and constructed as someone who is truly old by the centre members, in distinction from themselves who may be experiencing some normal ageing, but who are not really old – distinctions I discuss in more detail below. Furthermore, this shift in definition also promotes a systematic exclusion of Mrs Atherton from the category of full adult. Mrs Atherton is made old and is ostracised because of her behaviour (on to which oldness is read by her peers) and in turn is subjected to treatment such as speaking about her in the third person in her presence and searching her person without her consent for her keys, which would not be acceptable with other adults.

While these are extremely sensitive topics to broach and difficult ones to obtain Ella's or Mrs Atherton's own perspectives on, one day Mrs Atherton brought them up herself with me. In the late autumn towards the end of my fieldwork, I ended up helping her home in her wheelchair again after one of her infrequent trips to the centre. As we walked towards her bungalow, she told me that earlier in the day, before bingo, she had been planning to come to the centre but that she had not been sure if she should since she did not feel well and since people did not want her there. Although sadly this was largely true, I was surprised to hear her say so since she usually seemed so oblivious to the other members' coolness and animosity. I asked her why she thought that. She replied that it is not fair of her to come if she's not well because 'it puts on people' and that 'once you get to be nearly one hundred, you can't expect much'. In this way, Mrs Atherton attributes her difficulties at the centre to issues of health (not feeling well) and sociality (not feeling wanted). However, despite these vocalised pressures and the sheer exertion of wheeling herself to the centre, Mrs Atherton still tries to attend. I believe that this is because although she categorises herself as 'nearly one hundred' and not in a position to 'expect much', unlike her peers she does not conceptualise herself as an old woman. As such, she perceives the avenues of participation as still open to her, despite the other members' best efforts to exclude her. Mrs Atherton's situation makes all too evident the rupturing gap between epistemology and pragmatics in terms of the everyday experiences of ageing, selfhood and subjectivity.

## Monitoring

Percival (2000) has written about the paradoxes of gossip among older people living in sheltered housing in inner London and who attend community centres similar to those in Dodworth. His exploration of the social role of gossip and the close social surveillance by one's peers that it represents mirrors in some ways the dynamics I have been describing here. As with Percival's descriptions of gossip and the maintenance of social norms, the building of consensus about Ella and Mrs Atherton by centre members is able to simultaneously forge closeness and social distance among members (Percival, 2000). Where our work differs, however, is that Percival does not examine whether gossip contributes to the ways in which oldness is attributed among peers. Although gossip as social practice did figure in my research experiences, more relevant to the attribution of oldness described above is what I call 'monitoring'.

Monitoring is an unorganised, informal activity that I observed and indeed participated in during my time in the centres, such as the examples of Ella and Mrs Atherton. While ostensibly a meeting place in which to play bingo and whist, centre meetings are also centrally important sites for socialising, and offer a chance to catch up on the week's events in the village and on each other's lives. An important aspect of catching up on an individual as well as on a collective basis also involves keeping track of the state of being of members and of other village peers. This includes a great deal of attention in public meeting places being paid to how people appeared physically and mentally. Pallor of skin, manner of walking, relative ease or unease of movement, tiredness, alertness, decision-making ability, consistency in narrative, believability of narrative, ability to remember, ability to concentrate, maintaining good social skills and social comportment are characteristics attended to. Monitoring is thus the practice of paying keen attention to and of discussing in detail other people's physical and mental states. Although everyone was potentially subject to low-grade monitoring, including me, each centre and the luncheon club had figures around which monitoring was particularly focused and intense. Any perceived decline in others then becomes public property for the gossip circuit, passed by word of mouth from group to group, circulating through individuals, sometimes becoming part of the accepted community code about a particular person and at other times not making a lasting impression.

In several respects, my analysis of monitoring is indebted to Foucault's notions of discipline and power (1979). His work on the panopticon and the self-disciplining behaviours people consequently devise to evade the unseen observer are particularly relevant to monitoring. Self-disciplining is evident in the centres and in Dodworth in terms of pressure to demonstrate ongoing competence in the required fields, such as 'appropriate' social comportment. Foucault's work also elucidates how power is often exercised in indirect forms that silently permeate everyday lives and constrain the ways in which we act. Monitoring is very much akin to this sort of Foucauldian analysis of power. It is a set of practices that reaffirms narrow models of behaviour as normal and appropriate and censures others. Furthermore, it is based not on an authoritative source of power but rather a diffuse and circulating form as the social message becomes so internalised that people come to regulate their own behaviour for fear of being labelled as 'old'.

Where my analysis diverges from a Foucauldian perspective, however, is his emphasis on the inescapability of internalised social control and the extent to which people are utterly powerless or trapped by social rules and norms. I would argue instead that the experiences within the centres and in village life more broadly for older people in Dodworth are more complex, and at times more unpredictable, than this. For example, monitoring is not an evenly distributed practice. Some individuals did more of it than others and some days at the centres more monitoring occurred than on others. It is important to bear in mind as well that monitoring among peers happens over a period of time and in multiple locales of interaction: people run into each other outside the centre in their daily lives and there is a circuit of information that operates and maintains a flow of status reports about one another of the old Dodworthers throughout the village. As an overall pattern in the centres, however, monitoring was a widely pursued practice and is one of the building blocks of making and assigning old age among peers.

Monitoring is a sensitive subject because the construction of where old age begins seems to hinge implicitly on the extent to which individuals are perceived by the people around them to be physically able and mentally cohesive. By asking people to talk to me one to one about these cultural constructions and about other people, I was making the implicit explicit. Doing this with such a loaded label of 'oldness' often provoked deep unease. I found I had to tread very lightly when discussing this with people who took part in this research. This is because of the social stigma of being labelled or perceived as 'old' and the shift in power relations that often occur once this reassignment occurs. As such, I generally avoided explicitly asking about other individuals in these terms. Whenever possible, I did ask for their reflections on these topics but found it much more useful to pay close attention to what was said and implied in spontaneous circumstances and how situations developed over time among members at the centres.

Furthermore, an emphasis on monitoring could be misconstrued as meaning that the people I worked with all manifest the negative characteristics of decline that they watch for in each other and stigmatise once identified. This is not the case. I wish to be clear here that the participants in this research rarely manifested forms of stereotyped old-age behaviour that circulate freely in cultural constructions of old age. The people I came to know are not senile, overwhelmingly ill, forgetful, mentally slower and withdrawn, but instead, like younger adults, manifest varying degrees of vivacity, quick-wittedness, perception and activity depending on their individual personalities and situational context. What does transpire, however, is a social current of attention to, and remarking negatively upon, other individuals' mental acuity and bodily characteristics if they appear to change or are perceived to transgress a certain threshold. This threshold is the one that represents the frontier between what is described as 'slowing down' or normal ageing and 'getting past it', or real old age, a much more threatening prospect. Thus, through the practices of monitoring, centre members were policing the changes in their peers that could signal the manifestation of old age, a shift that had socially damaging ramifications if identified for the person concerned. Monitoring, then, is one way the gap between epistemology and pragmatics becomes bridged in everyday experience.

## Making and breaking norms of ageing

The practice of monitoring thus reveals a distinction made by older people in the centres between 'normal ageing' and 'real old age'. The accepted parameters of normal ageing as constructed by the older people I came to know allow for, and indeed anticipate, a certain amount of physical and mental changes that are due to the ageing process. These include the possible onset of, for instance, arthritis, diabetes, difficulties in walking and breathing, changes in vision and memory blanks. Some of these characteristics do not manifest themselves consistently within individuals but fluctuate over time, nor do they manifest consistently across my research population, although they are widespread. Such conditions are openly discussed and commiserated over and are not perceived as threatening the integrity of the individual nor as signalling the arrival of old age. While often a topic of discussion between individuals and within groups, such ailments are ultimately attributed to the inevitable ageing process and were often summarised with statements such as: 'Well, what can you do? It's just old age.'

Far more threatening, however, are sharp declines in mental acuity and associated shifts in social comportment. These are the conditions subject to the closest monitoring and suspicion and mark the onset of real old age in the perception of the older people I worked with. In group settings, members monitor each other closely for continuity in narrative accounts, for personal comportment, for ability to concentrate and perform tasks such as playing cards or keeping the record books properly and for respecting social conventions. Maintaining norms in these areas are signs of continuing good mental condition. The reason this becomes so critical is that full personhood and full adulthood is assigned to those individuals who meet the acceptable criteria of physical, social and mental performance. Variations from the norm are tolerated to different degrees in group settings, depending on the individual's behaviour and the individual's role in the group, but if consensus builds that someone is 'getting past it' into real old age, small but significant shifts in how that person is interacted with start to accumulate within the group. Those who are perceived to be 'getting past it', 'losing themselves' or manifesting real old age are interacted with in different ways and no longer seen fully as equals. This is in part due to the pressures of maintaining a consistent sense of self as well as group stability in an environment where the mind and body are under uncontrollable and unpredictable pressures due to the ageing process. The practice of monitoring that I describe within the centres is not limited to these sites in Dodworth, but mirrors wider social practices that transpire throughout village networks and call to mind Foucault's evocative description of the panopticon (1979). Negotiating these pressures, both inside and outside of the centres, are some of the most demanding experiences of growing older. The protective measures put in place to guard one's selfhood are vital and demonstrate what is at stake in the practices of monitoring that I describe.

A further factor in this process is that although some centre members are relative newcomers to the area, importantly, a significant majority has lived in Dodworth for decades and many members have known each other over a long period of time. As such, they have long-standing notions and memories of how someone 'is', as well as how they fit into the wider social landscape. Monitoring often occurs within the context of long-standing knowledge of one another and their place in the village, their personal and family histories, past grievances and long-standing relationships. In this way, the ramifications of monitoring are perhaps more severe and potentially threatening in a locale like Dodworth, with its low levels of anonymity, than in a setting with higher levels of residential mobility and less stable residence patterns, where transgressions of the boundaries of old age may not be as easily remarked upon. In a setting such as Dodworth, however, monitoring becomes another key element in the way old age and oldness are assigned intra-generationally.

## Conclusions

In an attempt to move away from the problematic terminology in the social scientific literature on demarcating when old age begins or who can be said to be old that has tended to focus implicitly on chronological age or physical ability, I have turned my attention in this chapter to ethnographic examples of how old age is forged through processes of social interaction among peers. While 'oldness' is a state of being that people in Western cultures agree exists, and 'old age' is a category that is readily used in daily discourse and living, what old age is and who is old, nevertheless, resists anchoring. Despite this, the boundaries of old age are codified according to deeply negative attributes, all of which threaten the integrity of the self, and ageing is perceived as 'an unwelcome movement out of personhood, as something to be hidden or disguised' (Hockey and James, 1993: 87). It is because of these negative connotations that no one feels as if they personally are old (Itzin, 1990) and why the radical disjuncture between how old age is defined by the dominant society and how it is actually experienced is deeply alienating for older people (Vesperi, 1985).

This chapter demonstrates that attending to this gap as it plays out in daily life reveals important insights into what is at stake for the ageing self, a selfhood that is at times made exceedingly vulnerable through negative social pressures. I have examined the complicated ways in which oldness is a relational concept and how the social category of old age is constructed, used and negotiated by older people themselves. While old age is culturally constructed, it is not something that is simply 'made' by younger adults and 'read on to' older people. Old age is also a social category which older people themselves, as socialised members of society, are engaged in making. This is not intentionally malicious behaviour but is rather what de Certeau identifies as everyday practices that usually reside in the 'obscure background of social activity' (1984: xi). By attending explicitly to the everyday of intra-generational relationships, I seek to bring the obscure into closer focus and to demonstrate some of the ways in which oldness is attributed by older people themselves about their peers in everyday life. This is not an exercise in placing blame. Rather, I wish to highlight the complicated and multi-directional ways in which oldness is made in order to better understand the processes at work in the cultural construction of old age.

One key point that emerges from this scrutiny is that although oldness is stigmatised as much by older people as it is by younger adults, older people use different criteria to demarcate old age and oldness. Where old age begins is not a linear frontier, not an imaginary line that before being stepped over one is 'not yet old' and after stepping over the same person is irrevocably 'elderly'. Old age is not a frontier whose edges, once breached, are irreversible. It is instead a complicated mixture of comportment, attitude and acuity, adjudicated on by other people in one's life. Old age as a culturally assigned category is created within the dialectics of interpersonal interactions and varies a great deal depending on one's own relative position. The older people I worked with made far more distinctions about who is old and what oldness is than most younger people would ever make or have a vocabulary to distinguish among. Furthermore, unlike the many attempts at categorising where old age begins and the different levels of it that I began this chapter with, older people in Dodworth do not emphasise oldness, chronological age nor physical ability but instead weigh mental acuity and social comportment more heavily in their assessment of their peers.

The intra-generational relationships recounted in this chapter, the distinctions between 'looking' and 'acting' one's age, the symbolic positions occupied by Mrs Atherton and Ella at the centre, the concrete practices people engage in with them and the language used to describe them demonstrate the culturally imagined boundaries of old age for older people themselves in Dodworth. These portraits also demonstrate how the process of attribution of oldness is not a fixed one. It can change, given different social dynamics, such as in Ella's case, and it is not necessarily a label that is internalised evenly, as in the case of Mrs Atherton.

The practice of monitoring is a second key point this chapter develops. While a gap may exist between epistemology and pragmatics in the application of the category of old age, older people in my research population watch for signs of oldness in their peers. I have demonstrated how monitoring becomes a critical element of how oldness is adjudicated on by one's peers and the extent to which relationships with peers play a role in the construction of old age. Monitoring also reveals the distinctions made by older people themselves about the boundaries and distinctions between 'real' and 'normal' old age. While a great deal of physical change and a certain amount of shifts in mental states are accommodated in older people's notions of normal ageing, the most important gauge of the onset of real old age is a decline in mental acuity and related shifts in comportment. Monitoring is thus a practice with salient and often deeply negative social ramifications and figures prominently in the everyday ways in which oldness is assigned and experienced among peers.

### Notes

1 'There's nothing [good] in getting old.'
2 'They'd give me hell.'
3 Interestingly, Paul Thompson writes about the high esteem in which self-control was held in working-class and middle-class Edwardian families in Britain. According to him, this was 'commoner in the north … the impact of evangelical puritanism on the industrial working classes may provide part of the explanation, but equally the hardships of industrial work itself may have left a deep scar on life within the family' (1992a: 43). Possibly the emphasis on self-control that I experienced among my research participants is a lasting influence of this ideal of personal comportment.
4 More typical is the saying that someone is or has 'a big age' (e.g. 'Well, she's a big age now') or that someone is 'getting on now'. While a way of acknowledging a person's chronological age, these phrases do not stigmatise in the same way that saying someone is 'getting past it' or 'old' does.

# 5

# Reconfiguring normative models of self

## Introduction

Having considered the category of old age and ways it is made in the previous chapter, this chapter addresses the ways in which normative forms of selfhood and subjectivity can come under pressure and begin to shift in older age. In Chapter 1, I laid out a processual approach to the self that emphasises the salience of interaction and intersubjectivity in the creation of self. Within this framing, the self is negotiated through a variety of settings and situations, shifting at times to accommodate them. What is emphasised in one's presentation of self depends importantly on the context of interaction and the other social actors present. Crapanzano comments on this when he writes of 'metapragmatic characterizations' (1992). By this he means that how the self and the other are characterised do not stem from inherent, essential traits of individuals, but are produced in the context of the moment of interaction and encounter – that what matters is not what the self 'means' but rather how the self is used and managed. In this way, Crapanzano argues for recognition of 'the self as a product of social interaction' (1992: 12). What I propose in this chapter is that while a theoretical understanding of selfhood as intersubjectively produced is an extremely useful one, in the case of older people it also helps reveal the social pressures they face to be consistent in their self-presentation, a lived dilemma that is not experienced to the same extent by younger people.

Such pressure to maintain consistency is in tension with a fluid model of self that is celebrated in the academic literature; debates have occurred over whether or not, and the ways in which, the self is continuously produced through social interaction and if discontinuity and rupture inform the self as much as continuity and consistency do (Battaglia, 1995a; Ewing, 1990; Quinn, 2006; Sökefeld, 1999; Strauss, 1997). I argue that these models do not always accommodate the experiences of older people as they do for younger and middle-aged people. So, for example, later in this chapter I discuss the relationship between 'the remembered self' and 'the inhabited self' to illustrate the pressures on the ageing self to negotiate shifting bodily and temporal frames that inform the self. This theme also continues in Chapter 6 where I consider the central place of narrativity in the construction of self and the ways in which this too might reformulate under the unique dimensions of older age. Ultimately, what I wish to consider in this chapter are the challenges that the ageing self presents to the working normative model of selfhood that circulates in Western cultural contexts.

My reflections here on ageing selfhood sit within a growing movement by other social scientists working on ageing who have begun turning their attention to related issues of identity, the ageing self and embodiment. Authors, mainly sociologists, have emphasised various perspectives: the extent to which age-related identity can be said to be newly flexible compared to a previous fixity, particularly with the rise of consumer culture, commodification and lifestyle markets (Blaikie, 1999; Featherstone and Hepworth, 1989; Gilleard and Higgs, 2000; Katz, 2005); critiques of the ways in which gerontological knowledge and discourse shape the experience of old age (Katz, 2005, 1996); a rise in attention to agency in old age (Tulle, 2004); tensions for older people living in an ageist society between inner and outer selves (Biggs, 2004; Bytheway, 2000), 'ageless' selves (Kaufman, 1986) and 'not feeling old' (Thompson *et al.*, 1990); and what a literary turn can reveal about the ageing self (Hepworth, 2000). This body of work has all been part of a significant attempt by social scientists to reinsert a sense of humanity into accounts of ageing and to bring current critical social theory into conversation with ageing studies.

Such burgeoning interest in ageing and identity in the social sciences has also been attuned to developments in social theory, which have witnessed an increased attention to the body. The literature on embodiment has demonstrated that the body is not simply 'a "thing" onto which social patterns are ... projected' (Jackson, 1983: 329). Rather, being-in-the-world is corporeal, somatic and embodied (Jackson, 1983; c.f. Csordas, 1990). Our bodies matter profoundly to our sense of self, our social lives with others and our everyday experiences (Shilling, 2003). This is a problematic that has been highly influenced by the work of key thinkers such as Merleau-Ponty, Bourdieu and Foucault, with serious attempts to engage with these bodies of work in the sociological literature on ageing appearing in the late 1990s and early 2000s (e.g. Gilleard and Higgs, 2000; Katz, 1996; Kontos, 1999; Twigg, 2004). Developments in this area have grown steadily since, with authors considering the ageing body across a range of social sites. This corpus of work includes older elite runners and the relations of bodily ageing, identity and ageing they make manifest (Tulle, 2004). It extends to clothing and how what we wear 'mediate[s] between the naked body and the social world, the self and society, presenting a means whereby social expectations in relation to age act upon and are made manifest in the body' (Twigg, 2007: 285) and in turn help to frame the ageing process. Dementia and selfhood have furthermore been a fruitful site for thinking through the ways in which agency is located not just in the mind, but in the body as well whereby the ability of the mind to express a functioning normal self is severely affected but an embodied active self might still express itself in various ways (Kontos, 2003). All of these authors, mainly sociologists, rightly emphasise that such focus on embodiment is not to essentialise ageing as a physiological concern, but instead to insist on the social and cultural parameters that shape and give meaning to bodily experience for all human beings, whether older or not. My reflections here help develop this body of work. I do so by wedding fine-grained ethnographic detail, which permits close consideration of the intimacy of people's subjective experiences, with the anthropological literature on self. In focusing on the self, and as I previously stated in Chapter 1, I do not simply mean identity or social roles. While these are bound up in issues of selfhood, it is instead the subjective 'I', the constellation of subjective realities created through interaction (Morris, 1994) that binds people to the social world and permits them to act in it, which is of interest to me here.

This, however, is not to say that questions of selfhood have been absent in the social science literature on ageing. Selfhood has featured prominently in two respects, namely in debates over 'inner' and 'outer' selves and in regards to dementia and Alzheimer's disease. However, as I discuss below, in both cases opportunities have been missed to better understand (ethnographically and experientially) perspectives on the ageing self and ageing subjectivity. This chapter redresses such a framing by examining how aspects of the self specific to old age but not specifically linked to illness or disability play out in everyday life. It also reflects on how some characteristics specific to the ageing self can enlarge wider debates about self and experience in anthropology.

## 'Inner' and 'outer' selves

A body of work exists that examines tensions for older people living in an ageist society between inner and outer selves (Biggs, 2004; Bytheway, 2000), 'ageless' selves (Kaufman, 1986) and 'not feeling old' (Thompson et al., 1990). This work focuses on a lack of self-identification as 'old' by older people and contributes to broader debates over continuity and discontinuity in later parts of the life course. One of the most prominent aspects in this literature is a debate focusing on the tension often experienced by the ageing subject between physical transformations – the outer self – and a continuous self-perception as 'young' – the inner self. Two texts, Kaufman's The Ageless Self (1986) and Featherstone and Hepworth's chapter on the mask of ageing (1989) are key references in this debate.

The central issue is the experiential rift that grows between one's increasingly 'old', external, physical self and a simultaneous feeling of continuity in one's self-perception as 'young' inside. This sets up a series of conceptual oppositions between an outer self (the ageing, physical body) and an inner self (a younger, unchanging essence located in an individual's spirit and mind). The tension between inner self and outer self is compounded by the negative social assumptions read onto the ageing body and perceived threats to selfhood such as a growing dependency on others, what Tanner (drawing from Phillipson and Biggs, 1998), has described as something that risks destabilising one's 'core self' (2001: 269). Silver reminds us, however, that shifts in subjective and psychological states are also gendered (2003: 388), a consideration that is not always drawn out in the ageless self debate.

What does emerge, however, in this debate is a vision of an inner self that is perceived as 'not old' in the face of external stereotypes of old age, which are projected onto an ageing body and that determine how society treats its older members (c.f. Gibson, 2000: 775). This leads to the belief that a self can be 'old' physically but remain 'young' in spirit (*ibid.*: 777). Kaufman writes that older people do not adopt an 'elderly' identity but instead maintain a sense of themselves in old age, a sense of self that does not centre around ageing but rather around this inner, still young, self. As Bytheway describes Kaufman's work, although 'her subjects are aware of popular conceptions, of how these conceptions [of 'old age'] relate to appearance and of the appearance of their own bodies', they choose instead to 'reassert and find meaning in the idea of a continuing "un-ageing" self' (Bytheway, 2000: 786), which is also felt to be the 'true' self. The concepts of self at work here resonate strongly with Taylor's dichotomy of public/private selves and also the self acting simultaneously as object and subject of Mead and Foucault that I discussed in Chapter 1.

In a related vein, Featherstone and Hepworth posit that increasingly in Western societies, the ageing process is understood as a mask that disguises and hides the youthful self beneath (1989: 148). They argue that ageing is a physical process that unjustly layers misrepresentative and misinterpreted symbols of foreignness onto the body, revealing the extreme Western valuation of the 'true' self as the younger self. This has two implications. The first is that the disjuncture between external appearance and an internal, subjective sense of self is likely to become more strongly marked in our awareness as we age (*ibid.*: 151). The second is that the stereotypes of ageing are rigid and permit little space for older people to express what they are actually experiencing: 'it seems to be very often the case that we fix older people ... in roles which do not do justice to the richness of their individual experiences and multi-facets of their personalities. The sanitised one-dimensional benign stereotypes "granny" and "grandpa" are good examples of this ageist trap' (*ibid.*). These stereotypes lock older people into one-dimensional roles and gloss over the other aspects of their experiences of becoming older. It also denies a multidimensional experience of time and self to older people, which middle-aged adults are able to enjoy without fear of censure, intensifying the process of transforming older people into the Other.

The explanatory model of inner and outer ageing selves and the mask of ageing has become a powerful one in the social science literature. However, criticism has been levied against it on the grounds that such a perspective promotes an ageist argument. Gibson, for example, has argued that:

> The idea of people being 'old' physically but 'young' in spirit, is based on an outworn Cartesian concept of a mind/body split ... This ageist attitude ... is unintentionally reinforced by those academics and professionals who insist that, although people must become 'old' in years, the youthful ghost can remain untainted, as it were, by the passage of years. Many gerontologists write as though they accepted the existence of the young ghost inhabiting an elderly machine (e.g. Comfort, 1977). Others appear to think that the ghost is ageless but the machine goes on ageing (e.g. Kaufman, 1986). Some, like Hepworth

(1991), suggest that the ghost is 'the real self' and remains young, whilst the machine – not the real self – continues to age. Biggs (1997) presents a variety of accounts which are all, basically, a version of the ageless ghost wearing the mask of the time-weary machine. (Gibson, 2000: 777)

In an article thinking through Gibson and other authors' challenges to this model, Bytheway posits that a vision of inner and outer selves reflects a subjective interpretation of one's own body in light of the fairly negative popular conceptions of old age. Rather than this model being a denial of ageing (as Gibson would have it), it involves the individual staking a claim to an inner, younger self which mutes the outer, older self, thereby asserting one's identity as still socially relevant (Bytheway, 2000: 786). In a further step addressing the accusation of ageism, Bytheway argues that rather than social gerontology being ageist, it has erred in the other direction. In other words, he says that the discipline asks questions that are framed only by age. This creates a dynamic whereby the discipline's research comes to centre on '*ageing* rather than *living* individuals: ageful rather than ageless' (2000: 785–6, emphasis original). Such a division into inner and outer is both made possible by cultural framings of self premised on a Cartesian dualism of mind and body, but it also challenges the division, as I elaborate below in my discussion of Pia Kontos's work on embodied selfhood and my own work on remembered and inhabited selves. It further parallels what M. Rosaldo identifies as a particularly Western concern with 'hidden inner selves' (1984: 147) whereby a gap emerges between 'the presentation' and 'the self', discussed in Chapter 1. I return to this debate later, but first I turn to a second significant theme in the literature on self and old age, that of the 'loss of self'.

## Self, dementia and Alzheimer's disease

Alzheimer's disease, dementia and the 'loss of self' that they precipitate has garnered a great deal of anthropological and sociological attention (see for example Chatterji, 1998; Cohen, 1998; Herskovits, 1995; Hinton and Levkoff, 1999; Kontos, 2004; Leibing and Cohen, 2006; Sabat, 2001) with a similar trend also evident in human geography (Andrews *et al.*, 2007: 155). This perspective on ageing, which emphasises threats to the self, is understandable given the existential rupture that a loss of self provokes and the cultural imagination that has come to associate 'senility' and 'dementia' with ageing. Contributions these authors have made include analysing personhood in Alzheimer's disease as contested space (Leibing, 2008); experiential accounts of Alzheimer's from the perspective of the sufferers themselves that is not simply a register of losses but which also highlights the abilities that continue (social and cognitive) despite the disease (Sabat, 2001); and accounts that critique the Cartesian dualism of mind/body as sustaining selfhood, arguing instead that a corporeal understanding of the self should complement a cognitive model of selfhood that has underpinned dementia care (Kontos, 2004, 2005).

Kontos is a prominent writer in this body of work and argues that in order to appreciate what happens to the self with advancing years (especially with onset of dementia as an effect of Alzheimer's disease), a closer look at the embodied nature of identity (2004, 2005) and at the materiality of the body and its expressions of selfhood (1999) is necessary. She argues that the framework for understanding the self in Alzheimer's has largely been influenced by a social interactionist perspective where the key emphasis in on the social nature of self (2005: 554). Kontos contends that 'confining what is essential about selfhood to the brain is to overlook how bodily sources of agency, grounded in the pre-reflective level of experience, are fundamental to the constitution and manifestation of selfhood and Alzheimer's disease' (2005: 555). Kontos further posits that 'individuals bring to social engagement, by virtue of their embodied nature, a degree of intentionality and creativity', which should be duly acknowledged in person-centred dementia care (2005: 557). Kontos proposes giving due importance to the body in understandings of selfhood. Her argument 'advocates the irreducibly embodied nature of human subjectivity and agency' (2003: 152). To develop an alternative framework that can 'embrace the "facticity of our embodiment"' (2003: 160), Kontos draws on Merleau-Ponty's ideas on intentionality and those of Bourdieu on habitus. This is in response to, and a critique of, the powerful emphasis that biomedical sciences give to 'link[ing] inseparably intention and mental capacity' (2003: 164). The increasing 'biologization' of understandings of the self, personhood and identity is also a concern for Leibing (2008) who links this tendency with larger shifts in post-modern societies towards globalisation, timespace compression and hence what she calls a flattening of the world. Leibing argues that this leads to a flattening and reduction of the several ways in which personhood can be conceived, leading to an emphasis on cognition and memory as markers of identity rather than also giving due recognition to embodiment, corporeality and the soul (2008).

While extremely valuable for the richness they bring to the conceptualisation of selfhood and subjectivity of those living with Alzheimer's disease, such an emphasis in the literature on the ageing self that focuses on dementia and Alzheimer's can unintentionally but problematically reproduce negative stereotypes of older people. While Alzheimer's disease is a pressing and devastating condition, it is also at an extreme end of a long spectrum of experience. It is, furthermore, a minority of older people who suffer with Alzheimer's and other dementia disorders: in 2006 in the UK, these affliction figures were 0.9 per cent of those aged 60–64, rising to 6.0 per cent by age 75–79, 12.2 per cent for those aged 80–84 and 24.8 per cent in those aged 85 and older (Parliamentary Office of Science and Technology, 2007). While these figures are not insignificant, they also indicate that even at the most severe levels of incidence, more than three-quarters of people (aged 85 and over and far more in the younger age brackets) are *not* suffering with dementia disorders. Thus, focusing on Alzheimer's and dementia is at the expense of a wide range of other experiences of self and subjectivity in older age that are less extreme, more commonplace and more representative of many older people's lives and the lives of many older-people-to-be. It risks reproducing a problematic vision of the self in old age only in terms of fragility and decay. Indeed, Ikels and Bealls identify a broader trend within the anthropology of ageing since the 1980s as centred on the study of physical decline, disability and care giving, interests that have

> nearly overpowered all other facts about age and aging for anthropology. The number of anthropologists working on some aspect of age-associated disability, be it on experiencing or interpreting illness, obtaining appropriate health care, or being 'burdened' by providing care, is probably about equal to the number working on all other aging-related phenomena. (2001: 126)

The focus on dementia raises the issue of how aspects of the self specific to old age but not specifically linked to illness or disability play out in everyday life and what such work can contribute to a fuller analysis of self across the life course. It is to this that I now turn my attention. I begin by considering some of the ways in which the older people I came to know described their own sense of ageing selfhood.

## Selfhood and staking claims to being active

Over the many months of fieldwork and multiple encounters in different social registers with people I came to know, key signifiers associated with a sense of self emerged from field notes and interviews. In this section, I wish to look in detail at one of these, the concept of being 'active'. I highlight the experiences of one individual, Emma, who I introduced in Chapter 3, and her family, whose accounts demonstrate particularly well what is at stake.

'Active' is a word some people in my research population use to describe themselves and their sense of self. It also serves in many ways as shorthand for asserting one's independence. 'Active' is, however, not purely physical: it is also social. Physical activity is considered widely by my research participants as essential to warding off the negative aspects of old age and helps people to 'keep going'. To maintain an active life and keep busy is also to symbolically protect oneself from perceptions of 'oldness' and instead to sustain and prolong the self as 'not old'. As such, 'doing' and 'not doing' are part of the way that boundaries of old age are marked. Keeping active and 'doing', not surprisingly then, were also key signifiers associated with a sense of self. Activity varies in people's narratives, such as those seen in Chapter 3, from Mary and Tom's constant travelling, to Vivienne's desire to 'mix' socially, to Emma's descriptions of how she still does all her own housecleaning even though she can no longer walk more than the shortest of distances. Decline in either activity or ability are perceived as a potential threat to one's conception of self.

When asked directly, people would often explain what 'being active' means to them in similar terms to how Ivy describes them here:

> CATHRINE: I wonder . . . you were describing yourself as very active . . . how would you explain what active means?
> IVY: Well, I can't be doing with sitting doing nothing. I must stay doing something, whether it's housework or sewing or anything like that. But I go out a lot, you see, as well.

CATHRINE: Where do you like to go?

IVY: Well, I like to play cards. And I like to go walking and, I do swim, but very occasionally now ... because it's too far away. Well you've got to go to Metrodome and you've two buses to catch, you see.

Ivy who was born in Scotland but moved to Dodworth in her twenties when she married a Dodworth man who worked for the Co-op stores, is quick here to emphasise that she is busy in the house and that she goes out often. She tells me that her activities outside the house are not just bingo and whist (which she does enjoy) but also include physical activities such as swimming and walking, both fairly unusual for her peer group. And yet, while activity (physical and social in this case) is important in Ivy's daily life and forms a significant element of her description of self, she acknowledges that it is also something which has certain limits, such as the difficulties of accessing facilities such as the local swimming pool at the Metrodome.

Sometimes the links between the self and activity are more subtle and connect back to a person's past self and past responsibilities, such as when I asked Emma if she feels like the same person now as she was twenty years ago:

Not really, I'm not. I'd do anything for anybody, but you can't as you get older, can you? ... You see, I had Mrs Lund, Mrs Tott and me dad all at same time and I came here [to the bungalow where her father lived] twice a week [to look after him]. I can remember ... me dad said he'd go on Meals on Wheels, you know ... and uh ... first day it was a mutton chop which he didn't like and second, what were second? It were something he didn't like so he stopped [Meals on Wheels]. And I were cleaning kitchen when she come with second meal and I says, 'Oh, I do feel awful', I says, 'I come every Thursday and I've always had his dinner ready', and she says, 'Oh, don't worry about that'. And I cleaned his bungalow while ever he lived, you know. Cause at Saturday, when he come home at Friday from our house, I come on a Saturday and uh I didn't leave while half past eight at night and uh I'd changed all cushion covers and uh, I'd put them all in a pillow case, ready for me husband bringing them back on a Monday when he fetched him.

Emma's father died over twenty-five years prior to this interview, but she helped look after him for sixteen years after her mother had died. Mrs Lund and Mrs Tott were two older neighbours who became close friends and who Emma had over to her house every Friday for dinner for many years when Emma was herself middle-aged. This narrative segment reflects some aspects of Emma's essential self-concept as someone who *does* things for other people, but this becomes curtailed by the physical changes of ageing: 'I'd do anything for anybody, but you can't as you get older, can you?', something that also impacts on her sense of who she is. Such reflections also reflect a highly gendered set of expectations of uses the body should be put to, which for Emma include cleaning, caring and washing. Housework, unlike paid work, is something that never goes away and so, on one hand, women of this generation have opportunities (if housework can be considered as such) to continue with normal bodily activities for longer. By contrast, this also means that when bodily limitations arise that disrupt the ability to carry out such work, these limitations also come to invade the private sphere in a much more immediate way than for other individuals in classed or gendered positions who have not performed such tasks across their lives.

Significantly, Emma's reflections came at a point in her life where her walking has seriously deteriorated and she can no longer walk to the shop at the top of the street. Her daughter-in-law now goes to the supermarket for her, supervises her medications and has organised a cleaner to help her manage her housework. These changes all intensified after the recent death of her husband, Ernest, and while they worked together as a very efficient team, Emma is finding it difficult to take care of things on her own and feels this keenly.

Doing and being active are linked to finding ways to fill or pass time, discussed previously in Chapter 3. On the one hand, this evokes Hockey and James (1993) who cite Ekerdt's (1986) work on the existence of a 'busy ethic' in old age as a way of 'softening' the marginalisation of retirement. While this may well be true in Dodworth, there are also strong local idioms that link activity with perpetuating health and well-being and which are tied to a deep cultural valuation of hard work and proficiency. Furthermore, if we are to take a paradigm of embodiment seriously and consider that the body and how it is used is not simply symbolic of something, but rather is partly constitutive of ones' being in the world, such rhetoric also needs to be taken seriously. The dilemma this presents to ones' sense of self when one cannot *do* what one *could do* becomes more apparent.

The importance of being active and maintaining ability are evident in a joking passage from Mary's interview. I had not yet asked her about activity or the self in the interview and yet she draws them both out in conversation. The segment starts with me asking Mary, who lives in her own home, if she had ever considered living in a council bungalow. She has and says that the advantage would be that it would be a one-storey building rather than two-storey. I then asked her if having a warden would be advantageous. Rather than answering me directly, she pointed out that they could have had a walking warden (a service provided for a fee by the council for people living in private homes) come to their home if they had wanted one:

CATHRINE: A walking warden?

MARY: Aye, aye and I told her not to come because I was fitter than her and now, well, she's been dead and buried ages. And she says 'Shall I put you down [on my list of people to check on]?' and I says 'You shan't!'

CATHRINE: When was this?

MARY: Tom was sixty-five [about ten years ago] ... now I'm not saying it's not a good thing. I think if anybody's on their own, yeah, but again, they can have said they're alright and they can be all wrong after. And then they're left while next morning, apart from they've got alarms. Um and when I first went to Tech for having me hair doing [she gets it done for free so the students there can learn how to], as I was coming in, the woman there, she held a woman's arm and walked her to the door and I thought 'Don't you dare offer to *me*!' But I think she knew, because she left me alone! [laughter]

In quick succession, Mary relates to me two different events and recounts bits of past conversations (which is not unusual; see also 'Shifting temporal frameworks' in Chapter 6). In the example of the walking warden, Mary did not want someone she felt was less fit and less able than herself coming to assess her own state of wellness. At the hairdresser's, Mary saw another older client who was less able being helped to the door and immediately took steps with her own body language to ensure that she would not suffer the same indignity. An important qualification here is that Mary is very physically mobile and extremely active, but she recognises that since she looks 'older' (she is in her mid-seventies now), she might be interpreted by others as 'needing help'. Part of maintaining her sense of self as active and independent is making light of such incidents and recounting them to me as funny stories but also at times resisting them when they occur in daily life.

The sort of potential decline in activity and the threat it holds that Mary wards off skilfully is seen in a second example about Emma before her husband died. She and I were sitting one day in her living room. Since her husband was out running errands, I asked if I could tape some of our conversation. I had interviewed them together previously, but he tended to dominate the conversation and I wanted to hear more about her perspective. We started talking about her brother-in-law's hip operation which she said he'd had 'done'. I asked her to elaborate:

CATHRINE: When they 'do it' what do they do?
EMMA: They put a new joint in, a new ball in, you know.
CATHRINE: And does it make life easier?
EMMA: It does, love ... There's a lot who can walk about better uh, but me you see, it made me a diseased artery in this leg [when she had her hip operated on], so me hip's been alright but it's me leg now.
CATHRINE: Is it frustrating?
EMMA: It is. You, you know you can walk so far and then you've to stop, takes me four times to stop to go up to doctors [about 275 yards from her home]. You wouldn't think that, would you ... because it's not far.
CATHRINE: Do you ever get angry about it?
EMMA: No, I just accept it.

Emma may just accept it, but the implications of her difficulties walking are much more difficult for her granddaughter's husband. A year and a half after taping this conversation with Emma, a revealing set of events occurred that added another layer of meaning to our exchange above. Her granddaughter Nicola and Nicola's husband Adrian had been living with Emma for a couple of months. They had recently moved to the area and Adrian had been unable to find employment and Nicola had only just found work, so they were staying with Emma until they could move into their own home. Since Adrian was out of work, he stayed home looking after their two-year-old son, Michael.

One day I went to visit Emma and while she was in the kitchen making us all a cup of tea, Adrian told me animatedly how upset and angry he had been with

Emma the day before. Since her hip operation, walking has been painful and difficult for her and she never took walks on her own in the neighbourhood unless it was to walk to the centre for bingo and tea, or to walk to the bus stop once a week to take the bus into Barnsley to visit a friend of hers. Despite this, she had repeatedly asked Adrian to let her take Michael on a walk through the neighbourhood in his pram, saying that she would be able to keep her balance with the pram and how much Michael would enjoy it. Reluctantly, Adrian finally gave in, faced with Emma's determination to do something on her own with her great-grandson whom she clearly adores, as well as her desire to help Adrian with child-minding. So, off Emma and Michael went on a particularly sunny and warm spring day. After nearly forty-five minutes, Adrian became alarmed since they had not yet returned and went out to find them. He discovered them much further away than he had ever anticipated (and further than he, Nicola, or I ever thought Emma could manage given our experiences with her difficulties getting as far as the centre or the doctor's) and found Emma 'struggling', in his words, to make it back to the house. As he described it to me, he 'flipped out' on Emma because he felt that she had been irresponsible, overreaching her own ability and putting his son at risk should something have happened. He told me heatedly that he could not *believe* she had done this and that he would not let her take Michael out on her own, ever again. By this point in the story, Emma was coming back into the living room with our tea and Adrian abruptly changed the subject. When Adrian went to the toilet later on, I asked her what had happened, but she did not get a chance to tell me any more than that she did not see what the fuss was all about before Adrian returned to the room.

This set of events shows some of the risks to the self entailed in trying to stay active. This supposed failure (in Adrian's opinion) on Emma's part to recognise that she was attempting too much had serious consequences for Adrian's interpretation of both Emma's ability and her judgement. This, along with other factors such as her repetition of stories (see Chapter 6 on narrative repertoires) and her increasing problems with memory recall led Adrian to the conclusion that Emma was 'getting past it'. Although an unfortunate choice of words on his part, this is not a surprising conclusion, given the ways in which 'old age' becomes attributed through multiple social interactions. Emma recognises that she can no longer walk as well as she used to be able to and says that she accepts it. But yet, this interaction with her family demonstrates that within her own self-understanding, she still perceives herself as capable of carrying out caring tasks such as looking after her great-grandson. Indeed, the walk with Michael was not just about physical activity and keeping active. It was also deeply symbolically significant in demonstrating her usefulness and ability to help out by attempting to play her part in assisting her grandchildren with looking after their own child. To then be challenged on both the physical and symbolic level by Adrian, to have both her ability to be active as well as her ability to be involved with the social life of the family doubted, was devastating on the level of self-perception as well as traumatically embarrassing for all involved. It undermined her role as woman, grandmother and great-grandmother by challenging her ability to care for her family. This is partly why Adrian could not tell me about the course of events in front of Emma and why I could not ask Emma about her perception of them in front of Adrian. Indeed, it was a testament to the strength of my relationship with her that I could ask Emma about the events at all.

## The remembered self versus the inhabited self

This then brings me back to the questions I opened the chapter with. What if selfhood and subjectivity are not experienced in the same way over the course of our lives? One way that I have come to understand this stems from the ways in which my research participants describe the difference between their remembered selves and their inhabited selves. Initially, this may sound like the debate I detailed above about inner, younger selves and outer older selves, with the 'true' self being the one that is internal, private and hidden from view. It might appear that the remembered self is the same as the inner, younger self of the mind and that the inhabited self is congruent to the external, older, physical self. However, this is not the case. The remembered self is spoken of by my research participants as both an inner essence, the 'me' of the past and as a physical body that was able to do things in the past that it can no longer achieve in the present. *Doing* is also perceived as a form of *being*, a quality which is now lessened in the present day because the ability to *do* is also curtailed. Heikkinen's (2000) work that we have seen previously in Chapter 1 reflects on a phenomenological approach to ageing and 'the relationship between human beings and the world', which is 'a bodily one: my body finds expression in my relationship to things existing in the world, I take a bodily orientation to them' (2000: 478). This is a highly useful perspective to my purposes here. Heikkinen, drawing on interviews conducted with twenty older Finns at age 80 and then the seventeen survivors again at 85, found that for her interviewees, whose social activities and daily routines had declined, a corresponding preoccupation with their bodies had emerged and that:

> The altered body becomes an unknown terrain that must be relearned … this kind of experience often seems to generate a nagging sense of insecurity, of not having control over one's life … our bodily experience and bodily awareness are part and parcel of our identity. When bodily changes are so profound as to destroy bodily continuity, people's ability to find meaning in life may be thwarted. (2000: 474)

Or, at the very least, altered. 'When far is too far away, high up is too high up and down is too far down and when your memory starts to fail, you begin to feel your relationship to the world is no longer fluent, natural, harmonious' (2000: 475) and the interconnectedness between body, sense of self and change through time (here perceived as linear decline) becomes more obvious.

In comparison with her material comparing bodiliness at age 80–85, Heikkinen found that by age 90, when she once again interviewed the cohort:

> Awareness of one's body seems to be almost inseparable from the perception of the ageing experience and being-in-the-world … [the interviewees] had become

accustomed to carrying their 'bodily burden' ... the experience of bodily change had disappeared, or ... its meaning had waned. The key characteristic of bodiliness now seemed to be that of existence. (2004: 574)

Heikkinen's work on bodiliness provides much food for thought with regard to the potential for an embodied transformation of self, but it also perhaps swings too far towards an extreme of bodiliness as existence. Her assertion that bodiliness as 'the whole of the individual's sense perceptions and feelings ... received without analytical thinking or deliberation' (Heikkinen, 2004: 575) by the age of 90 strikes me as overstated, a framing that strips people of all cognitive agency. It also leaves little room for individual variation, associating as it does the chronological age markers of 80, 85 and 90 with assertions of change that are applied homogenously across her research cohorts.

The mutual inscription of *doing* and *being* evident in both her work and my own, however, is perhaps not an accident. People's remembered selves in Dodworth are active and healthy, and able and not forgetful; able to go for long walks and able to do sums; able to drive out to the moors for a walk and a picnic; able to care for family members of all ages; able to get down on hands and knees and scrub the floor, able to do vigorous gardening, able to go for long bike rides and able to *run* up Pilley Hill, a steep hill in Dodworth (see figure 3). Some people's inhabited bodies can still do some of these things, but for those who cannot, the rupture in doing becomes a significant disruption in experiences of and expectations about the self.

The inhabited self, on the other hand, is spoken of with disbelief, such as in these two brief moments from my fieldnotes:

> May 2000: Anne asked me to give Evelyn my arm and to help her from the car to the garden gate while Anne went ahead to unlock the door. As I did, Evelyn laughed ruefully and said to me 'I never imagined I'd need *this!*', gesturing to her difficulty walking and needing me to help her maintain her balance the short way from the car to the door.

> Sept. 2000: Every Thursday morning at eleven o'clock, Doris walks by my house on her way up Pilley Hill to the Post Office on High Street to collect her pension and pick up a few groceries at the shop. It is a steep, arduous walk, but Doris gets a determined sort of pleasure out of it and always says that 'it keeps me legs going'. On my way to the Post Office myself one Thursday, I caught up with her and we stopped for a chat. Coming down the hill was an older man walking with a cane whom she knew and he joined us for a few moments. He told her 'I never thought I'd need one of these' as he waved his cane about and she replied that she used to be able to run up and down this hill, but no longer.

At other times, the inhabited body is spoken of by my research participants with even a certain amount of contempt, particularly when it is not obeying, almost like a new skin that does not fit very well but which one is obliged to put up with since it is the only one available. Heikkinen (2000: 479) has described a similar phenomenon, stating that age and illness bring along 'a whole host of annoying companions that are "part" of us'. With increasing age or illness, she says, we

**Figure 3** Pilley Hill, from Dodworth Bottom.

become more aware of our bodies and 'what used to be a natural part of "I" stands out as a new, alien and external experience' (2000: 479). As such, rather than the 'self' being continuous and unaltered with only the body changing, I believe that the consequences of bodily change are inherently central to people's notions of self. What I wish to highlight here is that rather than the inhabited ageing body masking the 'true', unchanging, self within, it appears instead that the inhabited self comes to be a source of deep frustration. This is because it is on the whole not seen to have any merits over one's younger, more reliable, remembered self. This is encapsulated in Emma's off-the-cuff comment to me one day that 'There's nowt in getting old, Cathrine' after our brief discussion of the 'water tablets' the doctor has prescribed, which make her need to urinate frequently, the painfulness of her swollen feet and the irritating necessity of incontinence pads. Bodiliness is not the whole of the self in these accounts, but bodiliness can come to be an assertive presence by comparison with its relative taken-for-granted absence in younger life.

These are, of course, gendered and classed bodies but those distinctions appear at times to flatten under the shared experience of bodily change. Differential access to resources (social, cultural and economic capital) that permit greater or lesser degrees of control and autonomy over the changing body are surely at work, as are the lifelong and gendered lessons we are taught about our bodies. This includes for example how, from a young age, girls have already learned to interpret the female body 'as an object of discrete parts that others aesthetically evaluate' (Franzoi, 1995: 417 in Clarke and Griffin, 2007: 703), in great 'contrast to the male body which is viewed as a tool for action and achievement' (Clarke and Griffin, 2007: 703). Such a model develops a binary of the female body as one evaluated on appearance ('body-as-object-orientation') and the male body on ability ('body-as-process-orientation') (Franzoi, 1995 in Clarke and Griffin, 2007). Clarke and Griffin's work is based on women aged between 50 and 70. My research, based primarily with older women and men in their mid-seventies, eighties and some in their early nineties, attests to the ways in which body as *disrupted* process comes to matter more to both genders as they move from middle age and late middle age (and again, I acknowledge the difficulties of discerning when this can be said to be) to older age. Despite this, gendered differences in how women and men are socialised into monitoring their bodies with women being taught to 'scrutinise, evaluate, present and control their bodies throughout their lives' (Clarke and Griffin, 2007: 701) continue to be an important consideration for the gendered nuances of these differences.

How people remember what they could *do* is also part of how they remember who they *were*. Although much of who they were remains despite their altering bodily and mental abilities, there is a sense of something of that self which is permanently resident in the past and has not been able to be maintained or brought with them into the present. Simultaneously, through narrative accounts, the remembered self is made retrospectively into a coherent, unitary self and divided off conceptually from one's inhabited self. In this way, a certain plurality of self emerges, a multiplicity that includes a difficult balance between 'who I was' and 'who I am', and which offers 'who I was' as a comforting point of reference even if one is facing difficulties and inconsistencies in the present moment.

## Memory blanks

The remembered self, while often linked to the physical body, can also be located in mental adroitness. Some of my research participants had developed strategies for protecting against the potential embarrassment and disorientation of memory blanks. Sally was a woman I knew who did this often. She would tell me how her 'brain's going' (connoting that her concentration and focus are impaired) and that 'my memory isn't what it used to be'. This perception and experience of such shifts in her memory had significant implications for her wider sense of self and was troubling her deeply. This was particularly true since she was painfully aware that she could not control or rely on her memory the way she had been able to previously, making for a deep rupture between her remembered self and her present-day self. This is not surprising as Crapanzano reminds us that '"brain" and "mind" are, in the West, two of the most preeminent *loci* of the self. They connote independence, autonomy, particularity, originality, individuality and thinghood' (1992: 111). The threat of losing control over one's 'brain' brings with it the threat of losing touch with one's own self and perhaps the threat of an erasure of self altogether.

Despite her struggles, Sally's coping techniques were usually enough to bridge the gaps in her memory and meant she could complete tasks and trips that she had begun. However, after a long and arduous trip to Skegness, a coastal town to the east of Dodworth, to try and visit an old friend, she realised that she was no longer able to find her way about. The slips of paper which she would rely on to jog her memory and keep in her pocket were no longer enough to protect her or to fully compensate for memory loss. The trip was a disaster. She got lost trying to find her friend's house and then lost again trying to get back to the bus station afterwards. The experience had shaken her. On another occasion, she greeted me at the door with: 'My brain's slowing down', and then went on to tell me that she had been searching for six hours in her sideboard and a briefcase in her bedroom for some important paperwork and money that she had carefully organised yesterday but had then forgotten where she put them. Finally, after all that time hunting in the sideboard, in the pantry and in the bedroom, back and forth and back and forth again, she found them in a top drawer of the sideboard. This sort of hunting saddens and frustrates her because it is so different from how she remembers herself to have been: efficient and, in her own words, 'intelligent'.

On a different day when I went to visit her, she told me how she had been on the phone with a friend of hers, Flo, who lives in Barnsley. Sally told Flo how she feels that she 'can't do what I could do ten years ago' and Flo agreed, saying how it makes her ill to think about it. Sally then elaborated for me, saying how:

> When you've worked all your life, since fourteen, scrubbing floors, black leading stoves,[1] *not* being able to do what you used to be able to do is a bit frustrating.

This hard labour of housework before ready access to modern domestic appliances is often evoked by many women as a landmark, an anchoring point, to demarcate how much life has changed since their youth. Sally seizes on it here to underline what a capable worker she used to be and the things that she was capable of achieving, something that is not obvious now to someone like me whose experience and knowledge of her is divorced from her younger self. She also uses it to emphasise that her own perception of changes in self.

I had arrived that day at her home while she was in the midst of sorting out a TV licence and her over-75 exemption.[2] Her National Health card[3] and pension book with her National Insurance number in it were out on the table and she was trying to fill out the exemption form. Sally kept flipping between one document and another, poring over them, distractedly trying to remember which of the two numbers she needed to use, trying to discern what information she had to provide on the exemption form and worrying that her National Insurance number was written incorrectly on one of the forms. She was becoming distressed. I offered to look at the forms for her which she immediately accepted. I realised that she had entered her National Health number on the TV form which asked only for her National Insurance number and that the National Health number was not relevant. Sally asked me if I would complete the form for her and kept saying how she was so 'thick' and that people always used to come to her to figure things out and fill forms in, but now … Without finishing her sentence and without making an overt link between the two topics, she started telling me instead about how when she was in her forties, she applied for and got a job as a quality control monitor in a knitwear factory to assess the spools of thread. She had had to learn all about 'facts and figures' and decimals and although it had been hard learning all this new material, her husband (proudly, she always mentions that he was an engineer) had helped by tutoring her in the evenings. She finally mastered it and conquered learning something difficult as well as saving the company many thousands of pounds over the years. When she finally retired, the factory closed six months later, which she attributes in her narrative to the incompetence of her replacement, and by which she reaffirms her own talent for numbers.

In the span of twenty minutes or so that it took from me entering the house, hearing about Flo, helping with the form and then listening to Sally's narrative about her former working life, she seamlessly created a web of meaning between how she remembers herself and perceived herself in contrast with the issues she is facing now in her life and how the two ways of being do not align. She was, in effect, telling me through her story about her past that the Sally I see before me struggling with the difference between a National Insurance number and a National Health number is not the same Sally as she was and as she still perceives herself to be, albeit faced with evidence that something is wrong with her 'brain'. Sally is experiencing a profound crisis in subjectivity. She is aware of the memory blanks she is having, knows the practical consequences of them and is reflexively considering their more existential implications for the self. In the face of this, she attempts to shore up her subjective position by evoking her remembered self.

An important further consideration in this social equation is the dynamic that grows out of my presence in her life (and these of the other people I came to know) as a student researcher who wanted to learn about old age and the self. Narratives are always addressed to, performed for and created by somebody, and my own role as ethnographer and listener is an important contextualising consideration in this research. In eliciting narratives and engaging in participant observation, I provided a forum for my research participants to construct their remembered selves by inviting them to do so. Ultimately, I was participating in the intersubjective work of fashioning the self. In Sally's particular case, my regular visits over a year meant that I became a conduit for her to work through some troubling contradictions in self. She had limited access to any other social forums where this could occur, with no living family members, friends dispersed throughout the country, having been unable to establish successful membership at any of the public meeting places for older people, and not having status as an 'old Dodworther'. While her circumstances are extreme, the themes that her narratives encapsulate are not.

## The uneven and multidirectional processes of selfhood creation

The literature on old age has long debated the issue of continuity through ageing and whether or not an individual can maintain a consistent sense of self in the face of social pressures that stigmatise older people as socially irrelevant (see for example Kaufman, 1986; Matthews, 1979; Myerhoff, 1979; Vesperi, 1985). While this has been an interesting and important avenue of enquiry, I think that attending more specifically to the punctuating events that many older people face (such as the loss of a spouse, changes in mobility, memory blanks) as part of everyday, daily life and listening to what older people say about what it is like to live through them reveals something more nuanced than an equation of continuity versus discontinuity. People's sense of self as it is lived and experienced in ageing is a process that is uneven, multifaceted and multidirectional and can prompt a profound reordering of an individual's daily life and sense of self.

Emma, whose self-concept as one who does for others is being challenged by her physical decline, which limits what she can do, is an example of this. She experiences the contradictory currents of selfhood in her dispute with Adrian. Emma's narratives about how she used to care for her elderly father thirty years ago and her desires to take her great-grandson for a walk are both expressions of the nurturing, caring, family woman she perceives herself to be (all socially normalised and culturally appropriate). This continuity in self-perception (from when she was looking after the grandfather of the family to being the great-grandmother now herself), however, coexists with her recognition that she can no longer do what she used to and indeed her statement that she is not the same person that she used to be. Unsurprisingly, although she often lives day to day with this contradiction, these conflicting feelings do not always happily coexist. A stark example of this is what transpired when she 'over-reached' her abilities and incurred Adrian's wrath, simultaneously reinforcing his image of her as 'old', something that has implications for her own feelings of self. These negotiations and emotions are too complex to limit to either/or categories of continuity or discontinuity of selfhood. Instead, an ethnographic approach that considers what Geertz calls the 'thick description' of personal history and cultural context helps portray the richness of lived experience of the ageing self. In this respect, Hollan's (1992) argument about the overemphasis on ideal-types of self and under-examination of the experience of these types in actual practice that I discuss in Chapter 1 resonates deeply with the argument about continuity and discontinuity in old age. His suggestions for a more flexible approach to the self, where the oppositions between different models of the self are far less clear than previously considered, are particularly relevant here. Inconsistencies in self-representation reflect the dynamics of narratives themselves, which are never self-contained, but produced in encounters between the self and others. These interactions occur in multiple settings and diverse registers, all of which selectively draw out various elements of the mosaic of the self being narrated as well as the agendas of the listener to whom the narrative is being recounted (Crapanzano, 1992), such as the fieldwork encounter itself.

However, older people are in a difficult position with regard to flexibility of the self. They cannot risk being perceived as inconsistent or too changeable in presentation of the self, as this risks being interpreted as 'losing the self' for older people in a way that younger people are not subject to. So, for instance, while Kaufman (1986) and Hazan (1980, 1984, 1996), among other authors, disagree on the extent to which continuity of the self through ageing is maintained, authors like Ewing, in the literature on the anthropology of self without specific interests in old age, have argued convincingly that all self-making includes an illusion of wholeness (Ewing, 1990). This illusion is unconsciously maintained in order to make social action possible, but an illusion, nonetheless, which masks discontinuity and fragmentation in the subjective experience of self.

While discontinuity emerges from time to time in the narratives of my research participants (particularly when different levels and moments of discourse are placed side by side), what was particularly striking in my research experiences was the rigidity and consistency in the content of older people's narrative accounts. I argue that this is a manifestation of social pressures experienced by older people whereby the premium placed on consistency of self-presentation becomes extremely high. The freedom to shift levels becomes endangered and threatened for older people, unlike Ewing's younger key informant, Shamim, upon which her conclusions are drawn. While representations of the self seem to become more fixed for older people and contradictions in self-representation clamped down upon, anxiety-producing situations can be seen as times when the delicate balance starts to slip. During the hospital trip with Olive and the encounter between Vivienne and the insurance salesman, both of which I discuss in Chapter 6, and the set of events surrounding Emma's walk with Michael in this chapter, situations that threaten to run out of control are often the same conditions under which the veneer of consistency starts to wear thin and things begin to unravel. Fluidity of the self is interpreted as evidence of 'real' old age.

## Conclusions

In order to widen a theoretical conceptualisation of 'the Western self', I have turned my attention to some of the conditions of self-making in the experiences of older people in Dodworth. This is an approach to the ageing self that privileges narrativity and temporality as key constitutive elements. It is also one that, enabled by participant observation, is able to consider a wide range of contexts and interactions over a period of time in the lives of the people I knew and not only those that take place in public spaces. While there is much in the experience of the middle-aged self that parallels older selves, and which is brought with us as we age, there are also different issues at stake in the presentation and creation of the older self that at times challenges a model of self based primarily on middle-aged adults. These go beyond the normal channels of exploration into the ageing self, which tend to centre around the 'mask of ageing' or around 'loss of self', due to dementia. Examples I have explored which challenge a universalised middle-aged normative self include the remembered self versus the inhabited self and memory blanks. I believe that these are critical considerations for understanding what is at stake in experiences of self when the once taken-for-granted ground-ings of the self (physical, social, emotional, cognitive) begin to shift underneath one's feet. As I described earlier, a vision of an inner, younger, mental self as divisible from an outer, older, physical self, is said to provoke a tension between physical change (the outer self) and self-continuity as young (the inner self) in the ageing person. This model mirrors the ways in which the Western self is conceptualised as an opposition between an inner/private self and external/public self, with the inner self privileged as being the seat of the 'true' self in the Western world. However, conceptualising the ageing self in this way does not permit discussion of the temporal register of aspects of selfhood that emerged from how older people talked about the self. The remembered self is spoken of by them as both an inner essence, the 'me' of the past and as a physical body that was able to *do* things in the past that it can no longer achieve in the present.

'Doing' and keeping active are perceived as a way of *being* by my research participants. When the inhabited body is not able to achieve the same amount of activity as the remembered body, the self of today is also implicitly described as somehow a lesser form or lesser version of one's remembered self. This version of self is not one whereby the uncompliant body becomes outer and external to the self, but is one whereby the uncompliant body actually becomes a point of reference that redefines one's self concept, particularly in reference to the past. In extreme individual circumstances, such as those faced by Sally with her memory blanks, a profound crisis in subjectivity can arise. Despite this, she persists, evoking her remembered self as a way to maintain some steadying influence in the slippage of her sense of self of today and highlighting the ways in which the past is unevenly written onto the present.

People tend not to reflect explicitly on the self under normal conditions and yet issues surrounding the assertion of selfhood and challenges to it permeate everyday life. This makes selfhood a topic particularly well suited to the ethnographic method. Using data from both my fieldnotes and interviews, I have drawn out and consolidated certain key signifiers that my research participants associate with a sense of self. This is, of course, not the totality of the experiences of self as, for example, I have already described how the self is also constructed in relation to the past and in relation to far-reaching change. However, in this chapter, I have explored how the people I came to know make manifest a sense of self that has a distinctive emphasis with regard to experience of and through time, and in so doing, complicate normative models of self at work in the West.

## Notes

1 'Black leading' is a cream polish used on cast iron fireplace surrounds. It is another example of an iconic everyday technology that, while mainly now defunct, is used symbolically to evoke a changed world order.
2 In order to operate a television legally in Britain, each household must pay for a TV licence, payable annually and costing £100 at the time of my research. At the time of this encounter with Sally, people over the age of 75 were eligible for discounts and those over 80 received them free; since this time, TV licences have become free for all aged 75 years and above.
3 Every person registered with a doctor in the UK has an identification number on these cards.

**6**

# Narrative forms and shapes

## Introduction

In line with previous chapters, this one continues the argument developing throughout this book of the ways in which 'old age' come to be attributed to older people and how this is experienced subjectively. I have so far explored this with regard to temporality, intra-generational relations and selfhood. In so doing, I have privileged narrative accounts and interpersonal interactions. This chapter shifts gears somewhat by turning its attention to distinctive characteristics of narrative style and activity among my research participants. I am especially interested here in the intergenerational dissonance that sometimes emerges between particular narrative styles employed by older people in comparison with those used by younger adults. While people of all ages use narrative *content* to build the self, the narrative *styles* of the older people I worked with often seem very different from that of younger people. This is not easily quantifiable and yet it is perceptible. I propose that how such narrative activity is received, interpreted and responded to by interlocutors of all ages forms a critical aspect of how oldness itself comes to be projected onto individuals in certain circumstances. The terrible irony of this, however, is that such projections threaten at times to undo the very work of staking a claim to the creation of self that narrativity usually achieves. Narrativity thus, at times, works against the expectations of narrators themselves.

I further propose that in the case of older people, such an effect is heightened by both the relationship of narrativity with time and also temporal stereotypes about older people, including the assumption that older people are 'lost' in the past. Indeed, as I have argued in Chapter 3, negative stereotypes of older people effectively employ different temporal relations as an indicator of oldness itself. Narrative accounts bring together experiences, feelings and perspectives from different temporal moments. Narratives also modulate through time and in light of unfolding events or in anticipation of future ones. This chapter thus builds on the arguments about the ageing self already presented and explores the dynamics of these and their implications for the construction and maintenance of the self. In particular, I examine the characteristics of narrative style used by the older people I came to know during the course of fieldwork; I consider the ways in which these characteristics challenge narrative conventions and temporal ordering; and I call into question my own initial supposition that these narrative styles were a creative form of resistance to social stereotypes.

Other researchers have commented on the extent to which older people engage in what Myerhoff has termed 'narrative activity', something she describes as 'intense and relentless' (1979: 33). Hazan writes that 'the "invisible social worlds" (Unruh, 1983) of the elderly are ... often based on ritualized forms of talk (e.g. story-telling, discussion groups, proverbs, etc.)' (Hazan, 1996: 27). My research experiences were similar in this respect to Myerhoff's and Hazan's. I spent a great deal of my time during fieldwork happily listening to such forms of talk and spontaneous narrative accounts, both inside and outside the interviewing context. I am interested in the dialectic between subjectivity, narrative activity and age stereotypes. The narrative characteristics that I examine here are the use of 'irrelevant' information in conversation; repertoires of personal information (or narrative grooves); and shifting temporal frameworks at work in narrative accounts.

Research in sociolinguistics and ageing has revealed linguistically embedded ways in which old age as a category is reproduced and inscribed on individuals and cohorts. Coupland and Coupland (1991), key writers in this area of study, highlight the ways in which diachrony (change over time) and decrement (progressive decline in health or competence) have been powerful organising tropes in research on language and ageing. This trope is one of deficit whereby research has emphasised the 'linguistic and communicative impairment' of older people and a co-commitment to investigating how 'older people's linguistic competence may be lacking ... and how their involvement in conversational interaction may be problematical' (1991: 3). They argue convincingly that although such perspectives are built into popular understandings of ageing, they are highly restrictive and partial and point alternatively to sociolinguistic research that focuses on some communicative patterns in which older communicators perform consistently better than younger (1991: 12–14). In distinction to deficit models, Coupland and Coupland promote instead a 'discourse analysis perspective (which) recognizes the constitutive potential of talk as a vehicle for *formulating* life positions and responses to them by old and young alike, interactively and relationally' (1991: 8; emphasis in original). This approach is one that they and I share and I am particularly interested in what Coupland and Coupland identify as the 'semiotic impact [of linguistic performance] ... which elderly characteristics, in fact, connote 'elderliness', to whom and with what evaluative weightings' (1991: 11). In the sections of this chapter that follow, I build on their insights by examining the connection between an interactive and relational perspective on narrative activity with the dynamics of differing temporal relationships and their implications for the construction and maintenance of the ageing self. I take it further by embedding such sensitivities about the constitutive power of talk in ongoing and unfolding experiences which ethnographic fieldwork makes possible.

My research in Dodworth set out to examine what old age 'is' from the perspective of the people living it. As such, asserting that there is something distinctive about older people's narrative lives and mannerisms and that they are different from those of younger people may appear as though I am reverting to an essentialist argument after trying so hard to lay out an interpretive, processual framework lodged in subjectivity. This is not the case. As outlined earlier, I take the self to be created in part through narration. This self in narratives of older people tends to be an ageless self, as described by Kaufman (1986), as people do not usually self-identify as 'old'. However, the forms of narration and the narrative style utilised by my research participants are distinct from those used by younger Britons. Furthermore, these forms of narrative style are also one of the ways in which the wider society being interacted with comes to label and interpret individuals as 'old'. This is partly because the particular non-linear and sometimes repetitive features of this narrative activity are interpreted in Western cultural contexts as signs of senility and the dreaded manifestation of a loss of self. This may be the case for a minority of older people suffering from patholo-gies. However, the people I knew in Dodworth and whose narrative accounts I describe here were emphatically not suffering from such conditions. Despite this, the patterns and rhythms of their narratives approximated the stereotyped assumptions about 'elderly people' that circulate in mainstream notions of old age, in terms of repetition and temporal flux, which meant that a conversation about the present day could quickly shift into a different temporal framework located in the past. As such, there is a two-fold issue at stake here in discussing the construction of self through narrative in terms specific to 'old age': first, there is the way that through narration the self is created, worked and reworked, with certain stories being used to say 'this is me'; second, there are the ways in which certain stylistic attributes of telling these stories (and not the content of the narratives themselves) are interpreted by younger interlocutors as characteristic of 'old age', with the corollary that people using such stylistic patterns are them-selves judged to be 'old'. The first aspect of narrative style that I discuss is what I call the use of 'irrelevant' information in conversations. I begin with one example, drawn from my fieldnotes, that comes from experiences I shared with a woman called Olive.

### 'Irrelevant' information

Olive and I first met in one of the local centres at the regular Tuesday night bingo teas and we gradually came to spend more and more time visiting together outside the centres. Olive, 73, had lived in Dodworth from the age of one, when her father had moved the family from Leeds (twenty miles away) to take work in a local coal mine. She had married a coal miner and had worked at a number of paid jobs herself outside the home while raising a son who, during my fieldwork, no longer lived in Dodworth. Olive still lived in the council house she had moved to with her husband many years ago, although he had died several years before I met her. When we were chatting one day on one of my regular visits with her,

Olive told me that she had no one to go with her to the hospital for an upcoming diagnostic test that was worrying her. The test was to assess her heart rate after she had experienced a series of troubling falls over the course of a few months. She was nervously anticipating the test and I said I would be happy to accompany her. Olive accepted, but insisted that I come for lunch first and that we would then go to the hospital together. On the appointed day, after eating a two-course meal together, which she had prepared for us, we went to the bus-stop around the corner from her home to catch the bus to the hospital. The bus, typically, never arrived so we walked back to her house to call a taxi instead.

This disruption to her plan made Olive anxious. When we arrived back outside her house, it was apparent that she no longer felt certain nor in charge. Instead of going inside her own home to call a cab, she went directly to the next-door neighbour's house in distress and to tell Linda (a middle-aged woman) all about what had happened. Linda came outside, rolling her eyes and smiling at me and went with us into Olive's house. Olive by this point was so flustered by the disruption to our plans and how late it was making us that she could not think how to call the taxi firm nor where to find the number. Linda used the telephone book to find the phone number and then Olive asked Linda to ring the taxi firm for her, which Linda did. The taxi seemed to take forever to arrive and Olive was increasingly tense because it was clear that we would be late for her appointment.

Then, when Olive and I finally got to the hospital, I had thought we were going to ask for directions to the department she needed. Olive however sped off in a different direction, saying that she knew there was a staircase nearby. I think, in retrospect, that this was because she remembered that there had been a help desk near one of the main staircases, but at the time, it seemed irrelevant especially as we had just passed the help desk and there was no staircase where she insisted there would be. I made her stop when I realised how far we had gone in the wrong direction. By this time, we were already ten minutes late for the appointment, which heightened the tension. I asked her the name of the department that we needed. She said she did not know. She started instead searching through her pocketbook without explanation. It turned out that she was searching for her appointment slip and once she found it, she gave it to me without looking at it. I read that the appointment was with the Cardiology department. While this was happening, she stopped a man at random in the hallway where we were standing, to ask him for directions, but instead began by telling him about the bus not arriving and having to take a taxi and that we were late, rather than asking him for directions to Cardiology. She started to tell him all about what a good neighbour Linda is and how Linda helps her out with little things when I suddenly put my arm around her shoulders. I think I meant to calm her and help her focus on asking the 'right' question of this stranger, but what in effect happened was that I took over the conversation so that she would not embarrass herself. I was afraid that he would judge her unkindly as old, senile and incoher-ent. By the gesture of my arm, however, I gave away much of my own prejudices about the boundaries of old age and about 'old' comportment and how both were being made manifest through the narrative style she had begun to adopt: 'irrelevant' information furnished in an inappropriate context with an uninterested interlocutor.

Although we eventually found our way to the correct part of the sprawling hospital complex, and frustratingly the test results were to come back as inconclusive, what struck me most in hindsight was my own assessment of Olive's rapid shift into behaviour and narrative style that is culturally codified as 'old'. However, it is worth restating that Olive is an adult woman. She has lived on her own for many years and continues to do so very confidently and independently. She is a regular member at social events for older people in the village and is not marked out as 'old' in any of those contexts. And yet, to witness the transformation in her composure when we arrived back at her house from the bus stop and then again in the hospital made a profound impression on me.

Olive, however, was understandably nervous about the state of her health and what the unknown test would be like or what the results might portend. Furthermore, the irritation of the bus not arriving meant the added expense and organisational nuisance of the taxi. Her reactions, however, extended beyond the bounds of nervousness into comportment that I read stereotypically as characteristic of 'oldness', which was compounded by the narrative style she adopted with the stranger that was off-topic and unfocused. Olive's shift in comportment was mirrored by her increasingly fractured discourse and in my perception of her use of 'irrelevant' information. This example shows how anxiety-producing situations can sometimes threaten the normal ordering of one's relationships with the world. When under too much pressure, the carefully constructed balance of order can start to crumble. This then is mirrored in a stigmatised narrative style. To regain some control, Olive appears to seek refuge in the reassuring narration of details of events. These details provide a sort of soothing framework, even if from the outside they appear jarring and 'irrelevant'. Such moments reveal a certain fragility of the self, but one that is probably much more evident to the outside observer than to the person herself.

A second example comes from a visit to Vivienne's house. When I arrived, she told me that her insurance representative was coming at 3:30 p.m. but that I should stay while he was there. He arrived ten minutes late. Vivienne had asked him to come see her because she was not clear about what money she had paid, and when, for additional coverage on her insurance policy and what the addition covered. She and he talked and argued over and around each other. It seemed as if she could not understand what he was saying and what the chronology was of when they had changed the terms of her policy. She was also concerned that his company had not provided her with a copy of the new policy. The rep, who was well dressed and in his late thirties, patronisingly said he had extra copies outside in his car but that he was sure he had given her a copy; had she forgotten? Vivienne eventually brought out two large envelopes with her policy, dated 1999–2000 and a number of receipts. The rep then, again patronisingly, went through the material and said triumphantly: 'and here's your policy that you want me to get from the car'. He made a big deal of saying that, 'You only get one copy', insinuating that she was forgetful when what Vivienne was actually asking was 'Why does the policy say it is valid from 1999 to 2000 if I only get one? Why doesn't it say 1999 onwards? And why don't I get a new version for each year, with a new date?' He seemed not to hear.

At one point in this increasingly heated conversation, Vivienne switched topics and said quite out of the blue: 'I was in Silkstone Common today, you're from Silkstone Common, aren't you? Mrs Yates organises a club there that I go to', as if he would know who Mrs Yates was. In the context of the conversation this was a complete non sequitur, a moment in which Vivienne steps outside of 'normal' parameters of conversation, providing the insurance rep with more fodder to persist in his condescending treatment of her as 'dotty'. He acted as though she knew nothing about official documents and that she was senile; as if she had never run a business and had to do all the insurance and accounting for the corner shop during all those years, and as if she had no meaningful past or experience to draw upon. Vivienne said after he had left that she felt as though he had treated her 'like you might treat a child'. She was flustered and angry about that but also that they would not cover a strand of pearls that were lost two years ago because she did not know if she had lost them inside or outside the house and he had 'even had the cheek to say that they could have fallen down behind the couch' as a way of getting out of reimbursing her for them. Vivienne told me how hard it is to do all this, manage all of these details on her own because, even though she used to do all of it before, at least she had her husband to talk it through with, before he died. I asked why does she not talk to her daughters about it and she said stridently: 'I like my independence; I've always done these things my whole life.'

For Vivienne, fully aware of how she was being treated by the insurance man but seemingly unaware of the differences in their narrative styles, the difficulties she encounters with him highlight both the narrative differences she manifests but also the way the rep positions her as little more than a child, stripping her of the temporal depth of experience she is immersed in. Looking back at Chapter 3, where Vivienne herself tells Mrs Parkin that she does not feel she has a future, this is in marked tension with the rep's treatment of her here, as though she does not have a past. Because the rep treats Vivienne as if she is in a timeless present does not mean that she herself believes this to be the case. But yet, arguably the cumulative effect of being treated as if one does not have a relevant past and one simultaneously feels for oneself as though there is no substantial future to look forward to (ambivalent as these feelings about the future may be), is a position distinct to older age in which a combination of social, cultural and biological forces come to shape subjectivity.

These two vignettes encapsulate the use of 'irrelevant' information in conversation. While I offer specific examples of encounters shared with Olive and Vivienne, this was a common pattern that I experienced multiple times. I have purposefully placed the word 'irrelevant' in inverted commas since my reflections on this narrative behaviour are premised on the disjuncture between the assumptions of younger and middle-aged individuals as to what is normal narrative comportment and the narrative activity that sometimes emerges in conversation periodically among my research participants. Effectively, what I am calling attention to are verbal faux pas that manifest in moments of particularly exacerbated anxiety. Although intermittent rather than continuous, these stressful moments formed a pattern that was repeated many times throughout my fieldwork. Indeed, the discomfort they occasioned was so marked that in my fieldnotes I came to refer to it as 'the cringe factor'. In these moments, I felt that my own everyday parameters of social discourse and narrative expectations were being disrupted in a way that did not usually happen when engaged in conversation with younger people. I, in turn, use these moments methodologically as markers indicating that such situations called for closer attention and analysis. What was it about the interaction that provoked such profound discomfort on my part? What could the dissonance reveal? Ultimately, I believe that such moments play a role in the ways in which oldness comes to be made and attributed (in conjunction with other elements such as prior interactions, physical appearance and other aspects of narrative activity) in interaction between generations and between individuals.

## Narrative repertoires

The second narrative style I wish to explore here became most apparent over time. As I came to know individual people better through the course of my fieldwork, accruing many hours spent with them in multiple settings and engaged in a variety of activities, certain narrative repertoires became familiar to me about each person and their life experiences. By using the phrase 'narrative repertoires', my aim is to call attention to the clusters of stories that each individual has and uses to place his or herself. Each cluster of stories becomes a node in a larger web of self-description through which people recount themselves from different perspectives: for example, as an individual, as part of a couple, as a family member, as a mother, as a worker. An individual's particular repertoire of personal narrative also highlights elements of his or her life story and his or her own beliefs. The repertoires permit narrators to position themselves within a wider temporal framework that expands far beyond the moments of today. Indeed, the cluster of stories relied upon in one's narrative repertoire serve as a sort of condensed memory, perfected through their oft-repeated performance.

Indisputably, people of all ages have stories about themselves and their lives that are favourite ones. They too rely upon these stories to communicate a sense of self and thus often repeat and perfect their narrative repertoires. The narrative dynamic I am describing here, however, is one that I had never experienced before so strongly as during my fieldwork when I was in constant contact and companionship with older people.[1] The content, stylistic presentation and regular use of these narrative repertoires are so consistent that I began to think of them as 'narrative grooves'. Narrative grooves are predictable, orderly and have their own rhythms and flows. The repertoires of stories that the people I interacted with are told each time anew, as if the listener has never heard them before and yet each time they are told they have a remarkably familiar structure and content. This is the case to such a degree that after several months of intensive immersion in the field, I was able to recite elements of individual's narrative grooves myself, or help the narrator recite her, or his, stories if blanks appeared. The repertoires are particularly well known to the family and friends of the individuals in question and, indeed, are so often repeated and familiar that they could serve as a code breaker for the pseudonyms of earlier chapters of this book, thus crippling the confidentiality arrangements I have with my research participants. Hence, although there is some overlap between the sources used here and in previous chapters, I have renamed all of my sources with new pseudonyms in this section in order to ensure protection of their identities. The necessity of doing this demonstrates the extent to which narrative repertories, a particular element of narrative style, also serve as iconic moments of self-construction: the stories and moments are told and retold so often and so consistently that the repertoires in turn become easily identifiable as belonging to certain individuals.

During my fieldwork, narrative repertoires occurred spontaneously in interactions I witnessed between the people I was working with and other individuals, as well as in everyday conversations with me. They also occurred in more formal settings, like interviews I conducted, or sometimes upon my first introduction. As such, narrative repertoires were not necessarily products of the interview setting where someone is asked to construct and recount a coherent life story. Instead, they would crop up at different moments of time spent together over many months and in a variety of settings. Repertoires were, however, used consistently to talk about the self. These repertoires of self are hardly ever about 'being old', or about 'the ageing self' since authors such as Kaufman (1986) and Matthews (1979) have aptly demonstrated, 'being old' is not a pivotal identity for older people. Rather, they are points of reference for positioning oneself in the flux of time in a social and physical landscape which has changed so profoundly. As outlined in Chapter 2, this change is both personal (the end of work, the move from a family home to a retirement bungalow, the death of a spouse) and collective or social (family structures, moral norms, the erasure of certain events and cycles of holidays). Because of this context, these repertoires can be seen as a way of staking a claim to some kind of social order, which one can still be a part of by maintaining its existence through the narrating of one's own experiences.

Some aspects of narrative repertoires are stock stories that each person has, that they will tell about events that transpired in Dodworth or that they remember from the past, such as the Old Mr Greenwood story that Mr and Mrs Crawshaw would often recount. For many years, Mrs Crawshaw volunteered as a waitress at yearly teas held for older village residents. One day, as Mrs Crawshaw tells the story, a:

> Yorkshire Traction [local bus company] conductress had come as part of entertainment for one of these teas and she stood up and she said ... um ... 'I'll tell you this story', she says. 'There were a man wanting to get on a bus at top o' Dodworth, you know,' and she says, 'He had a dog.' So she, the conductress, told him: 'You can't get on (this bus), I've got one dog on.' I guess they mustn't be allowed two dogs on the bus. And he says to her, 'Oh, shove bus up thee ass.' She

says: 'Thee shove dog up thee ass and thy can get on!' (Laughter) ... Ain't it
funny, that! It were true, that! That was Old Mr Greenwood that kept Blacker
Green Dam.[2]

This story was a favourite of both Mr and Mrs Crawshaw and it never failed to set
both narrator and listener off in peals of laughter. Heightening the narrative kick
of the story are the contextualising details of both Mrs Crawshaw's reputation as
someone who would never normally swear and the locally known and remembered figure of Old Mr Greenwood as well as the local place, Blacker Green Dam.
This ensures that, to a local listener, both a key character and place in the story are
known and not anonymous, part of memory talk that circulates freely in
Dodworth.

More commonplace elements of an individual's repertoire of narratives,
however, are events from their own lives, which have come to take on a sort of
iconic weight or significance in how that individual speaks about herself or
himself. I have chosen three examples of segments from three different individuals' repertoires to include here, but the reader should bear in mind that these few
short samples represent an enormous amount of narrative energy spent on them
in the course of daily life. Also, each narrator has a repertoire of several stories,
although I only recount one here. Most of these examples are compiled from my
fieldnotes rather than from taped interviews since my knowledge of the repertoires accumulated during the course of fieldwork. Each is written as a summary
of the narrative segment and is in the third person rather than in the first person
as most often narrated by their narrators.

### Mrs Phyllis Lockwood

When her ageing father became very unwell, Phyllis's brother Tom and her sister
Alice decided that they could not look after him in his own house any more. Alice
only had a two up, two down[3] and if Tom had taken their dad, it would have been
a daughter-in-law, not a daughter to look after him, so they were going to put
him in the workhouse. When Phyllis found out about their plans, she absolutely
refused to agree and would not permit it. Instead, she ran up to the Pit Houses on
Station Road where she knew Dr Leischman, the local doctor, was doing his
rounds. She waited outside the house he was visiting until he came out so that she
could ask him for an ambulance to bring her father to her house, but not until the
afternoon so that she would have a chance to bring the mattress downstairs for
him and get a bedroom set up in the lounge so that he would not have to use the
stairs. Her father used to like to smoke his pipe and look out the window, which
faced the lane to Stainborough and he could watch people as they went by. He
lived with them on Intake Crescent on Snow Hill for eighteen months,
bedridden, until he died.

The story is never contextualised in terms of how old Phyllis was when this
transpired, but rather she always says she was living on Snow Hill at the time.
This is shorthand for saying that she and husband were living with their five
children in a semi-detached council house in what was then the family home and
Snow Hill is a micro-place name for one part of the village. Other key aspects of

the story that are always included are that 'they' (sometimes identified as specific named family members, other times less specific) wanted to send her father to St Helen's (a workhouse in Barnsley up until 1931) but that she absolutely would not permit this; Phyllis' memory of running up the hill to the Pit Houses, half a mile away, to speak with the doctor; the vantage her father had out the window from her house and that Phyllis cared for him until his death. Unspoken here, but valuable background information, is the high social valorisation (and expectation) of daughters caring for their ageing parents; the deeply stigmatising threat of the workhouse in an area where poverty had been a living experience for many families; the role of Dr Leischman as iconic village figure whose presence still lived on many decades after his death; and Phyllis' self-presentation as someone who always 'speaks my mind'.

### Mrs Joyce Micklethwaite

In the years immediately following the war, Joyce worked at the Suba Seal Factory in Barnsley, which manufactured hot water bottles. This is where she met her husband. One day she had to get a particular piece of rubber for hot water bottles from the store room. She already had a child and he had two, but his wife had died, which is something that she did not know. That is why when he asked her out she thought he was being cheeky and said something rude to him in response. When she got back to her own department and told her girlfriend there what had happened, the girlfriend told Joyce to go right back and apologise because the man was a widower. She did and they went to the pictures in Barnsley on their first date, but it had been difficult to arrange. This was because women could only work Monday, Wednesday and Friday at the factory but he had twelve-hour shifts so it took them a little while to find a day when they could both go. She still remembers the first film they saw, called 'The Sound Barrier' (1952).

Joyce had a child out of wedlock during the war, which was a very difficult episode in her young life. This experience also contextualises the importance of her eventually coming to find a husband and establishing a nuclear family after the trauma of being a single mother in an era when this was not approved.[4] This holds such significance to her for how her life unfolded that when she tells this story, she always emphasises how she almost missed the chance of finding her husband. The details of how she had misunderstood the context of his asking her on a date and the fortuitous intervention of her co-worker, as well as the complications of actually being able to meet to go out together, owing to their competing work schedules, are crucial details for appreciating how much weight this part of her narrative repertoire holds in her presentation of self.

### Mrs Lucy Batty

The first time she met me, Lucy came up to me after bingo to tell me in a rush of information all about her son Eric who went on holidays at age 21 to France and was paralysed from the neck down in a diving accident, how she had to take care of him and turn him four times a day so he would not get bed sores, and feed him and clean him for the next twenty-three years. Before he was released home from the hospital, she had to go for a training course at the hospital to learn how to take care of him because his wife did not want to have anything to do with him after he was paralysed. She was there for two weeks but they wanted her to stay another week. She would not stay because there was no one to look after her husband and cook and clean for him. He was still working full time, she wanted to come back and he wanted her at home. Despite having to miss the last few days of training, every time the district nurse came to visit she was always so impressed at what a brilliant job Mrs Batty was doing with preventing bed sores and how well Eric was taken care of. Eric died on her birthday, her husband died on Christmas Day and then another relative, a daughter-in-law, died a few months later, all in one year. She had lost also another son years before to leukaemia.

Many times after that, Lucy told me the same story, a self-defining narrative, a set of memories condensed into a series of events that she seemed to feel were the most pressing things any listener needs to know about her. I remember being very taken aback by the bluntness of this story and also being startled that it was the sort of story that she would choose to tell a stranger, seeing that it seemed so personal and was also such a taboo topic. For Lucy, however, it was something she was proud of and she would say how: 'There's lots what say Mrs Batty's had a hard life.' Indeed, many people did say that, with her personal tragedies entering into village lore and collective opinion among her peers about the quality of her life. Matsumoto (2009) has written on the topic of painful self-disclosure in conversations between older and younger interlocutors and draws on work from Coupland and Coupland (1991) in his analysis. They found that younger people expect painful self-disclosure as 'a resource to first-acquaintance conversation' (1991: 127), but with Lucy, something else was at play. Long-term ethnographic research demonstrated in her case that this was a repeating story, a narrative groove, told not just by her but by many others in the village about her and her family. While Coupland and Coupland rely on organised interactions between younger and older people, engineered to elicit certain responses, Matsumoto focuses instead on painful self-disclosure narratives that are spontaneously recounted with humour and laughter among Japanese women. Matsumoto argues that by recounting the painful self-disclosure with humour, the women subvert negative stereotypical images of older people as 'grumbling' or as 'disengaged' (2009: 930–1), stereotypes that persist in Dodworth as well. In the case of Lucy, it strikes me that the recounting of the death of her child, his absence and the tragedy she has lived through, is part of filling in the gaps that are central to her subjectivity and letting those she meets know who she is.

In addition to the formulaic, recognisable ways in which these and many other stories like them got told, the narrative repertoires often justify or confirm personality characteristics that individuals perceive themselves as having. The repertoires point interlocutors in a certain direction. Sometimes, however, additions or refinements to the repertoire would be presented quite unexpectedly. For example, as stated earlier, Phyllis tells stories about how she is not and has never been afraid to speak her mind, a culturally valorised form of social engagement in the region, as described in Chapter 2. On one occasion we were sitting in her living room and I was telling her how I had had a long phone conversation the night before with my friend who had told me, for the first time, that she was getting divorced. Phyllis replied: 'Well, that's nowt fresh lass, everyone's doing it these days!' I mentioned that maybe it was not an entirely sad thing that they were separating since my friend's husband had a difficult side to him. This led to Phyllis reciting one of her repertoire stories about her husband and how she had been lucky to marry a good man who was not violent, who brought his wage home and who did not like to drink; how in those days once you got married, that was it – divorce was too expensive to even consider. If it was like today, though, she says maybe she would have ended up getting divorced, too, given the way marriages go through ups and downs. This was all part of her usual narrative repertoire, but then she told me an additional story that provided extra details, outside the normal parameters of the repertoire story, about the one time her husband had hit her. From my fieldnotes:

> Phyllis had been cooking chips on the coal fire and he came home and said something to her (she could not recall what) and she responded 'Go to hell!' He swung around and slapped her face. She threw the dinner down, got her coat and spat out at him that she was off to the police to report him. She says they never used to swear at each other and she does not know why she did ... except that she'd always been the youngest kid in her family and always got her way and was never afraid to speak her mind. Anyway, off she went (this is when they lived on Snow Hill), but before she got very far, she started to wonder if the cops would laugh at her because maybe he had the right to hit her, so she went to her sister's house where she told her sister what had happened, had a cuppa and a laugh and then decided after a while that she'd better go back before he started to worry. As she was coming up to her house he had started down to look for her and when they saw each other they started laughing and all was fine.

On the rare occasions when new unfamiliar details emerged to enrich stories that were part of narrative repertoires, as here, they served a dual purpose. First, they were startling, in that they were so new and not part of the normal 'groove'. This highlights just how unusual it was for the content of repertoires to alter or to be elaborated. Second, the emergence of new details also highlights an important distinction between narrative repertoires, which I have been discussing here with their particular content, stylistic presentation and regular use that distinguishes them from less formulaic accounts of self and pieces of biography that flowed in everyday conversation but were not part of the rehearsed repertoire. Both are important sources of information about the self, but the latter takes on a prominence in these narrative accounts that I am foregrounding here for the purposes of analysis.

The three examples of narrative repertoires I chose to use here are particularly life-changing events – the decline and death of a parent; the serious injury and dependence of a child; the first meeting of a spouse – but by no means are all repertoires so dramatic. Others describe more mundane events, such a story Mrs Crawshaw often tells about one time when her mother came to visit her at home when she was a newlywed. This was in the early 1940s, before the wide availability of automatic washing machines and Mrs Crawshaw had just washed her sheets using a peggy board and mangle, hanging them outside to dry. When her mother arrived, she asked whose sheets were outside. Mrs Crawshaw replied that they were hers. Her mother was appalled because she felt they were not white enough and insisted that Mrs Crawshaw bring them in and wash them again. As a new wife responsible for her own home for the first time, in a social setting that places great moral weight on domestic perfection, Mrs Crawshaw understandably felt chastened. The humiliation of such a perceived failure as a young and inexperienced woman is in unstated contrast to the expert in such matters that she has become, but is also a humiliation that bleeds through from sixty years ago, carried into the present day, to reappear time and again in this oft-recounted narrative repertoire. Indeed, this strong emotional tone is characteristic of many narrative repertoires. These memories that persist are also often the ones that carry so much significance and emotional weight. They come to stand as important landmarks in people's lives, ones that are turned to over and over. This repeat attention to certain events helps rework the stories as they are told, refining and perfecting their importance. This would account for the almost ritualised way in which they are recounted and how they come to be a repertoire, fixed in content and in style.

At first I attributed the use of narrative repertoires to the dynamics of fieldwork. My desire to spend time with older people and learn about their lives placed my research participants in a fairly unusual situation. They were faced with a young, foreign woman wanting to do what they did and go where they went. Furthermore, although I wished to spend time with them, my relationships with them were not predicated on a family or health care client–professional relationship. Although it was an unusual proposition that my presence in the field presented, I was usually perceived by the older people I worked with first and foremost as a student who had come all the way from North America to learn about their lives. People welcomed this and seemed to feel that I should be given the benefit of the doubt. Following from this set of assumptions about me and my role, I initially believed that this is why people kept telling me the same stories about themselves: since I was there to learn, they would tell me what they wanted me to know about their lives and their histories. I thought that the repertoires were returned to because (not knowing me and perhaps not wanting to tell me anything more personal) these well-rehearsed sets of stories were what they felt comfortable sharing in public contexts and with a relative stranger.

As fieldwork progressed and I came not only to know people better, and them me, I found that the repertoires of narratives did not lessen. Instead, I came to know the stories in more detail and to learn a larger number of them for each individual. As such, I could no longer attribute the heavy use of repertoires of narrative simply to the potentially awkward initial fieldwork dynamic but needed to consider other explanations for the presence of such a distinctive narrative form. One possible explanation is that within this particular intergenerational context, it is culturally appropriate to adopt this sort of positionality. In other words, older people adopt a narrative position as a sort of repository of knowledge in the face of younger, eager listeners such as myself. But there is also something about a playing with time that is happening here too that needs to be considered.

I said earlier that: 'The repertoires ... permit narrators to position themselves within a wider temporal framework that expands far beyond the moments of today. Indeed, such stories seem to be a sort of condensed memory, condensed and perfected through their oft-repeated performance.' I would like to elaborate further. The temporal framework of repertoires extends normally far into the past, but a temporal sleight of hand is to collapse the gap between 'now' and a 'then' of fifty or sixty years ago whereby the repertoires stitch events from a considerable duration of time ago onto the 'who I am now'. What is thus perceived by a younger interlocutor as older people talking about the past or being lost in the past *is not necessarily experienced by the older person in this way* and the relevance and salience of those experiences when younger can instead be seen as *much of who I understand myself to be today*. That is to say, there is a temporal foreshortening that occurs. Other authors have interpreted the frequent use of references to 'long-gone people and places' of older narrators as 'certainly giv[ing] the impression that the present self is not truly representative of the full identity a narrator seeks to construct' and that multiple references to the past suggests 'a separate identity from that of the present storyteller, as if the teller were back in touch directly with the person they were long ago', or even that 'when [older people] orient to and associate themselves with the past or focus on change, to some degree they dissociate themselves from their current identity' (Norrick, 2009: 906). Such perspectives are problematic, however, as they are grounded in the assumption that temporal foreshortening necessarily divorces the self of now from the self of then. While I have argued in the previous chapter for a distinction between a remembered and inhabited self in terms of embodiment, the key is that *both are held together* and it is the disjuncture between them that is frustrating rather than a disassociation between a self of the past and a self of the now. The self is a continuum, not bifurcated components.

## Shifting temporal frameworks

One afternoon, Anne and I were sitting together at her kitchen table having a cup of tea and catching up, having not seen one another for about a week. We had known each other by then for about six months and usually met at least twice a week, often for several hours at a time. I was telling her about things I had been up to or that I was worrying about: trying to find someone to remove the rotting timbers and the stone slabs that formed the kitchen floor in my house and replace them with a new floor before they collapsed; the wedding I had been to in Lyme Regis; and a part-time teaching job I had been commuting to in Hull.

In marked contrast to my talk about the present, Anne listened politely and then went on at length about how her husband had told her when they started dating and then when they were married that she could not go out with her girlfriends any more, especially not dancing. He felt strongly that once they were a couple, they would do couple things together. This was something she had trouble accepting at first, but eventually (and especially after having kids) she got used to. She told me how her granddaughter is enjoying her new job as an assistant at a nursing home and then started talking about the changes in her own life after marriage. This led to her telling me about what it was like when her husband at the age of 50 (over thirty years ago) had to quit his job on the railway and take another job, owing to his angina.

Her narrative about these past moments, events and worries in her life was not at all self-consciously different from when she was talking about the present or listening to me speaking about it, but rather was seamlessly integrated into our chit-chat about current everyday concerns. Although Anne may weave different historical periods in and out of her narratives, she is by no means 'lost' in the past and lives a very active, present-oriented life. She does, however, incorporate a great many past events from long ago into her narratives about the present, as do the majority of her peers.

Similarly, while Vivienne and I were eating fish and chips together after watching some of the summer Olympics on the television, she began talking about her mother and how sad it was that her mother had grown up in an orphanage, lost her husband at age 33, lost her son to the war, got her house taken away from her at age 56 when her husband (a miner) was killed in an accident at work and then fell and 'woke up' the cancer in her hip, which led immediately into Vivienne speaking about herself and all the disappointments in her life. Vivienne lost the brother she 'idolised', she put off getting married until she was 28 so that she could help take care of her mother economically (as a widow, her mother had a severely limited income) and medically because she was suffering with depression following her son's death in the war. Then, Vivienne and her husband worked hard in their own business in the corner shop for thirty-four years, but only had a few years together after retirement before he died. Vivienne was not recounting these pieces of her life story in the context of an interview, but rather spontaneously and over a shared meal, aspects of her life that she wanted to relate. Like Anne, her story was a very unselfconscious usage of the past, but here there was a seamless switch from talking about her mother's life and hardships to her own life and its disappointments, a temporal shift that was completely incorporated into the story and indeed an important characteristic of it.

The temporal frameworks bookmarking Anne's and Vivienne's narratives shift much more than those of my own, with a more marked movement between past and present and their mutual integration. This characteristic of narrative style of older people that I became accustomed to during my fieldwork is different from the one used by younger adults. It often seemed as though I and the older people I had come to know were speaking in different forms of the same language. By and large, I was employing a linear form whereby small-talk is about present-day occurrences, experiences, worries and pleasures. Conversation is carried out in a more or less reciprocal kind of exchange where both parties get a chance to contribute, which moves the conversation on to further topics. For the most part, however, my research participants used a much more temporally circular form of small-talk that brought in a great deal of information from the past and was recited from a repertoire of narratives that were often strung together in long chains, rather than interjected into a conversation where interlocutors alternated between being speaker and listener.

Sally, another woman I came to know very well during my fieldwork, made an off-handed comment to me one day about how 'losing the art of conversation' was one of the consequences of old age. While she did not elaborate further, I believe that more than any other of the people who participated in my research, she is aware of some of the narrative shifts that occur in old age. These narrative shifts are linked to shifts in temporal perspective. However, while Sally talks about them as a loss (not surprisingly, given her overwhelming concern with the experience of disconcerting memory blanks that disrupt her conversation, which I discussed in Chapter 5), she was alone among the older people I knew to do so. For this reason I have chosen to conceptualise these shifts as a reconfiguration in narrative style rather than as a loss per se.

## Conclusions

Some of the episodes I recount here may seem banal when considered individually, with microscopic attention to descriptive details in the recounting of unremarkable events of daily life. Through them, however, I have sought to demonstrate that as these episodes accumulate, patterns emerge that are lodged in cultural praxis and come to define the parameters within which daily life is lived and experienced by older people. Some of these patterns are imbricated with the ways in which experience is narrated and the temporal perspectives framing that experience, a narrative and temporal perspective that diverges from normative middle-aged models. In particular, I have looked in this chapter at three distinctive patterns of narrative style that emerged in my fieldwork: the use of 'irrelevant' information, narrative repertoires and shifting temporal frameworks. In all three examples, narrative conventions based on normative models of linearity, chronology and contextualisation are not obeyed. Other authors have written about how narrative conventions shape the stories that people tell about themselves. Such stories are

> influenced by the vocabulary and grammar of the language in which they are
> expressed, by the broader cultural conventions of context, style and genre of
> expression and by the other stories in circulation. In this way, individuals
> come to consciousness within a conventional narrational context and within a
> narrational space which they are expected to occupy. (Rapport and Overing,
> 2000a: 286)

The conventional narrational context that Rapport and Overing evoke here is based on a particular set of fundamental principles, ones they cite J. Bruner (1990) as outlining as 'time or sequentiality, narrative voice or "agentivity", narrative structure or canonicality and point of view or perspectivity' (*ibid.*: 287). Through the use of these predictable characteristics, individuals come to share a collective way of 'organizing, presenting and remembering information and so knowing the world. The narrative stock of a culture is thus seen as embodying what are socially recognized to be typical behaviour patterns' (*ibid.*: 287–8). These ways of knowing the world through shared conventions of narrative are discussed by the authors above as consistent for all members of a particular culture or society. However, my fieldwork data shows that some of the conventions of narrative accounts can change and do change with age, particularly a relaxation of the narrative rules about limiting repetition and linearity. Ironically, this then becomes a double-edged sword since the disjuncture between middle-aged conventions of narrative (concerning the past, present and future; orderly, linear and thus 'rational'; non-repetitive) and those of older narrators (holders of knowledge about the past, not necessarily linear, sometimes repetitive) ends up reinforcing the younger interlocutor's assumptions that older people are confused and unreliable sources of information about the present day, such as the insurance rep with Vivienne and my own fears on Olive's behalf.

Rapport and Overing point out that the narrative conventions highlighted by Bruner are based on a deeply structural and deterministic view of narrative; 'through our narrative acts we create meaning out of experience, but only in terms of pre-existing and prescriptive categories' (Rapport and Overing, 2000a: 288). They offer a different perspective on narrative, one that highlights individual experience and subjectivity. This approach looks at how 'individuals create space for themselves beyond the formal surfaces of public and collective performance' (*ibid.*: 289), a sort of

> ongoing engagement with narrative [which] amounts to a way of proceeding actively through life, fixing personal moments of being and giving them meaning ... Through narrational performances, conscious selves come to be maintained: selves with pasts, presents and futures; selves with world-views and identities; selves with relations and possessions; selves with knowledge, self-consciousness and understanding. (*ibid.*)

While I concur with their emphasis on the subjective meaning, Rapport and Overing's essay raises two issues for me. First, I am concerned with the implications of narratives that transgress the collectively held conventions of delivery and what this transgression means for how older people are categorised and perceived by younger audiences as 'old', and as we saw in Chapter 4, among older people themselves about their peers. Second, while I agree that it is through narrational performances that selves are constructed and maintained (selves with world views and identities, knowledge, understanding), my ethnographic data from older adults call into question Rapport and Overing's assumptions about the universality of 'selves with pasts, presents and futures'. As described earlier in this chapter and picked up again in terms of memory talk and temporality in Chapters 3 and 5, how the past integrates with the present and the role of the future can be configured differently for older people. This, in turn, has important implications for the relationship between narrational performance and the creation and reproduction of the self.

So, in particular, these three narrative styles reveal a series of different relationships with time. The first of these is the way in which rigid distinctions made been different temporal eras, 'then' and 'now' – for example in my conversation with Anne – lose their importance. Moving rapidly between temporal frames of plural pasts and the present, the boundaries between them become blurred and insignificant. Vivienne too uses this narrative style to include not only her own past but the even more distant past of her mother's biography, to reflect on her own pasts and present. Temporal foreshortening at this level of scale, slipping easily between all ten decades of the twentieth century in Vivienne's example, and six decades in the vignette from Anne, is something all of the older people I came to know used at different moments and in the flow of normal everyday conversation. There is a great deal of narrative travelling between pasts and present, all of which become mutually embedded. A temporally circular narrative form results, marking the older people I interacted with out as distinct from younger interlocutors. Problematically, though, these narrative styles are taken by members of the wider society with whom older people interact as 'proof' of oldness. This is because non-linearity, repetition and temporal flux are read by younger adults as a damaged form of temporal perception being made manifest in the narrative account, as evidence of 'old age'.

There is a second temporal aspect to these narrative styles, one that can also be negatively associated with 'oldness' by younger interlocutors. This is when narrative accounts are perceived as 'garbled' precisely because they do not conform to normative temporal and narrative conventions. In the example of 'irrelevant' information, this is due to temporal links not being made by the narrator to help situate the narrative for the listener. The 'now' of the conversation (such as about insurance details) shifts abruptly to a non-contextualised piece of information, an 'other now' (such as 'You're from Silkstone Common, aren't you?'). This non-linear gap could have been bridged according to narrative conventions in a way that would have smoothed this temporal fold, but instead, a pattern of seeming relaxation of this concern is more evident at times among older speakers.

Hazan, as I have previously mentioned, says that older people are caught between social stereotypes of older age as static and their own actual experiences of great change (1980, 1984). Similarly, evident in the insurance rep's behaviour towards Vivienne, is the idea that Vivienne is somehow atemporal or temporally compromised: his treatment of her, 'like a child', strips her in their interaction of a temporally rich subjectivity that has built up over a lifetime, particularly her knowledge and experience (as a small business owner) of contracts, paperwork, insurance policies and maths. He, instead, seeks to position her as void of past experience and lodged in some sort of timeless present. She resists this to the best of her ability but then, under the stress and frustration of the encounter, introduces a temporally jarring element into the conversation which no doubt reinforces this idea of her as an 'old woman' who is supposedly confused. In this way, both narrativity and temporality come into play as channels through which older age takes shape in relation to younger age, as the rep casually exercises his generational prerogative to denigrate Vivienne. Such practices do not simply marginalise older people as fringe members of society in a relatively powerless position, but shore up the assumption of a different, lesser category of being human in comparison to a normative vision of the middle-aged adult whose temporal positioning becomes the standard against which older people are judged and ranked.

## Notes

1 Heikkinen (2000: 471) comments similarly in her work with older people in central Finland how 'it was quite astonishing to hear some accounts of key events that had been given (in interviews) five years previously repeated almost word for word' five years on in a series of follow-up interviews that she conducted with people now aged 85.
2 A local place name for a small nearby fishing lake.
3 A type of house built across England in the 1800s and early 1900s that had two rooms on the ground floor and two rooms above.
4 Although, as some of her peers pointed out when discussing her story among themselves (and how they wished she was not as open about it as she is), these and all sorts of other things happened during the war that would not have happened under 'normal' conditions.

# 7

# Conclusions

There is a purple geranium that flowers every June in my garden, billowing up in great masses of green leaf and mists of purple, papery blossom from the brown detritus of last year's plant that has rotted down over the course of each preceding winter. Its annual growth, blossoming and eventual fading always tugs bitter sweetly on me, marking as it does the passing of yet another year spent immersed in the pressurised flow of the demands of work and family life, pressures that mean it has been too long since I have been able to return to Dodworth and spend any significant amount of time with the people I have written about in this book. The purple geranium is doubly meaningful in this regard as it was given to me by Margaret, an old Dodworther, from her own garden.

I have written in passing about Margaret and this plant before (Degnen, 2009). She had insisted that I come to her garden for some cuttings for my own garden, now that I had my own house on Holdroyd's Yard and was no longer renting the anonymous flat on the High Street, discussed in Chapter 2. She, like me, had a small garden, but unlike mine hers was full of beautiful plants in well-tended beds. We spent the better part of a morning there, digging up sections of established plants and wrapping them in damp newspaper so that they would transplant easily into my garden later in the day. As I came to learn, Margaret's own biography had many points of intersection with gardening and with individual plants in her garden beds. During the war, she served in the Land Army on the estate of a stately home 3.7 miles from Dodworth, working on the land. It was, however, the walled garden there that she remembered with particular fondness and she attributed her gardening skills to the time she served in the Land Army. As we went along at our task, Margaret recounted spontaneously to me where and from whom many of the plants in her own garden originated: this one from a favourite neighbour that she lived next door to thirty years ago; this a pink carnation that she had successfully rooted from a birthday bouquet given to her by a granddaughter three years ago; and the purple geranium which had come from her mother's garden and travelled with her every time she moved, transplanting sections of it into her new garden each time. The purple geranium has travelled with me, too, now in its third garden since she originally gave it to me in 2001.

At the time, Margaret was in her late seventies. Born and bred in Dodworth, Margaret was well known by other old Dodworthers although she had lived away for a period of time after marrying her husband, a builder, about twenty-two miles to the north in Otley. After her husband died, she returned to Dodworth to be nearer her children who had remained in the Barnsley area. While her three uncles had been miners, her father had worked as a train driver on the mineral railway. Evelyn, another old Dodworther, remembers how Margaret's father used to regularly walk past their house in Sovereign Wood to catch his train on the railway at the bottom of their garden, and she recounted the story to me again when the news came in 2002 – after my fieldwork ended but while I was still living in Dodworth – that Margaret had died. While writing this manuscript, I have received news too now of Evelyn's death as well as of Anne, Vivienne and of Emma.

The passage of years that the geranium's annual cycle marks as well as my simultaneous absence from Dodworth and from the people I came to know best there seems ever more poignant. On a recent visit back to Dodworth in 2011, I spent several hours talking with Anne's son, daughter-in-law and granddaughter, sharing memories of Anne and hearing first hand from them what her final months had been like. Woven into our conversation were many familiar elements of Anne's own narrative repertoires of self that I had come to know so well: her love of freshening up the decor at home with new coats of paint, her irrepressible determination and sense of humour and her central role as matriarchal heart of the family. Despite her absence, the narratives live on, woven as they are into the biographies of her family and friends, woven into their and my memories of her, stories which in her absence we now recount to each other.

I feel fortunate to still be connected to some of the Dodworth families who I first came to know in 1999–2000 via their oldest members. These enduring friendships and acquaintances speak volumes about the generosity of the older people I came to know. They were willing to disregard social patterns that make it otherwise difficult for younger and older people to meet, to find common ground and to develop friendships. The people I came to know gave me a chance to share aspects of their lives with them over a long period of time, educated me in what they felt I needed to know about Dodworth's past and present, welcomed me into their extended families and into their private domain. It was one of the happiest periods of my life. But yet, writing about my time in Dodworth and returning to visit when I can is painful. I miss my now deceased friends terribly. The cohort I knew so well during my fieldwork is now almost entirely gone. In a place like Dodworth where I was taught how remembering is three-dimensional and where I was schooled in the minute specificities of those memories, being physically in Dodworth and immersed in those accumulated memories (many of which were never my own first-hand memories in the first place) yet unable to speak with the people I cared about so much and who taught me what I know is a melancholic and bittersweet experience.

In moving this book towards a conclusion, there are several points I wish to make, some of which stem, in part, from the reflections provoked by the purple geranium. The first of these is one that will be familiar to many ethnographers: conducting intensive fieldwork over a period of many months and years comes to intertwine the biography and identity of the ethnographer with that of the people and places she has worked. Sometimes this transformative effect is dialectical, but it is probably fair to say that 'being there' via fieldwork tends to make a stronger impression on the ethnographer who has chosen to arrive and who can, equally, choose to leave. A great deal of reflection on the power inequalities of ethnography and representation has rightly occupied anthropologists since the 1980s and the debates over 'writing culture'. My own anthropological training that commenced as an undergraduate in the early 1990s was profoundly shaped by this disciplinary epoch. This, in conjunction with cultural practices in Dodworth that deeply valorise the immediate locale, has undoubtedly come together to intensify the sense of melancholy and indebtedness I feel when I write about old Dodworthers and Dodworth now that I am no longer there. Experience and knowledge gained via ethnography can (and should) thus bind ethnographers to people and places via ties of duty and reciprocity: having been allowed to share in daily life in the name of research, there is a duty of care to 'do right' via the accounts produced, recounted and published that come from that research. This I have always done to the best of my ability.

However, I find that as time passes, and as the lives of the older people I worked with have drawn to a close, this duty weighs ever more heavily. Having joined the older people I came to know towards the end of their lives meant that the time available to me (as an ethnographer, and gradually in many cases as a friend) to nurture those relationships, to return and catch up, to see what twists and turns life brings, has been largely limited to the concentrated period of time of my fieldwork. A number of my contacts and friends died during fieldwork and nearly all of the others are now also deceased. The future does not extend tantalisingly into an expansive range of possibilities as it might have had I not chosen to work with older people. There is no opportunity now to touch base, 'check back' and revise my ideas about what I think I know – instead, faced with a blank page while writing, the duty of care becomes heightened to 'do right' by the individuals I knew who are no longer here, a duty of care to their memories by trying to express on paper who they were and why their lives matter. This duty feels heavier now that they have died.

Second, ethnography in Dodworth and with older people also permitted and required certain things of me. It permitted me the chance to immerse myself in the life worlds of older people. This meant I was able to escape the normal order of things whereby older and younger people tend to inhabit different social circuits in late capitalist societies, unless brought together in care- or family-based relationships. This is, of course, why outsiders always assumed I was a granddaughter, nurse or care worker if they came across me spending time with the older people who feature in this volume. That we might be friends was never a possibility that sprang first to outsiders' minds. Indeed, such a state of affairs is symptomatic of one of the themes I have sought to elaborate on in this book: namely, how problematic is the social position older people find themselves imbricated in, some of the ways 'old age' becomes a lived reality and how older age takes shape in relation to other parts of the life course.

Ethnography further permitted me to juxtapose public and private realms of everyday experience and to consider a wide spectrum of contexts and interactions. It permitted me to consider the ways in which these coalesce and blend, sometimes easily and sometimes uneasily in narrative and personal experience. Ethnography permitted me to become saturated with both the banal and the extraordinary detail of everyday lives and in turn seek to analyse and explore how it is that 'old age' comes to be assigned and experienced. As such, I have been able to explore how it is that, for example, dementia is a minority experience but has attracted much scholarly attention, while other less sensational aspects of self more relevant to daily life have received relatively little.

Third, ethnographic research with older people required that I suspend, as much as was possible, my own expectations of narrative and temporal conventions. Indeed, the purple geranium is a reminder in particular of the temporal depth I was immersed in – a plant that had lived longer than I had was gifted to me by a woman recounting seven decades of gardening knowledge – and which rendered my own temporal frame shallow by comparison. As I have sought to demonstrate throughout this volume, this distinctive temporal register is significant and consequential for subjectivity and the ageing self, but it is also an accumulative pattern that only becomes fully perceptible with the time and effort that participant observation demands.

I did not set out to document the oral history of Dodworth, but as it is such a crucial point of interest and linchpin of sociability for many of my research participants, it is inevitable that so much of it winds its way through *Years in the making*. Its presence here attests to the significance of memory talk for older people that, unlike organised 'reminiscence therapy', which has become so prominent in institutional settings for older people (Bornat, 1994; Westerhof *et al.*, 2010), instead occurs spontaneously within the currents of everyday life, such as the personal stories linked together by Margaret around the purple geranium and the shared memories Evelyn had of Margaret's father. The local history of Dodworth is furthermore not something that is only of interest to older residents, but something that speaks to many younger people as well. I thus hope that one of the unintended consequences of my time in Dodworth and of this book – and for those less interested in the anthropological questions I grapple with in it – will be the aspects of oral history that it records. Such history, furthermore, stands in instructive contrast to the social reconfiguration being wrought by shifting patterns of socio-economic mobility which are unevenly distributed in the north of England, and which the new Dodworth estate discussed in Chapter 2 attests to.

Dodworth is a place where the past matters. This, too, exerts ethnographic requirements. Dodworth is a place where many older residents explain what Dodworth *is* by saying that it is no longer what it *used to be*. This in turn has consequences for the ageing self as old Dodworthers point to a wide spectrum of change in multiple aspects of everyday life, which include the physical texture of the village, domestic technologies, forms of transport, sociability, neighbouring, food provisioning, communal holidays, housing stock, the local authority, employment and standard of living to describe the extent of social and economic transformation over their lifetime. Some of these have been experienced throughout Britain but others are highly specific to the region and still others hold particular shape and inflection in Dodworth itself. It is difficult to overstate the sheer magnitude that talking about shared memories of Dodworth, its inhabitants, its locales and the surrounding area play in everyday casual conversation of my research participants. While some individuals are particularly adept raconteurs, it is a practice and a skill that nearly everyone I came into contact with exercised. In this respect, it is not limited to older village residents, although they are of course the focus of this book and their temporal scope heightens its effect. Contemporary Dodworth is a present infused with the past, animated by shared memories of what used to be where, who used to inhabit those spaces and how those people and places are connected to the current day. There is a regular and predictable referencing of the past in people's narratives about their everyday present lives and their everyday present concerns. As Anthony Cohen describes in his ethnography of Whalsay, everyday 'conversation ... spans and concertinas the centuries' via chat about characters from the past, place names and language used to navigate the terrain which is linked to personal and family names (1987: 3). So too in Dodworth. The past drenches the present, animating and orientating discussion of current events. Developing a facility in memory talk thus became an ethnographic requirement as I discuss in Chapter 3.

But yet, one of my dilemmas in framing this book was how to convey the significance of memory talk and the past without at the same time overstating the case or giving the impression that the present and future were not also pertinent concerns. This is particularly true given the distinctive temporal patterns and pressures older people face and which I have examined in Chapters 1 and 3. I puzzled over where exactly one begins to recount the story of a place and the people living there, temporally and experientially speaking, when in the course of normal local conversation multiple references are made to things like rows of houses torn down forty years ago, or to shops no longer in existence, or to people no longer living or to places that look very different today than they did before. Where, temporally and experientially speaking, does one begin the story of a place when despite their absences and rupture those same places and people from past times still assist in orientating present-day experience and meaning? Although no longer physically part of contemporary Dodworth, these remembered traces of Dodworth's past are evoked, made real again and persist as salient points of reference in contemporary life. In Dodworth, a place where the past matters to such an extent, describing contemporary life without also evoking this temporal richness would be remiss. As such, I have described a number of historical and contemporary aspects of Dodworth but the intermingling of 1999–2005 when I lived there cannot easily be parsed from socially alive memories of earlier layers of meaning that overlay everyday interactions in the village, inform people's sense of self and their experience of ageing, as becomes clear in Chapters 3 and 5.

My own ageing and position as researcher are another point worth consider-ing. I arrived in Dodworth, aged 27, as an unmarried foreign student. In the nearly twelve years that have passed since December 1999, I have married, become a mother, embarked on a career in British academia, become a British citizen and begun to witness the gradual ageing of my own parents and in-laws. Much of my professional success, such as publications and being hired as a lecturer, stems directly from my fieldwork experiences in Dodworth. Indeed, I owe an unpayable debt in this respect to both the people of Dodworth and the people of Sheshatshiu, Labrador where I conducted my first fieldwork, for my Masters degree (Degnen, 2001). Having myself grown from one series of life positions into others – student to lecturer, childless to mother and so on – means that my ethnographic persona has also changed. Very soon, when working with older people in their seventies, eighties and nineties, I will no longer be of their grandchildren's generation but in the generation of their children, and eventually – 'all being well', as many old Dodworthers would say – approaching older age myself. How this shift in my own positionality impacts on ethnographic possibil-ities and requirements, as well as the shift in the generational cohort of the older people I hope to work with in the future, will in, and of itself, be intriguing.

It also begs the question of what the ethnographic canon might look like if it were not based so heavily as it is on accounts of relatively young people.[1] This is not to say that the anthropological literature is only populated by younger scholars as of course it is not. I do posit, however, that it is younger scholars at the beginning of their careers whose in-depth ethnographic accounts have dominated the canon. This is due in large part to the disciplinary rite of passage of first fieldwork. There are important exceptions to this general rule, but as a general pattern, subsequent periods of fieldwork are never again as long or as in-depth. Consider what anthropology might look like were the really crucial, unmissable, rite of passage to be 12–18 months of fieldwork at age 60, at the cusp of retirement. If this were the case, would temporality, for instance, have been less of a background concern to the discipline (Munn, 1992) and instead a more prominent framing of enquiry and analysis? What else might emerge as points of concern and interest in cultural analysis and theory, given this different genera-tional grounding? Would the temporal sleights of hand I refer to in Chapter 6 and the temporal foreshortening in narrative accounts be more familiar in both personal experience of ethnographers and thus better reflected in ethnographic accounts?

This point about ethnography and generational perspective is linked to one of the driving forces behind this book. I have sought to problematise the ways in which older people come to be treated in certain contexts as less than fully adult. For example, as discussed in Chapter 6, certain elements of narrative style, such as what I term narrative repertoires, are interpreted by interlocutors as character-istic of 'old age' itself. The unfortunate outcome is that people using such stylistic patterns themselves come to be judged and labelled as 'old' and narrative style thus becomes another element in the construction of old age. This parallels issues raised in Chapter 4 about how 'old age' is made. It is also evident in episodes such as Vivienne's encounter with the insurance representative and her launching into 'irrelevant' information, a loosening of comportment which is reflected in her language but which risks being interpreted against her as attributes of 'oldness'.

Throughout, I have sought to widen a theoretical conceptualisation of the self via an approach that privileges narrativity, temporality and interpersonal interactions as key constitutive elements. While there is much in the experience of the middle-aged self that parallels older selves, there are characteristics in the presentation and creation of the older self that at times challenges a model of self based primarily on middle-aged adults. Examples of this include what I have called the remembered self versus the inhabited self and the reconfiguring power of memory blanks for one's notion of self. The ageing self also serves as a reminder to theorists of the limits of models of self that are premised on fluidity and flexibility. While all social actors may experience discontinuity and fragmentation in the subjective experience of self but paper over it with an illusion of wholeness (Ewing, 1990), the ageing self is under particular pressure in this regard. Owing to the risk of coming to be labelled as 'really old' and the consequent lessening of status as full adult (such as I demonstrate in Chapter 4 in my discussion of Ella and Mrs Atherton), the premium on consistency in self-presentation for older people becomes extremely high and contradictions in self-representation clamped down upon. Indeed, it is precisely the ways in which distinctive temporal frames and distinctive narrative activity (both content and style) come to shape, and in turn be shaped by, the ageing self that I have sought to demonstrate in this volume. With regard to distinctive temporal frames, I have examined a number of key points: a sense of urgent timeliness; intergenerational and interpersonal tensions over relationships to the past and to time; the importance of fixed schedules in contrast with 'empty' time; the salience of temporal markers such as silver and golden wedding anniversaries; and relationships with the future. Turning my attention to narrative activity, I considered the ways in which the use of 'irrelevant' information, narrative repertoires and shifting temporal frameworks unseat narrative conventions based on normative models of linearity, chronology and contextualisation. Both temporality and narrativity provide insight into what is at stake ontologically (in terms of how people come to know, experience and dwell in the world) and subjectively (in regards to the self) in everyday life as people grow older.

Finally, anthropologists before me have identified and resisted related pressures on the ageing self, namely the association of loss with older age. Indeed, the need for such an approach should not be surprising given the Freudian perspective on ageing and the self discussed in Chapter 1 that is framed around loss and injury. For example, two anthropologists who have each made path-breaking contributions to the ethnographic literature on ageing are Kaufman (1986) and Myerhoff (1979). Both authors positioned their work on ageing as a move against the emphasis on loss: 'old age has come to be associated with predominately negative stereotypes – decline, loss and disease. Because of all the assumed losses – reduced sensory awareness, deaths among relatives and friends, lowered social and economic status due to retirement, for example, aging is often viewed as negative and problematic' (Kaufman, 1986: 4). Kaufman, as I have explained in Chapter 5, focused instead on how an identity of an ageless self 'operates as a source of meaning in old age' (*ibid*.: 14) and 'discovered … that though sociocultural demands for change are inevitable in late life and do present dilemmas of being and action, people, in describing the meaning of their lives, are able to create continuity of self. This process enables them to cope with demands for change and, thus, is a critical resource for remaining healthy' (*ibid*.: 6). As such, a vision of life for older people emerges from her work as one not based on losses, but one whereby new meaning is created by perpetual work on the self and identity building. Similarly, Myerhoff states that old age is often described as

> only a pathetic series of losses – money, freedom, relationships, roles, strength, beauty, potence and possibilities … We are rarely presented with the views of old people about themselves and given an opportunity to hear how aging is experienced by them, 'from inside the native's head', so to speak. This approach, basic to anthropology, yields the 'aging as career' concept, to replace the usual 'series of losses' notion that results when younger people regard the elderly from their own perspective. (1979: 250–1)

Both authors propose useful and sensitive ways of reframing ideas about old age that focus on cumulative building throughout one's lifetime rather than decay. This in some respects mirrors my own point about how older selves are 'years in the making'. However, conceptualising old age as a time of loss is not something that only younger people do, as Myerhoff suggests, but also something that older people themselves engage in at times. Denying the experience of loss is to silence and erase portions of the wide range of important experiences that inform one's sense of self in older age. There are profound consequences of loss that many of my research participants spoke openly about. Loneliness in particular is one of these and stems most often from the loss of spouse and the sense of alienation (to varying degrees) from one's family. Shifts in what the body can do is another, as I considered in Chapter 5. Like monitoring, discussed in Chapter 4, loneliness and loss are difficult topics to address since cultural assumptions about older people embrace on the one hand an image of old age as lonely and depressing and on the other hand, an emerging ideology of 'good agers' who are busy, social and happy and who have 'taken control' of their ageing. In light of these assumptions of 'good ageing', people who experience and express loneliness are often perceived as having only themselves to blame (c.f. Oliver, 2007), a highly individualistic premise. This is a model that does not sit easily with me as I take experience and meaning to be fundamentally social processes that do not occur in a vacuum of individual isolation. But ultimately, I also believe that none of these visions of old age (loss and decline versus 'good' ageing) encapsulate the entirety of experience of the people I came to know. I do not wish to portray the lives of my research participants as being held hostage to either. Despite this, a sense of loss had very real impact on the minutiae of daily life for many of my research participants and was a pressure that reconfigured everyday experience. To leave it unspoken would be misrepresentative of the everyday experience of many of the people I spent my time with and must not be muted for the sake of preserving a solely positive portrait of ageing. Indeed, seeking balance in representing the positive and negative aspects of experience, so to speak, is precisely what I mean by 'doing right' by the people I came to know and whom I write about in this volume.

So, indeed, sometimes the people I came to know in Dodworth felt worn down by the demands older age presented them with. At times like these, they might tell me 'there's nowt in getting old, Cathrine', as Emma did in Chapter 5 and Iris did in Chapter 4. This commonplace expression often signalled a frustration with one's uncompliant body or with circumstances rendered more difficult owing to older age. And yet, such frustrations are not what stands out in my memory when I think of Emma, Iris, Vivienne, Albert, Anne, Tommy, Evelyn, Margaret, Ernest, Mary, Tom and all their peers that I came to know in Dodworth. What stands out for me instead is how full of ideas, questions, fun, indignation, humour, directness, memory talk, emotions, contradictions and opinions they were. It is this vitality that I want to keep in focus and to see fuller recognition of in accounts of older age. *Years in the making* stems from my desire to see reflected in the ethnographic literature more of the perspectives and everyday experiences of older people. I further wished to consider what their distinctive positionality might contribute to anthropological perspectives on self, subjectivity, time and narrativity. This book originated in a deep frustration with the casual ways in which older people's subjectivity is often denigrated and eroded. Countering such dismissive gestures, though, is the very vitality of the people whose lives and perspectives I have recounted here, both of which have been deeply inflected by their relationships with the place and people of Dodworth, past and present.

## Note

1 I am indebted to Peter Phillimore for his suggestion and our discussion of this point.

# References

Abelmann, N. (1997) 'Narrating selfhood and personality in South Korea: women and social mobility', *American Ethnologist*, 24 (4): 786–812.

Adam, B. (1990) *Time and Social Theory*. Cambridge: Polity Press.

Adam, B. (2010) 'Future matters for ageing research', *Workshop Imagining the Future*. CPA London, OU Centre for Ageing and Biographical Studies and Centre for Policy on Ageing, London.

Alexander, B., Rubenstein, R., Goodman, M. and Luborsky, M. (1991) 'Generativity in cultural context: the self, death and immortality as experienced by older American women', *Ageing and Society*, 11: 417–442.

Andrews, G., Cutchin, M., McCracken, K., Phillips, D. and Wiles, J. (2007) 'Geographical gerontology: the constitution of a discipline', *Social Science & Medicine*, 65 (1): 151–168.

Arber, S. and Evandrou, M. (1993) 'Mapping the territory: ageing, independence, and the life course', in S. Arber and M. Evandrou (eds) *Ageing, Independence and the Life Course*. London: Jessica Kingsley Publishers.

Barnsley Chronicle (2002) 'Survey reveals town's "most deprived" tag', *Barnsley Chronicle* (12 April), p. 11.

Battaglia, D. (1993) 'At play in the fields (and borders) of the imaginary: Melanesian transformations of forgetting', *Cultural Anthropology*, 8 (4): 430–442.

Battaglia, D. (1995a) 'Problematizing the self: a thematic introduction', in D. Battaglia (ed.), *Rhetorics of Self-Making*. Berkeley: University of California Press.

Battaglia, D. (1995b) 'On practical nostalgia: self-prospecting among urban Trobrianders', in D. Battaglia (ed.), *Rhetorics of Self-Making*. Berkeley: University of California Press.

Bender, J. and Wellberry, D. (1991) 'Introduction', in J.Bender and D. Wellberry (eds) *Chronotypes: The Construction of Time*. Stanford: Stanford University Press.

Biggs, S. (1997) 'Choosing not to be old? Masks, bodies and identity management in later life', *Ageing & Society*, 17 (5): 553–570.

Biggs, S. (2004) 'Age, gender, narratives, and masquerades', *Journal of Aging Studies*, 18 (1): 45–58.

Blaikie, A. (1999) *Ageing and Popular Culture*. Cambridge: Cambridge University Press.

Bornat, J. (ed.) (1994) *Reminiscence Reviewed: Perspectives, Evaluations, Achievements*. Buckingham: Open University Press.

Bourdieu, P. (1977) *Outline of a Theory of Practice*. Cambridge: Cambridge University Press.

Bourdieu, P. (1984) *Distinction: A Social Critique of the Judgement of Taste*. London: Routledge.

Boyarin, J. and Boyarin, D. (1995) 'Self-exposure as theory: the double mark of the male Jew', in D. Battaglia (ed.), *Rhetorics of Self-Making*. Berkeley University of California Press.

Bruner, E. (1984a) *Text, Play, and Story: The Construction and Reconstruction of Self and Society*. Washington, DC: American Ethnological Society.

Bruner, E. (1984b) 'The opening up of anthropology', in E. Bruner (ed.), *Text, Play, and Story: The Construction and Reconstruction of Self and Society*. Washington, DC: American Ethnological Society.

Bruner, E. (1986) 'Experience and its expressions', in V. Turner and E. Bruner (eds) *The Anthropology of Experience*. Urbana and Chicago: University of Illinois Press.

Bruner, J. (1990) *Acts of Meaning*. Cambridge: Harvard University Press.

Bulmer, M. (1975) 'Sociological models of the mining community', *Sociological Review*, 23 (1): 61–92.

Bytheway, B. (2000) 'Youthfulness and ageless: a comment', *Ageing and Society*, 20: 781–789.

Carrithers, M. (1985) ' An alternative social history of the self', in M. Carrithers, S. Collins and S. Lukes (eds) *The Category of the Person: Anthropology, Philosophy, History*. Cambridge: Cambridge University Press.

Cave, A. (2001) 'Language Variety and Communicative Style as Local and Subcultural Identity in a South Yorkshire Coalmining Community', Doctoral thesis, Sheffield University.

Chatterji, R. (1998) 'An ethnography of dementia', *Culture, Medicine and Psychiatry*, 22 (3): 355–382.

Clarke, L. and Griffin, M. (2007) 'Becoming and being gendered through the body: older women, their mothers and body image', *Ageing & Society*, 27 (5): 701–18.

Clark, M. and Anderson, B. (1967) *Culture and Aging: An Anthropological Study of Older Americans*. Springfield, IL: C. C. Thomas.

Cliggett, L. (2005) *Grains from Grass: Aging, Gender, and Famine in Rural Africa*. Ithaca, NY: Cornell University Press.

Cohen, A. (1987) *Whalsay: Symbol, Segment and Boundary in a Shetland Island Community*. Manchester: Manchester University Press.

Cohen, L. (1994) 'Old age: cultural and critical perspectives', *Annual Review of Anthropology*, 23: 137–158.

Cohen, L. (1998) *No Aging in India: Alzheimer's, Bad Families, and Other Modern Things*. Berkeley: University of California Press.

Comfort, A. (1977) *A Good Age*. London: Mitchell Beazley.

Coupland, J. (2009) 'Time, the body and the reversibility of ageing: commodifying the decade', *Ageing & Society*, 29 (6): 953–976.

Coupland, N. and Coupland, J. (1991) 'Language and later life: incipient literatures', in N. Coupland, J. Coupland and H. Giles (eds) *Language, Society and the Elderly: Discourse, Identity and Ageing*. Oxford: Blackwell.

Cowgill, D. and Holmes, L. (1972) *Aging and Modernization*. New York: Appleton Century Crofts.

Crapanzano, V. (1992) *Hermes' Dilemma and Hamlet's Desire: On the Epistemology of Interpretation*. Cambridge, MA: Harvard University Press.

Crow, G. (1994) *Coal, Culture, and Community*. Sheffield: PAVIS Publications.

Csordas, T. (1990) 'Embodiment as a paradigm for anthropology', *Ethos*, 18 (1): 5–47.

Cumming, E. and Henry, W. (1961) *Growing Old: The Process of Disengagement*. New York: Basic Books.

Dawson, A. (1990) 'Ageing and Change in Pit Villages of North East England', Doctoral thesis, University of Essex.

Dawson, A. (2002) 'The mining community and the ageing body: towards a phenomenology of community?', in V. Amit (ed.), *Realizing Community: Concepts, Social Relationships and Sentiments*. London: Routledge.

de Certeau, M. (1984) *The Practice of Everyday Life*. Berkeley: University of California Press.

Degnen, C. (2001) 'Healing Sheshatshiu: community healing and country space', in C. Scott (ed.), *Aboriginal Autonomy and Development in Northern Quebec-Labrador*. Vancouver: University of British Columbia Press.

Degnen, C. (2006) 'Commemorating coal mining in the home: material culture and domestic space in Dodworth, South Yorkshire', Available online at: www.hrionline.ac.uk/matshef/degnen/MSdegnen.htm.

Degnen, C. (2009) 'On vegetable love: gardening, plants, and people in the north of England', *Journal of the Royal Anthropological Institute*, 15 (1): 151–167.

Dennis, N., Henriques, L. and Slaughter, C. (1956) *Coal is Our Life. An Analysis of a Yorkshire Mining Community*. London: Eyre & Spottiswoode.

Diamond, T. (1992) *Making Gray Gold: Narratives of Nursing Home Care*. Chicago: University of Chicago Press.

Dumont, L. (1980) *Homo Hierarchicus*. Chicago: University of Chicago Press.

Edwards, J. (1998) 'The need for a "bit of history": place and past in English identity', in N. Lovell (ed.), *Locality and Belonging*. London: Routledge.

Edwards, J. (2000) *Born and Bred: Idioms of Kinship and New Reproductive Technologies in England*. Oxford: Oxford University Press.

Ekerdt, D. (1986) 'The busy ethic: moral continuity between work and retirement', *The Gerontologist*, 26 (3): 239–244.

Estes, C., Lee, P., Gerard, L. and Noble, M. (1979) *The Aging Enterprise*. San Francisco: Jossey-Bass Publishers.

Ewing, K. P. (1990) 'The illusion of wholeness: culture, self and the experience of inconsistency', *Ethos*, 18 (3): 251–278.

Fabian, J. (1983) *Time and the Other: How Anthropology Makes Its Object*. New York: Columbia University Press.

Farmer, B. (1996) *A Nursing Home and Its Organizational Climate: An Ethnography*. Westport, CT: Auburn House.

Featherstone, M. and Hepworth, M. (1989) 'Ageing and old age: reflections on the postmodern life course', in B. Bytheway, T. Keil, P. Allat and A. Bryman (eds), *Becoming and Being Old: Sociological Approaches to Later Life* London: Sage.

Foucault, M. (1979) *Discipline and Punish: The Birth of the Prison*. New York: Vintage Books.

Frankenberg, R. (1957) *Village on the Border*. London: Cohen and West.

Franzoi, S. (1995) 'The body-as-object versus the body-as-process: gender differences and gender considerations', *Sex Roles*, 33 (5/6): 417–437.

Freeman, M. (1997) 'Death, narrative integrity, and the radical challenge of self-understanding: a reading of Tolstoy's Death of Ivan Ilych', *Ageing & Society*, 17 (4): 373–398.

Geertz, C. (1984) '"From the native's point of view": on the nature of anthropological understanding', in R. Shweder and R. LeVine (eds) *Culture Theory: Essays on Mind, Self and Emotion*. Cambridge: Cambridge University Press.

Gell, A. (1992) *The Anthropology of Time: Cultural Constructions of Temporal Maps and Images*. Oxford: Berg.

Gibson, H. B. (2000) 'It keeps us young', *Ageing & Society*, 20 (6): 773–779.

Gilleard, C. and Higgs, P. (2000) *Cultures of Ageing: Self, Citizen, and the Body*. Harlow: Prentice Hall.

Gray, G. (1976) 'The South Yorkshire coalfield', in J. Benson and R. Neville (eds) *Studies in the Yorkshire Coal Industry*. Manchester: Manchester University Press.

Gubrium, J. (1975) *Living and Dying at Murray Manor*. New York: St Martin's Press.

Gubrium, J. (1993) *Speaking of Life: Horizons of Meaning for Nursing Home Residents*. New York: Aldine De Gruyter.

Hallowell, A. I. (1955) 'The self and its behavioral environment', in *Culture and Experience*. Philadelphia: University of Pennsylvania Press.

Hamby, P. and Wyatt, S. (1997) *Honest Dodworth 2*. Dodworth: Dodworth Publications.

Harvey, D. (1989) *The Condition of Postmodernity*, Oxford: Basil Blackwell.

Hazan, H. (1980) *The Limbo People: A Study of the Constitution of the Time Universe amongst the Aged*. London: Routledge & Kegan Paul.

Hazan, H. (1984) 'Continuity and transformation among the aged: a study in the anthropology of time', *Current Anthropology*, 25 (5): 567–578.

Hazan, H. (1990) 'The construction of personhood among the aged: a comparative study of aging in Israel and England', in J. Sokolovsky (ed.), *The Cultural Context of Aging: Worldwide Perspectives*. New York: Bergin & Garvey.

Hazan, H. (1996) *From First Principles: An Experiment in Ageing*. Westport, CT and London: Bergin & Garvey.

Heikkinen, R.-L. (2000) 'Ageing in an autobiographical context', *Ageing & Society*, 20 (4): 467–483.

Heikkinen, R.-L. (2004) 'The experience of ageing and advanced old age: a ten-year follow-up', *Ageing & Society*, 24: 567–582.

Henderson, J. and Vesperi, M. (1995) *The Culture of Long-Term Care: Nursing Home Ethnography*. Westport, CT: Greenwood.

Hendricks, J. (2008) 'Coming of age', *Journal of Aging Studies*, 22 (2): 109–114.

Hendricks, C. and Hendricks, J. (1976) 'Concepts of time and temporal construction among the aged, with implications for research', in J. Gubrium (ed.), *Time, Roles, and Self in Old Age*. New York: Human Sciences.

Hepworth, M. (1991) 'Positive Ageing and the Mask of Age', *Journal of Educational Gerontology*, 6: 93–101.

Hepworth, M. (2000) *Stories of Ageing*. Buckingham: Open University Press.

Herskovits, E. (1995) 'Struggling over subjectivity: debates about the "self" and Alzheimer's Disease', *Medical Anthropology Quarterly*, 9 (2): 146–164.

Hinton, W. L. and Levkoff, S. (1999) 'Constructing Alzheimer's: narratives of lost identities, confusion and loneliness in old age', *Culture, Medicine and Psychiatry*, 23 (4): 453–475.

Hobsbawm, E. J. (1968) *Industry and Empire*. New York: Pantheon.

Hockey, J. (1990) *Experiences of Death: An Anthropological Account*. Edinburgh: Edinburgh University Press.

Hockey, J. and James, A. (1993) *Growing Up and Growing Old: Ageing and Dependency in the Life Course*. London: Sage.

Hodges, M. (2008) 'Rethinking time's arrow: Bergson, Deleuze and the anthropology of time', *Anthropological Theory*, 8 (4): 399–429.

Hollan, D. (1992) 'Cross-cultural differences in the self', *Journal of Anthropological Research*, 48: 283–300.

Holland, D. and Kipnis, A. (1994) 'Metaphors for embarrassment and stories of exposure: the not-so-egocentric self in American culture', *Ethos*, 22: 316–342.

Hunt, A. (1978) *The Elderly At Home: A Survey Carried Out on Behalf of the Department of Health and Social Security*. Office of Population Censuses and Surveys, Social Survey Division. London: HMSO.

Ikels, C. (1997) 'Long-term care and the disabled elderly in urban China', in J. Sokolovsky (ed.), *The Cultural Context of Aging: Worldwide Perspectives*, 2nd edition. New York: Bergin & Garvey.

Ikels, C. and Beall, C. (2001) 'Age, aging, and anthropology', in R. Binstock and L. George (eds), *Handbook of Aging and the Social Sciences*, 5th edition. San Diego and London: Academic Press.

Ingold, T. (1993) 'The temporality of the landscape', *World Archaeology*, 25 (2): 152–174.

Itzin, C. (1990) 'As old as you feel', in P. Thompson, C. Itzin and M. Abenstern (eds) *I Don't Feel Old: The Experience of Later Life*. Oxford: Oxford University Press.

Jackson, A. (1987) *Anthropology at Home*. London: Tavistock Publications.

Jackson, M. (1983) 'Knowledge of the body', *Man (N.S.)*, 18 (2): 327–345.

Jameson, F. (1989) 'Nostalgia for the present', *South Atlantic Quarterly*, 88 (2): 517–537.

Jeffrey, C. (2008) 'Waiting', *Environment and Planning D: Society and Space*, 26 (6): 954–958.

Johnson, C and Grant, L. (1985) *The Nursing Home in American Society*. Baltimore: Johns Hopkins University Press.

Johnson, S. (1971) *Idle Haven: Community Building Among the Working Class Retired*. Berkeley: University of California Press.

Katz, S. (1992) 'Alarmist demography: power, knowledge, and the elderly population', *Journal of Aging Studies*, 6 (3): 203–225.

Katz, S. (1996) *Disciplining Old Age: The Formation of Gerontological Knowledge*. Charlottesville: University Press of Virginia.

Katz, S. (2005) *Cultural Aging: Life Course, Lifestyle, and Senior Worlds*. Peterborough, ONT: Broadview Press.

Kaufman, S. (1986) *The Ageless Self: Sources of Meaning in Later Life*. Madison: University of Wisconsin Press.

Kaufman, S. (2000) 'In the shadow of 'death with dignity': medicine and cultural quandaries of the vegetative state', *American Anthropologist*, 102 (1): 69–83.

Kayser-Jones, J. (1981) *Old, Alone, and Neglected. Care of the Aged in Scotland and the United States*. Berkeley: University of California Press.

Kondo, D. (1987) 'Creating an ideal self: theories of selfhood and pedagogy at a Japanese ethics retreat', *Ethos*, 15 (3): 241–272.

Kontos, P. (1999) 'Local biology: bodies of difference in ageing studies', *Ageing & Society*, 19 (6): 677–689.

Kontos, P. (2003) '"The painterly hand": embodied consciousness and Alzheimer's disease', *Journal of Aging Studies*, 17 (2): 151–170.

Kontos, P. (2004) 'Ethnographic reflections on selfhood, embodiment and Alzheimer's disease', *Ageing & Society*, 24 (6): 829–849.

Kontos, P. (2005) 'Embodied selfhood in Alzheimer's disease: rethinking person-centred care', *Dementia*, 4: 553–570.

Kusserow, A. (1999a) 'De-homogenizing American individualism: socializing hard and soft individualism in Manhattan and Queens', *Ethos*, 27 (2): 210–234.

Kusserow, A. (1999b) 'Crossing the great divide: anthropological theories of the Western self', *Journal of Anthropological Research*, 55 (4): 541–562.

Lamb, S. (1997) 'The making and unmaking of persons: notes on aging and gender in north India', *Ethos*, 25 (3): 279–302.

Lamb, S. (2000) *White Saris and Sweet Mangoes: Aging, Gender, and Body in North India.* Berkeley: University of California Press.

Laslett, P. (1989) *A Fresh Map of Life: The Emergence of the Third Age.* London: Weidenfeld & Nicolson.

Lawler, S. (2008) *Identity: Sociological Perspectives.* Cambridge: Polity Press.

Leach, E. (1961) *Rethinking Anthropology.* London: Athlone Press.

Leibing, A. (2008) 'Entangled matters – Alzheimer's, interiority, and the "unflattening" of the world', *Culture, Medicine and Psychiatry*, 32: 177–193.

Leibing, A. and Cohen, L. (eds) (2006) *Thinking about Dementia: Culture, Loss, and the Anthropology of Senility.* New Brunswick, NJ and London: Rutgers University Press.

Liddington, J. and Norris, J. (1978) *One Hand Tied Behind Us: The Rise of the Women's Suffrage Movement.* London: Virago.

Lloyd, D. and Swallow, F. (eds) (1924) *The North Country and Yorkshire Coal Annual.* Held at John Goodchild's Wakefield Archives, Wakefield, West Yorkshire.

Lockwood, D. (1966) 'Sources of variation in working-class images of society', *Sociological Review* (14): 249–267.

Luborsky, M. and Sankar, A. (1993) 'Extending the critical gerontology perspective: cultural dimensions. Introduction', *The Gerontologist*, 33 (4): 440–444.

Luckmann, T. (1991) 'The constitution of human life in time', in G. White and J. Kirkpatrick (eds) *Person, Self, and Experience: Exploring Pacific Ethnopsychologies.* Berkeley: University of California Press.

Mageo, J. (2002) 'Toward a multidimensional model of the self', *Journal of Anthropological Research*, 58 (2): 339–365.

Marriott, M. (1990 ) 'Constructing an Indian ethnosociology', in M. Marriott (ed.), *India Through Hindu Categories.* New Delhi: Sage Publications.

Matsumoto, Y. (2009) 'Dealing with life changes: humour in painful self-disclosures by elderly Japanese women', *Ageing & Society*, 29 (6): 929–952.

Matthews, S. (1979) *The Social World of Old Women: Management of Self-identity.* Beverly Hills, CA: Sage.

Mauss, M. (1985 [1938]) 'A category of the human mind: the notion of person; the notion of self' (translated by W. D. Halls), in M. Carrithers, S. Collins and S. Lukes (eds), *The Category of the Person: Anthropology, Philosophy, History.* Cambridge: Cambridge University Press.

McHugh, E. (1989) 'Concepts of the person among the Gurungs of Nepal', *American Ethnologist*, 65 (1): 75–86.

Mines, M. (1994) *Public Faces, Private Voices: Community and Individuality in South India.* Berkeley: University of California Press.

Moody, H. (1988) 'Toward a critical gerontology', in J. Birren and V. Bengston (eds), *Emergent Theories of Aging.* New York: Springer.

Morris, B. (1994) *Anthropology of the Self: The Individual in Cultural Perspective.* London: Pluto.

Munn, N. (1992) 'The cultural anthropology of time: a critical essay', *Annual Review of Anthropology*, 21: 93–123.

Murray, D. (1993) 'What is the western concept of the self? on forgetting David Hume', *Ethos*, 21 (1): 3–23.

Myerhoff, B. G. (1979) *Number Our Days.* New York: Dutton.

Myerhoff, B. (1984) 'Rites and signs of ripening: the interweaving of ritual, time and growing older', in D. Kertzer and J. Keith (eds), *Age and Anthropological Theory.* Ithaca: Cornell University Press.

Ochs, E. and Capps, L. (1996) 'Narrating the self', *Annual Review of Anthropology*, 25: 19–43.

Ochs, E. and Capps, L. (2001) *Living Narrative: Creating Lives in Everyday Storytelling*. Cambridge: Harvard University Press.

Okely, J. (1996) *Own or Other Culture*. New York: Routledge.

Oliver, C. (2007) *Retirement Migration: Paradoxes of Ageing*. London: Routledge.

Office of Population, Censuses and Surveys (1934) *Census of England and Wales 1931, Industry Tables*. Table 3. London: HMSO.

Office of Population, Censuses and Surveys (2001) *KS01 Usual Resident Population: Census 2001, Key Statistics for Urban Areas*, www.statistics.gov.uk/StatBase/ssdataset.asp?vlnk=8271&Pos=2&ColRank=1&Rank=224 (accessed 11 January 2011).

Ortner, S. (2005) 'Subjectivity and cultural critique', *Anthropological Theory*, 5 (1): 31–52.

Parliamentary Office of Science and Technology (2007) *Postnote: Alzheimer's and Dementia* (February), Number 278.

Peacock, J. and Holland, D. (1993) 'The narrated self: life stories in process', *Ethos*, 21 (4): 367–383.

Pearson, G. (1983) *Hooligan: A History of Respectable Fears*. London: Macmillan.

Percival, J. (2000) 'Gossip in sheltered housing: its cultural importance and social implications', *Ageing & Society*, 20 (3): 303–325.

Phillipson, C. and Biggs, S. (1998) 'Modernity and identity: themes and perspectives in the study of older adults', *Journal of Aging and Identity*, 3 (1): 11–23.

Pickard, S. (1995) *Living on the Front Line: A Social Anthropological Study of Old Age and Ageing*. Aldershot: Avebury.

Quinn, N. (2006) 'The self', *Anthropological Theory*, 6 (3): 362–384.

Rapport, N. and Overing, J. (2000a) 'Narrative', in N. Rapport and J. Overing (eds) *Social and Cultural Anthropology, the Key Concepts*. London: Routledge.

Rapport, N. and Overing, J. (2000b) 'Moments of being', in N. Rapport and J. Overing (eds), *Social and Cultural Anthropology, the Key Concepts*. London: Routledge.

Rapport, N. (2002) '"Best of British": an introduction to the anthropology of Britain', in N. Rapport (ed), *British Subjects: An Anthropology of Britain*. Oxford: Berg.

Reed-Danahay, D. (2001) '"This is your home now!" conceptualizing location and dislocation in a dementia unit', *Qualitative Research*, 1 (1): 47–63.

Rees, G. (1993) 'Class, community and the miners: the 1984–85 miners' strike and its aftermath', *Sociology*, 27 (2): 307–312.

Rodman, M. (1992) 'Empowering place: multilocality and multivocality', *American Anthropologist*, 94 (3): 640–656.

Rosaldo, M. (1980) *Knowledge and Passion: Ilongot Notions of Self and Social Life*. Cambridge: Cambridge University Press.

Rosaldo, M. (1984) 'Toward an anthropology of self and feeling', in R. A. Shweder and R. A. LeVine (eds), *Culture Theory: Essays on Mind, Self and Emotion*. Cambridge: Cambridge University Press.

Rosaldo, R. (1993) *Culture and Truth: The Remaking of Social Analysis, 2nd edition*. Boston: Beacon Press.

Rowles, G. (1983) 'Place and personal identity in old age: observations from Appalachia', *Journal of Environmental Psychology*, 3 (4): 299–313.

Ryden, K. (1993) *Mapping the Invisible Landscape: Folklore, Writing, and the Sense of Place*. Iowa City: University of Iowa Press.

Ryvicker, M. (2009) 'Preservation of self in the nursing home: contradictory practices within two models of care', *Journal of Aging Studies*, 23 (1): 12–23.

Sabat, S. (2001) *The Experience of Alzheimer's Disease: Life Through a Tangled Veil*. Oxford: Wiley-Blackwell.

Savishinsky, J. (1991) *The Ends of Time: Life and Work in a Nursing Home*. Westport CT: Bergin & Garvey.

Shield, R. (1988) *Uneasy Ending: Daily Life in an American Nursing Home*. Ithaca, NY: Cornell University Press.

Shilling, C. (2003) *The Body and Social Theory*, 2nd edition. London: Sage.

Shweder, R. and Bourne, E. (1984) 'Does the concept of the person vary cross-culturally?', in R. Shweder and R. LeVine (eds) *Culture Theory: Essays on Mind, Self and Emotion*. Cambridge: Cambridge University Press.

Silver, C. B. (2003) 'Gendered identities in old age: toward (de)gendering?', *Journal of Aging Studies*, 17 (4): 379–397.

Sökefeld, M. (1999) 'Debating self, identity, and culture in anthropology', *Current Anthropology*, 40 (4): 417–447.

Somers, M. (1994) 'The narrative constitution of identity: a relational and network approach', *Theory and Society*, 23 (5): 605–649.

Spiro, M. (1993) 'Is the western conception of the self "peculiar" within the context of the world cultures?', *Ethos*, 21 (2): 107–153.

Stewart, K. (1988) 'Nostalgia – a polemic', *Cultural Anthropology*, 3 (3): 227–224.

Strangleman, T. (2001) 'Networks, place and identities in post-industrial mining communities', *International Journal of Urban and Regional Research*, 25 (2): 253–267.

Strathern, M. (1981) *Kinship at the Core: An Anthropology of Elmdon, a Village in North-West Essex in the Nineteen Sixties*. Cambridge: Cambridge University Press.

Strauss, C. (1997) 'Partly fragmented, partly integrated: an anthropological examination of "postmodern fragmented subjects"', *Cultural Anthropology*, 12 (3): 362–404.

Suzman, R., Willis, D. and Manton, K. (eds) (1992) *The Oldest Old*. New York and Oxford: Oxford University Press.

Sykes, S. (1989) 'In the Shadow of the Hill: A Comparative Summary of the Pre-industrial Development of Stainborough and Dodworth Townships. Volume 1 and 2', Masters thesis, University of Sheffield.

Szurek, J. (1985) 'I'll Have a Collier for My Sweetheart: Work and Gender in a British Coal Mining Town', Doctoral thesis, Brown University.

Tanner, D. (2001) 'Sustaining the self in later life: supporting older people in the community', *Ageing & Society*, 21 (3): 255–278.

Taylor, A. J. P. (1965) *English History, 1914–1945*. Oxford: Oxford University Press.

Taylor, C. (1989) *Sources of the Self: The Making of the Modern Identity*. Cambridge: Cambridge University Press.

Taylor, I., Evans, K. and Fraser, P. (1996) *A Tale of Two Cities: Global Change, Local Feeling and Everyday Life in the North of England: A Study in Manchester and Sheffield*. London: Routledge.

Thompson, E. P. (1967) 'Time, work-discipline, and industrial capitalism', *Past and Present*, 38 (1): 56–97.

Thompson, P. (1992a) *The Edwardians: the Remaking of British society*, 2nd edition. London: Routledge.

Thompson, P. (1992b) '"I don't feel old": subjective ageing and the search for meaning in later life', *Ageing & Society*, 12 (1): 23–47.

Thompson, P., Itzin, C. and Abendstern, M. (1990) *I Don't Feel Old*. Oxford: Oxford University Press.

Threlkeld, J. (1989) *Pits 2: A Pictorial Record of Mining*. Barnsley: Wharncliffe Publishing.

Threlkeld, J. (1993) *Pits 1: A Pictorial Record of Mining*. Barnsley: Wharncliffe Publishing.

Townsend, P. (1981) 'The structured dependency of the elderly: a creation of social policy in the twentieth century', *Ageing & Society*, 1 (1): 5–28.

Tulle, E. (ed.) (2004) *Old Age and Agency*. Hauppauge, NY: Nova Science.

Turner, V. (1985) *On the Edge of the Bush: Anthropology as Experience* (ed. by Edith Turner). Tucson: University of Arizona Press.

Twigg, J. (2004) 'The body, gender and age: feminist insights in social gerontology' *Journal of Aging Studies*, 18 (1): 59–73.

Twigg, J. (2007) 'Clothing, age and the body: a critical review', *Ageing & Society*, 27 (2): 285–305.

Tyler, K. (2012) *On Home Ground: Whiteness, Class and the Legacies of Empire*. Basingstoke: Palgrave Macmillan.

Unruh, D. (1983) *Invisible Life: The Social Worlds of the Aged*. Beverly Hills, CA: Sage.

Vanhoozer, K. (1991) 'Philosophical antecedents to Ricoeur's time and narrative', in Wood, D.(ed), *On Paul Ricoeur: Narrative and Interpretation*. London: Routledge.

Vesperi, M. (1985) *City of Green Benches: Growing Old in a New Downtown*. Ithaca and London: Cornell University Press.

Walker, A. (1981) 'Towards a political economy of old age', *Ageing & Society*, 1 (1): 73–94.

Westerhof, G. J., Bohlmeijer, E. and Webster, J. D. (2010) 'Reminiscence and mental health: a review of recent progress in theory, research and interventions', *Ageing & Society*, 30 (4): 697–721.

White, G. M. and Kirkpatrick, J. (eds) (1985) *Person, Self, and Experience: Exploring Pacific Ethnopsychologies*. Berkeley: University of California Press.

Williams, R. (1975) *The Country and the City*. St Albans: Paladin.

Williamson, B. (1982) *Class, Culture and Community: A Biographical Study of Social Change in Mining*. London: Routledge & Kegan Paul.

Winterton, J. (1993) 'The end of a way of life: coal communities since the 1984–85 miners' strike', *Work, Employment and Society*, 7 (1): 135–146.

Woodward, K. (1991) *Aging and Its Discontents: Freud and Other Fictions*. Bloomington: Indiana University Press.

Woodward, K. (1995) 'Tribute to the older woman: psychoanalysis, feminism, and ageism', in M. Featherstone and A. Wernick (eds), *Images of Aging: Cultural Representations of Later Life*. London: Routledge, pp. 79–96.

# Index

Note: 'n.' after a page reference indicates the number of a note on that page.

EU authorised representative for GPSR:
Easy Access System Europe, Mustamäe tee 50,
10621 Tallinn, Estonia
gpsr.requests@easproject.com

www.ingramcontent.com/pod-product-compliance
Lightning Source LLC
Chambersburg PA
CBHW052009270326
41929CB00015B/2853